Studying Singapore

C.M. Turnbull and
History of Modern Singapore

Studying Singapore's Past

C.M. Turnbull and the History of Modern Singapore

Edited by

Nicholas Tarling

NUS PRESS
SINGAPORE

© 2012 Nicholas Tarling

Published by:

NUS Press
National University of Singapore
AS3-01-02, 3 Arts Link
Singapore 117569

Fax: (65) 6774-0652
E-mail: nusbooks@nus.edu.sg
Website: http://www.nus.edu.sg/nuspress

ISBN 978-9971-69-646-7 (Paper)

National Library Board, Singapore Cataloguing-in-Publication Data

Studying Singapore's past: C.M. Turnbull and the history of modern
  Singapore / edited by Nicholas Tarling. – Singapore: NUS Press, c2012.
  p. cm.
  Includes bibliographical references and index.
  ISBN: 978-9971-69-646-7 (pbk.)

  1. Turnbull, C. M. (Constance Mary) – Authorship. 2. Turnbull, C. M.
(Constance Mary). History of Modern Singapore, 1819–2005. 3. Singapore
– Historiography. 4. Singapore – History. I. Tarling, Nicholas.

DS610.34
959.570072 — dc23   OCN781234324

Cover image: View of electronic tramcars plying along North Bridge Road and High Street (Courtesy of the National Archives of Singapore).

Printed by: Mainland Press Pte Ltd

Contents

Introduction

WHEN THE SAD NEWS OF MARY TURNBULL'S death arrived in 2008, the idea of a Nachschrift at once emerged. That it has taken so long to produce does not imply any reluctance to contribute. Contributors were simply anxious to do their best.

It was in keeping with her sustained role in teaching as well as research that the Nachschrift should include work by younger scholars as well as those more senior.

Books of this kind need a focus even apart from the inspiration provided by the person whose memory they honour. Mary taught in Kuala Lumpur and Hong Kong as well as in Singapore, so much in the early years in KL that she claimed she could "count students instead of sheep to get to sleep".

Though her 1962 thesis was on the Straits Settlements and their transfer to the Colonial Office in 1867, and it was subsequently turned into a major book, her latter-day research turned her towards the Commonwealth more than Southeast Asia. In particular, she worked on Malcolm MacDonald, though finding his biography, as she put it, "so complicated, with such voluminous archives spread over many continents and a long span of time", that it did not "lend itself to in-depth research in any one area".

It was, however, in Singapore that she made her strongest mark, in particular by producing what became the most widely-used history of Singapore. The focus of the Nachschrift is thus primarily on Singapore, but that provides only a partial definition of its perimeter.

Mary was a scholar who enjoyed controversy and expected debate. It is not at all inappropriate that contributors felt free to comment on her work, if need be critically, as well as to appraise its impact. In some sense, the tribute is an evaluation, but the evaluation is also a tribute. And, just as it is appropriate to cover topics close to her heart, it is not inappropriate to add topics she did not pursue, or to point to evidence she did not utilise.

All those factors shape this book and help to give it coherence. We hope it not only provides a tribute to a distinguished historian, but also adds to the historiography of Singapore and to the debate among the issues that it raises.

The volume opens with P.J. Thum's entertaining and informative story of her life. That is followed by Karl Hack's discussion of *A History of Modern Singapore, 1819–2005*, the third edition of which appeared after her death in 2009. He argues that it was "a teleological exercise in endowing a modern 'nation-state' with a coherent past that should explain the present".

Kevin Blackburn then discusses the book from a rather different point of view: if you were a musicologist, you might refer to its "reception history". When Singapore history was introduced into schools in 1984, the Ministry of Education's textbook drew on the chronology and themes she suggested. Her work thus helped generations of students to formulate their ideas about Singapore and its past, though now it is but one of several books on the subject.

P.J. Thum returns in a more critical vein as a third commentator on the work. Turnbull relied on English-language sources which he argues result in an incomplete picture of Singapore's history. Using the vernacular press, he argues, provides a fuller understanding of Chinese attitudes to the colonial government's post-war proposals on education, of student activism, and of episodes such as the Hock Lee bus strike.

Next follow two chapters that take the reader back from the closing years of colonial rule to the founding of modern Singapore. One comes from John Bastin, who was heading the History Department in KL when Mary countered insomnia by counting all those first-years, and is, of course, the world authority on Raffles. Raffles had promised to give the public a memoir on Singapore, but was hampered by the loss of his papers in the wreck of the *Fame*. Bastin believes that the *Historical Sketch* re-published here was, however, largely his work. Anthony Milner's paper argues that Raffles and other British officials of the period, with their concept of reconstructing a Malay "nation" under British tutelage, helped in the propagation of racial thinking among "the Malays".

Two more chapters move us back nearer to the end of the colonial period, the time, of course, when Turnbull began her own career as a civil servant. Kelvin Ng writes of the British Military Administration, which she claimed destroyed the goodwill that existed at the time of liberation. The reoccupation period, Ng argues, indeed had lasting consequences. Tony Stockwell writes of Governor Franklin Gimson, whom

Malcolm MacDonald thought might be too "starchy" for Singapore. The chapter reminds us of the trans-colony experience that senior imperial officials had, both, perhaps, an advantage and a disadvantage.

The last two chapters consider two aspects of what may be called the foreign policy of Singapore as a "nation-state", even though they begin in the colonial phase. Jason Lim discusses the overseas Chinese trade missions to China and Taiwan in 1956–1957, concluding that they had little success, but further polarised the Chinese community with respect to the question of citizenship. In the final chapter of the collection, the editor offers, by way of comment on Singapore's international position, some account of its stance on the future of other small neighbours of the two larger countries of the "Malay world", West New Guinea/Irian, Portuguese Timor, and Brunei.

Writing that, and collecting the other chapters from his fellow contributors, continually brought Mary's presence to mind, not only her writings, but the contacts and correspondence scattered but enjoyed over the greater part of half a century. Though she was demonstrably still sharp of mind and crisp of speech at the conference marking the editor's 75th birthday, age was soon to overtake her. The loss cannot be redeemed by a tribute, except to the extent that it stimulates interest in her work and in the historiography to which she contributed.

1

Constance Mary Turnbull
1927–2008:
An Appreciation[1]

P.J. Thum

Early Life

Constance Mary Turnbull was born in West Lyham, Wooler in Northumberland on 9 February 1927, where her family had farmed the land for several generations. It was a difficult time for her family and for the country as a whole. Britain was still struggling to recover from the effects of the First World War. Having sold many foreign assets to pay for the war effort, and lost many others through enemy action, Britain had suffered a severe loss of foreign exchange earnings. This left the British economy more dependent upon exports, and more vulnerable to any downturn in world markets. But the war had permanently eroded Britain's trading position in world markets though disruptions to trade and losses of shipping. Overseas customers for British produce had been lost, especially for traditional exports such as textiles, steel, and coal. Churchill's restoration of the gold standard in 1926 had also made British exports more expensive. For a farming family, dependent on the vagaries of the market and the land, it was a struggle to survive.

With the development of exciting new opportunities in the motor and the electrical goods industries, many people left the land and headed to the cities to seek their fortune. Among them was Turnbull's father,

David Turnbull, who sold his farm and moved the family to Coventry, then the centre of the motor industry, in 1929. An early memory of Turnbull's demonstrated how common this occurrence was. The teacher in her Church of England primary school asked the class how many of them had been born in Coventry. Out of the 50 students in the class, only five raised their hands.

The family struggled on, living a simple existence amidst the Great Depression. When she was four, her mother, Edna Turnbull Williamson, got a job as a supply teacher. With Turnbull not yet due to start school, she was shipped off to the Isle of Man, where her mother's family were from, to live with her grandparents. She would later remember those "six idyllic months in the Isle of Man" with great pleasure.[2]

At the outbreak of war in September 1939, all the schoolchildren were evacuated eight miles to the south, to the Warwickshire town of Leamington Spa. While it later would be home to the Free Czechoslovak Army, at the time it was considered sufficiently far from the major industrial and military centres to be safe. However, nothing happened over the next eight months. It was the time of the Phoney War, as British and French troops sat entrenched on the Maginot Line, and the Germans on the Siegfried Line. They sat and stared at each other all winter. As time dragged on, people started drifting back home, and it was finally decided to send all the children back to school.

In the summer of 1940, however, bombing raids on Coventry began. The city not only contained major metal working industries, including cars, bicycles, and aeroplane engines, but since 1900 had developed a large munitions industry. Coventry was, therefore, in terms of what little international legal precedent that existed governing the subject, a legitimate target for aerial bombardment.[3]

Like many of the industrial towns of the English West Midlands which had been industrialised during the Industrial Revolution, industrial development had occurred before zoning regulations had come into existence. Many of the small and medium-sized factories were woven into the same streets as the workers' houses and the shops of the city centre.

However, there also existed large interwar suburbs of private and council housing, which were relatively isolated from industrial buildings as a result of being built after the zoning regulations had been made law. It was in one of these that the Turnbull family resided — on Harefield Road — and as a result, they managed to escape unscathed from the massive "Coventry Blitz" of 14 November 1940. It destroyed over 4,000 homes and over three-quarters of the City's factories. Turnbull's house had its windows blown out and its roof knocked off, and a few houses around hers had suffered direct hits, but none of her neighbours were killed.

All the schools that survived the bombings were closed, and Turnbull was sent to Bangor, Wales, to live with her great-aunt. For the rest of the year, she attended Bangor High School with her cousins and led a "normal sort of existence".[4] When the local children spoke to them in Welsh, she and her refugee classmates would retaliate by speaking to them in French. She attributed her good knowledge of French and her ability to spell the name of one of the villages to which she was sent (Llanfairpwllgwyngyllgogerychwyrndrobwllllantysiliogogogoch) to this beginning.

The next spring, the schools reopened, and Turnbull returned, just in time for another two massive raids on 8/9 April and 10/11 April. But by that stage, the city had adapted. The schools remained open and her studies continued.

As the war dragged on, food became scarce. Hunger was a constant companion, although she never starved. Small pleasures like peanut butter (which, inexplicably, was never rationed) were treasured. Spread on a small loaf of rationed bread, shared with a friend, it tided her over between breakfast and dinner.

In later life, Turnbull would not speak much of this traumatic stage of her life, except to tell the occasional humorous anecdote. One of her favourites was to explain how, in the aftermath of the Coventry blitz, the Germans invented the word *coventrieren*. Mistaken in their belief that they had wiped Coventry off the map, *to coventrate* meant to destroy utterly. Turnbull would always relate this anecdote with great relish, her wartime defiance rising again to the fore.

This spirit of defiance helped her when in the middle of the war, her secondary school's headmistress gathered the pupils and told them that in order to beat Hitler, they were all going to have to get A's in every subject at their School Certificate Examinations.[5] A gasp went around the room, as nobody at Stoke Park School had managed it even in peacetime. However, when the results were announced, Turnbull had done her part. Studying in bombed-out classrooms with no tables or chairs, she still managed to get all A's and win a county scholarship. "I don't think Hitler ever knew that," she wryly commented much later in life. "I think there were other reasons why he lost the war."

With her unprecedented success, her school sent her to Oxford at age 16 for an interview. Sitting in the waiting room, she was surrounded by girls from public schools, all of whom had been polished and prepared for the interview and were full of self-assurance and confidence. In the interview, an eminent female historian looked down at Turnbull and told her she "had never heard of this Stoke Park School". Turnbull was told she was too young to apply and to come back the next year.

Entirely put off by her experience, Turnbull elected instead to go to Bedford College at the University of London, where she studied under an even more eminent female historian — Dame Lillian Penson, later the first female Vice-Chancellor of the University of London.

Graduating in 1947, she joined Imperial and Chemical Industries as a Training and Personnel Officer the following year. Then at the zenith of its power, ICI was a product of the same interwar industrial expansion that had shaped Turnbull's early life. Formed just three months before Turnbull was born, its range of products included pharmaceuticals, chemicals, explosives, fertilisers, non-ferrous metals, and paints, and looked towards a future of human mastery over the physical world.

Turnbull also yearned for a better, brighter, more promising future. She found the poverty and rationing of post-war London depressing. It was dreary, dull, and grey. Opportunities for women in post-war Britain were few and far between. Turnbull quietly resented the restrictions the economy and society placed upon her, and her heart longed for adventure and fun.

Malaya

In 1952, having arrived early for an appointment in London, Turnbull walked into the Appointments Board office near Euston Station and said to the person in charge, "Have you got something exciting a long way away where the sun shines?"

Working hours having just started, the lady was still opening the post. She had just opened a letter from the Colonial Office asking for six women to be recruited. She offered it to Turnbull, saying, "What about Kuala Lumpur?"

"Well, that sounds perfect." Turnbull replied.

Surprised at her quick response, the lady asked, "Where is it?" Neither of them knew, nor did anyone else in the office, so they had to get an atlas out to find it.

A huge amount of manpower was being consumed with the Malayan Emergency and they were short of Administrative Officers to run the District Offices throughout the Federation of Malaya. As Britain had already committed to independence in the Federation of Malaya, the

Colonial Office was reluctant to recruit more men to the service as they would be permanent staff and would have to be reassigned to other colonies after Malayan independence. At the same time, the local University of Malaya had been established in 1949 and was just about to produce its first graduates. It was expected that these people would form the backbone of the future civil service.

As such, it was decided that they would recruit six women just to tide over the manpower shortage, freeing up the men to work in the rural District Offices at the frontline of the Emergency. Turnbull was offered a three-year contract, which she gladly accepted. Her family, largely on the basis of the film *The Planter's Wife*, had formed an alarmist picture of life in Malaya during the Emergency.[6] They did their best to dissuade her, but she was not to be talked out of it.

When the Chief Secretary of the Federation of Malaya, Sir David Watherston, learnt women were being recruited, he cancelled the scheme. Watherston argued the natives would never work under women. Turnbull, however, had already been despatched, and thus became one of only two female officers ever in the Malayan Civil Service.

Coming from grey, spartan England, Malaya seemed to Turnbull a technicolour land of plenty. She arrived in the midst of tremendously exciting times. With perfect timing, she had arrived just as the worst of the Emergency was over, and in time to observe all the milestones of Malayan independence.

Her posting in Kuala Lumpur was to the Establishment Office, similar to what she had been doing before with ICI. Her predecessor was tremendously happy to see her, as it freed him to take up the District Officer post in Ulu Rompin, Pahang, a dangerous and critical post. Turnbull's work, though confining her to Kuala Lumpur, enabled her to have a deep understanding of the workings of the government throughout the Federation. Among her responsibilities was to report back all cases of accidents, illness, hospitalisation or death. Due to the Emergency, there were a large number of casualties. All of them had to be reported as quickly as possible to enable families to be informed before the standard 72-hour press embargo ended. It was a sobering duty.

An opportunity to escape Kuala Lumpur came during the 1955 Federal Elections. These were the Federation's first national elections, and it was very important that they were run smoothly and fairly. A shortage of Presiding Officers in Kelantan and Trengganu required many of the administrative officers to be sent out. Turnbull would forever retain vivid memories of how they were crowded into two little Douglas C-47 Dakota airplanes, with everyone in a merry mood as it meant three days away from the office and all the files. In Kota Bharu, those who were posted north of the Kelantan River then got into a jeep, dropping off along the way until only two of them remained, destined for the town of Tumpat, Kelantan, just a few miles from the Thai border.

As the town was a traditional Muslim fishing village, it was decided Turnbull would speak to women voters and her colleague, the men. Also, the polling was scheduled from 10 a.m. to 10 p.m. to allow the fishing fleet to go out. It was expected that the bulk of the voters would then turn up later in the day. However, when the polls opened at 10 a.m., there was already a massive queue of people, who waited quietly and patiently for their turn to vote. So vividly was the experience lodged in her mind that years later, Turnbull could still recall the individuals who arrived who were not on the register, describing each of them and how she worked out why each of them had not registered. In each case, she would tell them they could vote in the next election if they registered. "*Lain kali*," she said, meaning "next time". Unfortunately, her Malay was not up to scratch. "*Lain kali*" means "another time", and so as the polls were closing, all of them showed up again, thinking that she had meant that if they came back at the end of the day, she would sort out their problems and enable them to vote.

The Alliance swept to victory, winning 51 out of 52 seats and 81% of the total vote. The Alliance leader, Tunku Abdul Rahman, had built a solid consensus out of an extremely diverse multi-ethnic state. Recalling Britain's own indecisiveness in the 1950 and 1951 elections, she felt that Malayans had really given the British a good lesson in democracy and statesmanship.

University of Malaya

In 1955, with her contract ending, and no possibility of renewal, Turnbull cast about for a new direction. By chance, she met Cyril Parkinson, Professor of History at the University of Malaya. Parkinson, who would later become famous for creating Parkinson's Law, was looking for someone to teach British history at the University of Malaya. He offered her a one-year post, which suited Turnbull. She had been thinking of returning to Britain to take a doctorate on Malayan history. The year would be a perfect time to gather materials for her thesis. However, one year would turn into two, and two into a lifelong career.

The Federation government were happy to release her a few weeks early, and so on 30 September 1955 she finished her work, attended a small farewell party in her honour, got in her car and drove through the night to Singapore.

The overnight trip symbolised the change she encountered in Singapore. Officers at the Federation civil service were filled with worries about their future, but the staff and students at the University of Malaya looked forward with hope and optimism for a better tomorrow. Turnbull felt liberated, leaving a conservative bureaucracy to teach and engage with energetic and lively students.

The energy and excitement of Singapore both thrilled and scared her. The clarity of the Federation's political situation, starkly divided between "White" areas declared free of terrorists, and the dwindling "red" areas where communists lurked was in her past. Reading the English newspapers and listening to the politicians, it seemed as if Singapore seethed with subversion, with communists indistinguishable from nationalists, terrorists from patriots. Policing was much stricter and the hand of the state lay much more heavily upon the people. To her eyes, Singapore's greater law and order barely restrained the anger and bitterness of its subjects.

She was unable to access the Chinese world, although she did give it a good try. Among her papers is a beginner's course in Chinese that she never was able to complete. She also sympathised with the poverty of the population, the housing shortage that forced so many into little spaces, the mass unemployment, and the discrimination that the non-English-speaking faced.

However, she was horrified by the riots, the explosions of mass anger against the unfeeling government and the European elite. Although never personally in danger, the raging heat of resentment and bitterness scared her. Her instinctive sympathy for the British point of view, supported by the one-sided reporting of the *Straits Times*, and a war survivor's abhorrence of violence, ensured she would always condemn the explosive manifestations of the independence struggle. Without any ability to access the Chinese-speaking world, it would remain inscrutable to her, the language and culture a barrier she never was able to overcome.

Still, she contributed in her own way to the independence struggle. A visionary, Parkinson recognised that the University had to train independent Singapore's future administrators. He thus argued that the University should admit as many capable students as possible. The other departments did not share his vision, believing that the University was best served by limiting places to only the very best. However, Parkinson's own department stood behind him and admitted as many students as they could. Turnbull and her colleagues complained to one another about being overworked, but recognised that they were working for the common good. As a result, the greatest proportion of independent Singapore's administrators had history degrees and had been taught by Mary Turnbull. By Turnbull's own reckoning, she worked twice as hard for Malaya when she was at the University as when she was in the Federation, and by all accounts, she did twice as much good.

Furthermore, Parkinson felt it was a ridiculous state of affairs that the University of Malaya taught a British and European history syllabus that was virtually identical to any British university. He devised a scheme to divide Malayan history amongst his department to research. From this came the beginnings of modern Malayan historiography. Turnbull chose the Straits Settlements as her speciality. From this research would later come her PhD thesis, "The Movement to Remove the Straits Settlements from the Control of India, Culminating in the Transfer to the Colonial Office in 1867". This would then become a book, *The Straits Settlements, 1826–67: Indian Presidency to Crown Colony*, the first in a long and distinguished career.

Published in 1972, it was immediately recognised as "by far the best work done on the early history of the Straits Settlements". Khoo Kay Kim, writing in the *Journal of Southeast Asian Studies*, wrote that, "On a foundation of meticulous research", she had "traced the development of Straits society as a whole".[7] It remains the standard work on its subject. The depth of her research is illustrated by her discovery that the personal papers of Governor Orfeur Cavenagh (1859–1967) were in the possession of his grandson in western Canada. She personally went to convince his grandson to grant her access. They are now at the University of Victoria, BC.

One reason for her choice of this subject, as she always acknowledged, was convenience. Colonial documents in Singapore before the transfer to the Colonial Office in 1867 had been transferred to the Raffles Museum, while documents after 1867 had remained in the individual government offices. When the Japanese captured Singapore, they preserved the Museum, but many documents in government offices were lost during the Occupation. With paper in short supply afterward, many more documents were lost to looters. A rumour went around that some hawkers at the wet market were wrapping their fish and vegetables in governor's despatches from the late 1800s, but no one was ever able to confirm this.

Thus, between the surviving documents, and research carried out in England during the summer vacations, Turnbull was able to complete her work over several years, finally submitting her thesis to the University of London in October 1961. Throughout this time, she carried a full teaching load as well. When the University of Malaya was divided into two in 1960, she moved to the Federation campus in Kuala Lumpur but carried on uninterrupted in her work.

Family

Shortly after she had arrived in Malaya in 1952, a party was being held at the hotel where Turnbull was temporarily being housed. Some female colleagues asked to use Turnbull's room to change for the party, and invited her along as well.

Throughout the Emergency, there had been an unwritten rule that Kuala Lumpur was a neutral zone for both sides of the conflict. Consequently, there were no terrorist attacks on the capital itself, and anyone coming into KL who was legally entitled to carry guns surrendered them at the main police station. As a result, most of the local expatriate population poured into KL to relax at the weekend.

Amongst those arriving in KL that weekend to attend the party was the tall, dark Leonard Rayner. He strode into the party with two empty gun holsters on each hip, looking from all accounts like John Wayne. Surveying the room, his eye alighted on Turnbull and he asked her to dance. The cowboy turned out to be an accountant who worked for a coal mining company in Batu Arang. Ten years later, they were married.

By this time, he was based in Singapore, having started his own firm there, and was also Advisor to the Confederation of British Industry. Turnbull thus moved back to Singapore, where she and Leonard raised two daughters, Susannah (b. 1963) and Penelope (b. 1965).

However, motherhood did not slow Turnbull down. She continued to work and travel, but now she brought her two daughters along with her. In the days before jet travel, mass tourism and package tours, the lone indomitable woman and her two toddler daughters visited India, Africa, and Europe.

The political circumstances in Singapore continued to worry her from time to time. During the 1964 riots, Rayner, a member of the Volunteer Corps, was called up to active duty. The University and schools were closed and under curfew. During the day, Turnbull would obtain a curfew pass to go check on Rayner's office. Sorting the mail, it seemed that it largely consisted of letters from potential business partners in Australia and Canada who did not want to get involved in Singapore due to its uncertain political climate.

Hong Kong

Within a few years, that climate began to turn against her. With the civil and security services thoroughly Malayanised, attention turned to the University. Europeans found their contracts restricted, their movements monitored, their lives made much more difficult. Suspicion fell on the University as a potential hotbed of radicalism and subversion. The humanities largely escaped unscathed, but the social sciences and other departments with many western academics were heavily scrutinised. On one occasion, the entire student body of the Political Sciences, Philosophy, and Sociology departments were summoned to the National Theatre, where they were warned of being overly influenced by their western tutors.

Singapore was moving forward and the government was determined to cast off its colonial past. The Rayners' house, originally leased from the government in the colonial era, was in danger of being terminated as the government wanted to turn it into a diplomatic residence. The girls' school, Raeburn Park, was scheduled for closure. Originally the school for port employees' children, it was situated on prime land in Tanjong Pagar. It was to be demolished as part of the port's expansion.

By 1971, Turnbull was the last expatriate left on the staff of the University, there for the sufferance on contract and not having a pleasant time at all. "The wrong gender and the wrong colour" in her words, she had none of the contractual rights that her colleagues did — no sick pay, no annual leave, no permanent contract. The University's obsession with shaking off colonialism even extended to forcing staff to teach their own ethnic background, regardless of their own speciality. Turnbull was forced to teach British history, of which she had comparatively little knowledge and had even less interest.

A post came up in the University of Hong Kong. They were starting a Master's programme in Comparative Asian Studies, and they wanted to put the emphasis on Southeast Asia to balance their traditional strength of China studies. The Head of the History Department encouraged her to apply. The opportunity was too good to pass up. She applied and got the post.

It was with a certain amount of sadness but a much greater amount of relief that Turnbull departed Singapore for Hong Kong. She found the University of Hong Kong to be a relief after the University of Singapore. Ironically, she experienced more freedom in the colony than in the independent country, as it was operating free of political involvement. The enormous restrictions and stultifying, politicised atmosphere of the

University of Singapore had made it impossible for her to pursue her research. Her ties to Singapore remained strong: Rayner would remain in Singapore to oversee his firm for several more years, she had many friends there, and many fond memories.

A History of Singapore

Her strongest link, however, was the book which would make her name synonymous with Singapore history. She had already begun work on it in the late 1960s, but between family, work, and moving, it took her the better part of the decade to finish. She returned to Singapore to continue her research at every opportunity: Christmas, Easter, the long summer vacation were all spent in Singapore, partly at home with her family but mostly in the library and archives.

Part of the rationale for the book was the lack of a truly Singaporean history; Singapore had never been conceived of as an independent state. It was tied up with Johor, with Malaya, with the Straits Settlements, and with the wider British Empire, but never properly addressed on its own terms. A stronger rationale, however, was the political movement at that point in time, led by the People's Action Party (PAP) government, which declared that Singapore *had no* history, that the past was irrelevant, that Singapore's history started now. History had become unfashionable, portrayed as a colonial relic, an albatross around the neck of a young nation that yearned to fly free and forge its own destiny. It was even removed from the primary school syllabus in 1972, in favour of more "practical" subjects that prepared students to be part of the workforce in the future. As a historian, these events made Turnbull deeply uneasy and she believed them to be misguided and unconstructive. With her book, she set out to demonstrate the importance of Singapore's past to its present, to create the field of Singapore history, and to prove the PAP wrong.[8]

Published in 1977, reviews were excellent and praised her for creating the new field of Singapore history. Reviewing the book for the *Journal of Southeast Asian Studies*, Yeo Kim Wah praised her ability to separate Singapore from the Malayan mainland, presenting it on its own merits: "Skilfully synthesizing information gleaned from primary and largely secondary sources, Dr. Turnbull has succeeded in presenting the first scholarly and highly readable general history of Singapore."[9] However, he also felt that her book was best in the first few chapters and went downhill from there. The final chapter, discussing contemporary Singapore, felt weak, and her analysis appeared superficial. Turnbull took these criticisms to heart, and when the next edition came out in 1988, the reviewer specifically praised her added chapters, which pulled no punches and delivered even-handed and insightful criticism of the PAP's later years.[10]

Yeo, in summing up his review of the first edition, agreed with Turnbull's introduction that the book was a beginning, not an end. It paved the way for further scholarship, and looked forward to a time where a definitive history would inevitably be published.

To Turnbull's amazement, over 30 years later, her book remained the standard text on Singapore history (and it still is today). The longevity of her work is testament to the quality of her research and writing.

However, it is also due to the purposeful promotion of her work by the Singapore government as orthodoxy. When the Singapore government finally woke up to the importance of a national education programme, it was Turnbull's understated, matter-of-fact historical narrative which became the basis for the official "Singapore Story".

Turnbull's work was more than convenient. Her values, born of the Great Depression, forged by Hitler's relentless bombing, and sharpened by the poverty of post-war Britain, emphasised stability, hard work, and thrift. These values influenced her work and were exactly the values that the Singapore government wished to inculcate. Her conservative approach to history, which told the story based upon the lives of politicians and leaders, mirrored the government's view of their achievements.[11]

However, the institutionalisation of her work as orthodoxy has also meant that the "Singapore Story" inherited its weaknesses. In particular, it rejects the possibility of alternative contexts to Singapore history. Turnbull herself, having been witness to much of Singapore's history, gave greater weight to personal experience and was doubtful of the merit of other perspectives. Her staunch defence of that approach has helped to legitimise the exclusion of other equally valid frameworks for Singaporean history.

In the introduction to her original 1977 edition, Turnbull had been careful to distinguish her history as a "sympathetic personal interpretation", writing that

> It is difficult to see that any 'standard' history of Singapore can be written for some time to come, since the diversity of cultural background and experience is so great that no foreigner or Singaporean of any one community can speak for the society as a whole ... it is presented in the hope that its limitations, omissions and faults may spur

historians, sociologists, political scientists, anthropologists and others to fill in the gaps and correct misconceptions, in order that we may ultimately come to a greater understanding of the background of this young nation.

Over 30 years later, however, in the introduction to the third edition of *A History of Singapore* (re-titled *A History of Modern Singapore, 1819–2005*), Turnbull specifically dismissed some of the challenges to her historical narrative as "infantile" and others as wistful nostalgia. She went so far as to explicitly criticise those who promoted an "alternative" history to the PAP version (and, indirectly, her work):

> Such 'vibrant diversity' was not music to the ears of investors, nor were the strikes, mass rallies, protest demonstrations and violence which accompanied it, and Singapore was to take the more prosaic path of eschewing ideology in favour of practical common sense in providing the security, jobs, housing, schools and other amenities of comfortable living.

However, she also expressed some worry at the pace of Singapore's growth and its costs. Just as chickens grown in battery cages develop health problems, stress, and aggression, Turnbull perceived that Singapore's crowdedness and relentless devotion to growth was "terrifying" and causing damage to its people.[12]

Ever aware of her responsibilities as a teacher, Turnbull had fought with her publisher (Oxford University Press) about the pricing of the book, forcing them to lower it substantially. She was not, however, able to do anything about the drab cover they put on it. This was not something she would permit in her next book, which followed shortly after. *A Short History of Malaysia, Singapore, and Brunei* was published in 1979. Turnbull designed it as a basic textbook that integrated all of the British possessions in maritime Southeast Asia. It had a colourful cover and was priced attractively. Once again, it was well received, being praised for being "a clear synthesis of the great mass of events and developments that occurred", "very readable", and "of immense value" to teachers and students from undergraduates downwards.[13] At the same time, its structure remained premised entirely on the British colonial framework as a temporal and spatial reference.

Turnbull produced numerous journal articles and reviews, including a chapter about Malacca under British colonial rule in *Melaka: The Transformation of a Malay Capital, c. 1400–1980* in 1983. The second edition of

A History of Singapore was released in 1989. This time, she personally chose the cover illustration, an image of early Singapore.

She retired from the University of Hong Kong in 1990, a full Professor and Head of the History department. She and Leonard threw themselves into making a life for themselves in England. Leonard wanted to retire to the country, so they to chose to live in Sulgrave, Northamptonshire, near George Washington's ancestral home. It was not too far from London, where their children were, and convenient to Coventry, where her mother was.

Freed from the constraints of teaching and administration, her output multiplied. She kept up her research, holding visiting fellowships at Durham University and Cambridge University. A chapter on regionalism and nationalism in Southeast Asia was published in 1992 as part of the *Cambridge History of Southeast Asia*.

In 1993, she was asked by Singapore Press Holdings, owners of the *Straits Times*, to produce an official history for their 150th anniversary on 15 July 1995. No history had been produced at the centenary as Singapore had been under Japanese Occupation, and the newspaper was eager to make up for it.

With less than two years to prepare and write the book, it was very rushed. It marked probably the most personally traumatic year of her life. Leonard contracted leukaemia, and Turnbull had to put all her work on the *Straits Times* history on hold while she looked after him in his final months. After his passing, with little time to grieve, she worked flat out, getting up at 5 a.m. and working until midnight every day. Already 67, she also had to take on gruelling travel to interview people and carry out research overseas. One trip involved a 13-hour flight to Singapore, a couple of days there for research and interviews, then a flight to Australia for one day, then back to Singapore for a few days, before flying back to Britain — where she promptly collapsed from the strain.

In addition, her house was burgled and many family heirlooms were stolen. On a trip north to visit friends and family, her car was burgled and burnt by the thieves to cover their tracks. In February 1995, on her birthday, she was diagnosed with colon cancer. She kept going. Following an operation, she was given the all clear and the cancer never returned. Also in 1995, she was appointed to a Visiting Professorship at the School of Oriental and African Studies, University of London, and never missed her teaching duties. In 1995, right on schedule, *Dateline Singapore: 150 Years of the Straits Times* was published.

1999 saw two more contributions to collaborative works: "Formal and Informal Empire in Southeast Asia" in volume 5 of the *Oxford History of the British Empire*, and "The Malayan Civil Service and the Transition to Independence", in *Administering Empire: The British Colonial Service in Retrospect*. She also wrote eight entries for the *Oxford Dictionary of National Biography*.

The same year, alone in Sulgrave, Turnbull decided to move to Oxford and reconnect with academia. She was very active in the University community, attending many seminars and conferences. She also joined the local history society and enjoyed tramping about the county, visiting sites of historical interest. Her vitality despite her advancing age was a constant source of surprise to all who met her.

Not to rest on her laurels, her work took on new directions. In 2007, she presented new work on British colonialism and its role in the creation of the Johor Empire (which was published posthumously in 2009). A conference in her honour was held shortly after her 80th birthday that same year, celebrating and critiquing the continued dominance of *A History of Singapore* in the field of Singapore history.

Working tirelessly to the end, she submitted the final proofs to *A History of Modern Singapore, 1819–2005* just two weeks before she passed away. It was published in 2009, reasonably priced, with a paperback cover, and an attractive cover photo contrasting old and modern Singapore that she had personally selected.

A tireless advocate and friend of Singapore, she also spent much time and effort promoting Southeast Asian studies in Oxford. She was a friend and mentor to many Singaporean students who passed through. But with typical grace and humility, she always felt surprised when they came to her doorstep, looking to meet the Grand Old Lady of Singapore history. A teacher to the end, she would read and critique their work, and tell them stories of Malaya as it had been, when she stepped off the airplane, a young woman looking for a little sunshine and adventure.

Notes

1. Material drawn from the obituary in the *Straits Times* was written by the author, from John Gullick's obituary in the *Journal of the Malaysian Branch of the Royal Asiatic Society*, and from Mary Turnbull's interview with the Oral History Unit, National Archives of Singapore. Many thanks to Susannah and Penelope Rayner for their assistance.
2. Mary Turnbull, interviewed by Sashi Jayakumar, 12 February 2006, Oral History Unit, National Archives of Singapore.

3. Frederick Taylor, *Dresden: Tuesday, 13 February 1945* (London: Bloomsbury, 2004), p. 117.

4. Turnbull, 12 February 2006, Oral History Unit.

5. Taken at 16, they were replaced by the GCE O Levels in 1951.

6. Starring Claudette Colbert, it was actually filmed in Sri Lanka.

7. Kay Kim Khoo, "Review of 'The Straits Settlements, 1826–67: Indian Presidency to Crown Colony'", *Journal of Southeast Asian Studies* 4, 1 (1973): 147–8.

8. Turnbull, 12 February 2006, Oral History Unit; C.M. Turnbull, *A History of Modern Singapore, 1819–2005* (Singapore: NUS Press, 2009), p. 1.

9. Kim Wah Yeo, "Review of 'A History of Singapore, 1819–1975'", *Journal of Southeast Asian Studies* 10, 1 (1979): 227–9.

10. Hugh Wilson, "Review of 'A History of Singapore, 1819–1988, 2nd ed.'", *Journal of the Malaysian Branch of the Royal Asiatic Society* 63, 2 (1990): 91–3.

11. See, for example, C.J.W.-L. Wee, "The Vanquished: Lim Chin Siong and a Progressivist National Narrative", in *Lee's Lieutenants*, ed. Lam Peng Er and Kevin Y.L. Tan (Singapore: Allen & Unwin, 1999); Albert Lau, "The National Past and the Writing of the History of Singapore", in *Imagining Singapore*, ed. Kah Choon Ban, Anne Pakir, and Chee Kiong Tong (Singapore: Times Academic Press, 1992); Kah Seng Loh, "Within The Singapore Story: The Use and Narrative of History in Singapore", *Crossroads* 12, 2 (1998): 1–21; Hong Lysa, "Making the History of Singapore: S. Rajaratnam and C.V. Devan Nair", in *Lee's Lieutenants*, ed. Lam Peng Er Lam and Kevin Y.L. Tan (Singapore: Allen & Unwin, 1999); Hong Lysa, "The Lee Kuan Yew Story as Singapore's History", *Journal of Southeast Asian Studies* 33, 3 (2002): 545–57.

12. Turnbull, 12 February 2006, History Unit.

13. Kay Kim Khoo, "Review of 'A Short History of Malaysia, Singapore and Brunei'", *Journal of the Malaysian Branch of the Royal Asiatic Society* 55, 1 (1982): 89–90.

2

Framing Singapore's History

Karl Hack

*Interest in the history of Singapore as a separate entity is a relatively modern pheno-
menon, and until recently her story has been treated as part of Malayan history.*

— C.M. Turnbull, "Introduction to the First Edition", in
A History of Singapore (Singapore: Oxford University Press, 1989,
first edition 1977), p. xii

*... during the Ice Age, Southeast Asia was a single huge continent — a land-mass
which included Indo-China, Malaysia and Indonesia. After the Ice Age ended there
was a dramatic rise in sea-level that split up the continent into the archipelago of
islands we see today.*

— Stephen Oppenheimer, *Eden in the East: The Drowned Continent
of Southeast Asia* (London: Weidenfeld and Nicolson,
1998), p. 17

Introduction: Turnbull's Reframing of History

MARY TURNBULL IS MOST ASSOCIATED WITH *A History of Singapore* (1977 and
1989 editions), and with its posthumously published replacement, *A History
of Modern Singapore, 1819–2005* (2009). This chapter argues that these
works should be seen not just as the superbly crafted national histories
that they are, but also as prime examples of how a geographical space's
history can be framed, and reframed, over and again.

In *A History of Singapore* Turnbull talks about having written the history of a "young" Republic and "nation" that is referred to in anthro-
pomorphised form as "she": as if state and nation are evolving life-forms.[1]

17

When Turnbull began writing these books in the early 1970s, she self-consciously set out to provide an authoritative, empirical, chronologically organised history for a country which had only been born on 9 August 1965: with Singapore's traumatic exit from Malaysia.

As such, *A History of Singapore* framed the entire of the island's history with reference to the post-1965 nation it would lead to. The work is, in essence, a teleological exercise in endowing a modern "nation-state" with a coherent past that should explain the present. This is history with a purpose, both in providing for a new market and academic discipline ("Singapore history"), and in helping the process of creating the embryonic object of discussion: Singapore. In stark terms, when Turnbull wrote, the very idea of "Singaporean" (as opposed to overseas Chinese, Malayan, British subject and other categories) was still being formed. Even the ruling People's Action Party (PAP) had assumed, before 1965, that the island's inhabitants would and should become "Malayans".

Turnbull's most famous works therefore embody a paradox. They adopt Rankean form — the empirical, chronological, story of how a nation and state evolved — to describe the origins of a nation that was palpably an objective, rather than a fact, when the work was conceived. They fit a pattern of "domesticated" western academics (notably those who taught in the University of Malaya) writing to the "nation-state" agenda of the first couple of decades after 1965. In this, Turnbull followed the approach of fellow University of Malaya lecturer K.G. Tregonning, with his 1972 book, *A History of Modern Malaysia and Singapore*.[2]

There is some similarity here between the role of the *Sejarah Melayu* (*Malay Annals*) and that of these new "Singapore" histories. The *Sejarah Melayu* aimed to provide a suitable genealogy and origin for the Melaka-Johor-Riau Sultanate rulers, during a 17th century when they had long ago lost Melaka, and were threatened by rising Dutch power in the Straits.[3] The new histories of the 1970s also aimed to give Singapore a past or "genealogy" that would be meaningful and useful for the present.

This past could have been traced back to the 14th century, or beyond that to geological times. The history of a place can be as old as the events that formed its rocks, climate, fauna and flora. Turnbull could have begun her national history anywhere from geological time to 1965, and could have emphasised its long history as part of the Malay maritime world. Instead, her preoccupation with the roots of the post-colonial state led her to favour 1819, as a break with that Malay world.

In Turnbull's uncompromising words, "Modern Singapore was founded in 1819 on the initiative of one individual, Sir Stamford Raffles."[4]

In Turnbull's mind, it is the arrival of Sir Thomas Stamford Raffles, the East India Company, and the policy of free trade, which is the departure point for the modern state, and for the polyglot mix of immigrants that would evolve into the modern, cosmopolitan "nation". She acknowledged that there was a pre-existing settlement under the tutelage of the Temenggong, a subordinate Malay ruler in the Johor-Riau Sultanate. But that settlement of a few hundred — with an *orang laut* or sea people majority ruled over by feudal Malays[5] — was pre-modern. In this story, the modern nation is traced back to the imposition of free trade and British control, and to a decisive break with Malay traditions. Where Malay *Sejarah* or stories/genealogies seek to project royal descent ever further backwards, to Alexander the Great or even Adam, Turnbull cuts the family tree off at 1819. It is as if she looks at an immense canvas, and then decides to frame just the bottom right-hand portion of it.

Turnbull's approach to Singapore's history was thus forged to suit the needs of a particular postcolonial, post-1965, post-"exit-from-Malaysia" era. Her consequent commitment to the national and chronological approach remained unwavering to the end. In 2006, she visited the National University of Singapore (NUS) to discuss the third edition of her Singapore History that would appear posthumously as *A History of Modern Singapore, 1819–2005* (2009). At the NUS, she attended a seminar, sitting alongside two Singaporean scholars who had very different approaches to history.

First, there was Hong Lysa, then of NUS, who saw the various "histories" of the island as discourses, each with political and other motives. Hence, she saw Turnbull's work as helping to underpin a PAP narrative in which a modern state is formed in 1819, and in which the PAP from formation in 1954 had struggled heroically to forge a nation, against wrong-headed communists, chauvinists, and liberals. By contrast, Kwa Chong Guan, of Nanyang Technological University's Institute of Defence and Strategic Studies (now part of the Rajaratnam School of International Studies), suggested that Turnbull's works artificially and microscopically focused on just a short stretch of Singapore's history. Instead, he offered the image of a maritime centre with over 700 years of history. This was how he was already teaching Singapore history to students on the National University of Singapore's Scholars Programme, through an optional Singapore Studies module. I also inserted this longer timeframe into the History courses at Singapore's National Institute of Education (NIE, part of the Nanyang Technological University), from the Academic Year 2001–2002. Where previous lecturers' courses had stressed that their courses addressed "the country's past since 1819", the first Singapore history examination paper I set reflected the still-contested nature of the longer framework. It included the question: "Does Singapore have any useable history before 1819, or is almost everything before 1819 mythstory and travellers' gossip?"

By 2005, a range of courses at both the Nanyang Technological University and the National University of Singapore gave significant space to discussing the pre-1819 period. They also added new themes such as heritage, and tackled some old themes (such as immigration and the plural society) in new ways; for instance, through topics such as "Chinatown" as heritage site, and prostitution and opium.[6] At NUS, the range of courses now allowed students to opt for innovative approaches, or still study the more traditional history in the module "Singapore: The Making of a Nation".[7]

The teaching of Singapore history at university had entered a period of experimentation, and this was also reflected in publications. In 2009, Kwa Chong Guan joined other scholars in publishing a book which could be considered as a companion volume for courses on Singapore's history as a global city. This was Kwa Chong Guan, Tan Tai Yong and Derek Heng's *Singapore: A 700 Year History from Early Emporium to World City* (Singapore: National Archives of Singapore, 2009). This illustrated history is designed to appeal to everything from advanced school students, to undergraduates doing the increasing number of "Singapore Studies" survey courses available at NUS. The other two authors were senior NUS historian Tan Tai Yong, and America-based Singaporean archaeologist and historian Derek Heng.

Singapore: A 700 Year History neatly encapsulates the "700 versus 200 years" debate on Singapore history. It could be seen as a companion text to Kwa Chong Guan's Singapore Studies module at NUS of the time (SSA211, "The Evolution of a Global City State", Academic Year 2011–2012). It also encapsulates the tension between seeing the island's history as a series of very different manifestations as a maritime centre, or as mainly the background to or evolution of the modern nation. The 700-year school is supported by archaeological excavations from 1984 onwards, and by the writings of those involved in them, such as John Miksic and Derek Heng. Elsewhere, the latter has argued for "Casting Singapore's History in the Longue Dureé", by accepting that there has been an oscillation back and forth between two different ways of functioning as a "Melaka Straits region port settlement". At some points, Singapore has functioned as an entrepôt embedded in a bigger structure (East India Company, British Empire or Malaysia). At other times, it has struck out as an autonomous polity (Temasek, modern Singapore).

In this longer framework, periods of relative decline, such as the 17th to 18th centuries, are re-inserted into the island-story of being a rising and falling maritime port settlement. Hence, Peter Borschberg's *The Singapore and Melaka Straits: Violence, Security and Diplomacy in the Seventeenth Century* (Singapore: NUS Press, 2009) traces how Europeans and others saw the island in a period when it hosted little more than a local maritime official of the wider Johor-Malacca Sultanate.

In short, there are "700 versus 200 years" and "origins of the modern state versus long durée" framings for Singapore's history. The longer versions lend themselves to the inclusion of more abbreviated stories from disparate times. For Heng, it is as if a painter includes several vignettes from different times on one canvas, which is nevertheless given coherence by a central theme or image of river, sea and trade.

For Kwa, Heng and others, the initial thrust was towards claiming some sort of continuity between these periods. That continuity, however, consists more in place — the opportunities and dilemmas thrown up by sitting at the meeting of the monsoons on the Melaka Straits — than of institutions or even a "nation". In 2010, I pushed this idea a little further, suggesting that the multiple experiments with how to respond to this dilemma were to some extent distinguished by their disconnection, their very variety.

This argument for the history of Singapore as a series of reinventions appears in Karl Hack and Jean-Louis Margolin (edited with Karine Delaye), *Singapore from Temasek to the 21st Century: Reinventing the Global City*. Abandoning the idea of uninterrupted chronology, its introduction argues that Singapore as a location has hosted diverse and partly discontinuous experiments on how to achieve centrality in the Straits: how to become a, or preferably the, pre-eminent entrepôt for central Southeast Asia and the Melaka Straits. Hence, *Singapore from Temasek to the 21st Century* offers chapters on the 14th-century Temasek experiment, Raffles' vision of Singapore as the place where British leadership would revive Malay culture and trade, and the attempt to make Singapore and its inhabitants "Malayan". It emphasises differences between these periods; for instance, the island's truly multicultural population before 1870s, compared with Chinese predominance after the vast immigration from China in the 1880s–1920s.[8]

In this approach, the very nature of the island's history is seen as lying in this constant need to reinvent its role and comparative advantages, in order to retain centrality in flows of people, trades and goods: a centrality other Straits cities would happily steal away. In this approach, the "continuity" between the 14th and 21st centuries is not one of institutions or peoples, but rather of this need to reinvent in order to adapt to the rapidly shifting geostrategic and geo-commercial context around Singapore.

These very different ways of framing Singapore's history were already taking form by the 2006 workshop at NUS, at which Turnbull defended her approach — and narrative national history — against the demands of Kwa for a 700-year global city frame, and Hong Lysa for a more critical approach to the post-war story of PAP success. Understandably, Turnbull's reaction was to defend the need for a narrative framework, and to argue that only limited changes were needed to her existing work, for instance by increasing Malay perspectives in the foundation of Singapore, and by adding a last chapter to update the story for 1990 to 2005.[9] In the resulting book, she repeated her defence of 2006, that "Narrative history has fallen out of fashion of late, in favour of a thematic approach ... But this does not displace the need for a chronological story, which gives due weight to each stage in turn and attempts to place individuals within a framework of evolution over time ..."[10]

The problem is that the choosing of the "framework" is vital, and in her earlier career, Turnbull herself had not made the evolution of the "modern" nation-state her main framing device. Instead, her various books frame Singapore's past in different ways. Her *The Straits Settlements, 1826–1867: Indian Presidency to Crown Colony* (London: Athlone, 1972) firmly locates Singapore as an East India Company dependency, and a cosmopolitan administrative headquarters for the "Straits Settlements" (Penang, Malacca, and Singapore). Penang — not Singapore — was the headquarters of government for that unit from its establishment in 1826 until 1832, and of judicial administration until 1856. The Chinese, though quickly becoming the largest single group in the population, did not predominate this period in the way they later would, even in Singapore itself. Indeed, for this period, a more significant proportion of the total Chinese were settled "Straits Chinese", or Peranakan whose ancestors had intermarried with "Malays".

So in this book, Turnbull describes something qualitatively different to the modern state, or to the Singapore that emerged after the 1870s, with the vast expansion in Chinese immigration, and in the state's capacity to rule directly (rather than indirectly through revenue farms and Chinese leaders). Though this book originated in a thesis on the 1867 transfer of the Straits Settlements from East India Company to Colonial Office control, it aimed to "trace the development of Straits society as a whole". Furthermore, one of the last pieces Mary wrote returned to this Straits theme, covering "Penang's Changing Role in the Straits Settlements, 1826–1946". This article appeared posthumously, in a 2009 book which originated in a project on "The Penang Story". Had Penang been allowed to choose, it would probably never have agreed to leave its "Straits" union with Singapore in 1946 in favour of the Malayan Union. But having been forced into that Malayan framework in 1946, like Singapore, its "Straits" period became overshadowed. Recent politics framed the narration of the past, and Mary found herself writing about Straits Settlement Penang as part of a more localised project on "The Penang Story".[11]

Mary's first book, on the Straits Settlements, meanwhile, was able to take a specifically "Straits" framework. It framed Singapore as a part of a bigger Indian-based system, with which its links were nevertheless slightly tenuous. Hence, there was a mere monthly steamer service to Calcutta as late as 1864.[12] Turnbull also traced how the Straits Settlements developed into more than a mere outpost and trading station for the East India Company. Given its location and the frailty of links to India, it began to embed itself into the region, interpenetrating the Malay Sultanates on the peninsula.

The result of this trend was that a distinctly "Straits" period in Singapore history also saw the beginnings of a "Malayan" trajectory within it: the era contained within it its own antithesis. This too is reflected in Turnbull's *The Straits Settlements*, which sees frustration at East India Company limits on intervention in the peninsula as one cause of demands for a transfer to London control. It also reflects in her edit and re-release of L.A. Mills, *British Malaya 1824–67* (Malayan Branch of the Royal Asiatic Society, 1961). This work framed the Straits Settlements as part of the wider area of Southeast Asia. Thus, in the early period the Settlements were both part of an East India Company centred world and its trade networks across to China, and yet also the emerging commercial centre of the "Malayan" interests of the company.

Ironically, then Turnbull's early career did not focus on Singapore per se, nor suggest that the past should be narrated as the origins of a distinct Singapore "nation" or "state". Indeed, the next logical step for Turnbull might have been a history of the island as a part of "Malaya", or Malaysia. She was a lecturer at both branches of the University of Malaya (in Singapore 1955–1960, and Kuala Lumpur 1960–1963), and then at the University of Singapore (1963–1971) after the two branches became separate universities. So she served in the universities at the time of the PAP's rise (it formed its first government in June 1959), and at the height of political moves to make Singapore more "Malayan". This was the period when almost all Singapore politicians craved merger with Malaya, but could see little immediate hope of achieving it. Hence, the moves to make the island more "Malayan", including an anthem sung in Malay, a stress on learning Malay in schools, and in 1957, an agreement that a Malayan representative would have the casting vote on a new Internal Security Council (ISC) when Singapore achieved full internal self-government (June 1959). Turnbull thus joined the University of Malaya and its successor at a time when a whole series of scholars — such as C.N. Parkinson (Raffles Professor of History 1950–1958) with his *Heroes of Malaya*, and Wang Gungwu (who was experimenting with distinctively "Malayan" poetry) — felt themselves a part of "something important": and above all else, something "Malayan".[13]

This "Malayan" trajectory had become a significant and increasing driving force in the island's history as long ago as the 1920s–1930s, by when the causeway to the mainland had opened (1923). I have traced elsewhere, in my "The Malayan Trajectory of Singapore's History", how this comprised several overlapping strands in education, infrastructure, demographics, economics and politics, which by the 1940s–1960s led most commentators to assume that Singapore's only viable route to independence was as part of a wider Malayan framework. This, however, was to be one framework that most scholars, Turnbull included, would downplay after Singapore's independence. It simply did not fit what happened on 9 August 1965, when Singapore and Malaysia parted ways.

It also did not fit with Turnbull's experience after 1963, as a young academic situated in the University of Malaya's original Singapore campus, now newly restructured as the separate University of Singapore. The University of Malaya itself had initially been intended to have just one, Johor-based campus. Had that happened, separation would have been an academic nightmare. Instead, financial limitations meant that the when the new university first opened in 1949, it was based at the old Raffles College campus in Singapore. Then, local demand led to the opening of a second campus of the university in Kuala Lumpur, in 1959. Though the two campuses were initially seen as complementary, both wanted to cover an increasing range of subjects. Both were tending towards becoming full universities in their own right, and they eventually split in 1962. By 1963, Mary was part of the new University of Singapore. Within a couple of years, she would also find herself in the new independent state which politicians such as Lee Kuan Yew had proclaimed a virtual impossibility throughout the 1950s and up until 1965: Singapore.

Turnbull thus experienced Singapore's first tumultuous years after separation, before moving from the University of Singapore to the University of Hong Kong in 1971. Turnbull only abandoned Straits and Malayan frameworks for emphasis on a "Singapore" one at this stage. In fact, *The Straits Settlements* first appeared in 1972. By the early 1970s, however, she was being encouraged to write a history of Singapore by Oxford University Press, which felt the unexpected state needed its own country study. In this context, she reframed her approach. The result, in 1977, was *A History of Singapore, 1819–1975*. She had made the personal and intellectual journey from framing the island as part of the "Straits", through looking at the early formation of its identity as a part of a wider "British Malaya", to "Singapore" as something distinct. In this, she reflected the mood of the time. H.F. Pearson's *Singapore: A Popular History 1819–1960* (Singapore: Eastern Universities Press, 1961) had been followed by Donald and Joanna Moore's *The First 150 Years of Singapore* in 1969 (Donald Moore, 1969).[14] Where pre-1914 writers had almost always written of the "Straits" or "British Malaya", authors now seemed impatient to throw off old names for new.

Just how far Turnbull's writing was being remoulded by the needs of the nation-state can be seen when we remember that, for the vast majority of the 156 years that Turnbull's 1977 volume covered, Singapore was formally a part of the Straits Settlements, whether as an adjunct to British India (1826–1867) or as a Crown Colony (from 1867 until de facto ending by Japanese Occupation in 1942, and de jure dissolution in April 1946).[15] She had in fact written about a period that covered "Straits" Singapore, Singapore as part of the Japanese empire, and Singapore as a post-war colony whose separation from Malaya was seen as temporary, with barely a decade of self-consciously separate "Singapore" history on the end (1965–1975). Singapore's history of being rooted in larger frameworks — and of overlapping pulls towards such frameworks as the Indian, Straits, South Seas and Malayan — had not changed: historians had.

Alternative Frames

We have already seen that the history of "the place that we now call Singapore" can be framed in multiple ways, notably as the "Straits", "Malayan", and Singaporean, and on a small canvas covering 200 years or a larger one covering 700. We have also seen that the latter raises questions of what you put in the frame, whether you attempt a coherent narrative, or incline to sketch disconnected vignettes onto one canvas: more like a patchwork quilt made from old dresses. Even if we agree with Turnbull that a narrative or chronological account is invaluable — necessary even — we can argue about when that should begin, and about how different periods should be brought together. Her act of writing as if there is a distinct "Singapore" narrative is, for periods before 1946 at least, a "political" one, and downplays other ways in which Singapore could be framed. This section will now go further, and suggest a series of more radical ways in which Singapore history has been, or could be, reframed.

1819 and All That: The "Singapore Story" Template

We start off with the framing device commonly used when the PAP projects history, and in school education since history returned as a major school subject in the 1980s. This is the "Singapore Story", as scholars soon dubbed the quasi-official version of Singapore's history which dominated from the 1990s. This narrative was put to the public most dramatically in a 1997 sound and vision show entitled *The Singapore Story*. Thousands visited this at Suntec City. It was subsequently refracted into a video which showed at the Singapore History Museum (today's National Museum of Singapore) until 2003. It focused on times of threat and tribulation, notably the war, the Hock Lee Riots and economic and security frailty, and the 1964 riots and communal dangers. It sought to project a vision of a vulnerable and potentially chaotic society that needed strong rule and nation-building, and the idea that this "story" was an objective reflection of "facts". Hence, its use of video close-ups of violence, of documents, and of the feeling of direct exposure to the evidence. In short, while carefully constructing a narrative intended to impart messages, it sought to suggest it was more truth imminent in evidence than story-telling.[16]

Variants of this "Singapore Story" with lessons attached were subsequently integrated into education, as "National Education" in schools from 1998, and into ministerial pronouncements. This reached its apotheosis in Lee Kuan Yew's *The Singapore Story: Memoirs of Lee Kuan* Yew (Singapore: Times, 1998), and *From Third World to First* (Singapore: Times,

2000). Lee had stood down as Prime Minister in 1990 after leading the country from when the PAP first won power in 1959. His resignation was a planned transfer of power to a nurtured second and third generation of leadership, with Lee subsequently retaining influence first as "Senior Minister" (1990–2004), and then as "Minister Mentor" (2004–May 2011).[17] Older PAP leaders now sought to enlist history — as the wartime generation started to pass away — to show why only the PAP's approach could have worked. It is no surprise that these works tell a story in which a small cadre of leaders is seen as treading the only possible path to success — through self-discipline and international investment — surrounded on all sides by a swampy morass from which they are assailed by liberals, communists, communalists and others, whose foolish visions could only have led only to disaster.[18]

This "Singapore Story" has informed most post-independence writing on Singapore's history.[19] Preoccupation with it has led university academics to detail key events with painstakingly researched books, notably on merger and separation.[20] Even anti-establishment histories and individuals have usually failed to escape its gravitational pull. For, in framing themselves as contestations of the PAP-state's "Singapore Story" many have, ironically, condemned themselves to orbit around it. For instance, Lee Kuan Yew's left-wing comrade Lim Chin Siong — who left the PAP to form the opposition Barisan Sosialis party in 1961 — is usually judged as either undercover communist (Lee's label for him) or (as he claimed) idealistic young trade unionist. A Discovery Channel documentary on Singapore's history, first shown in 2005, thus included a clip of Lim saying he was not a communist (a reaction to the "Singapore Story"), but nothing of Lim's own ideas.[21] At the time of writing, Lim's own speeches and memoirs remained mostly untapped,[22] though Kevin Tan was writing a biography. It seemed, belatedly, as if Lim's story might finally be told on his own terms, not just as an echo of the PAP narrative.

From 1998, the "Singapore Story" was entrenched. First, there was the major public exhibition on the "Singapore Story", emphasising the war years, the subsequent PAP struggle for independence and against communism, ethnic chauvinism and economic peril. Second, "National Education" based around this narrative — and attached "lessons" about how Singaporeans must behave — was integrated into school curriculums, at first as separate lessons, and ultimately infused across subjects. Students were also taken on "Learning Journeys" to wartime and business sites to reinforce the story's messages. There was an insistent state desire that students at all levels be imparted lessons through social studies at Primary

School, and history at Secondary, such as "We Must Ourselves Defend Ourselves". There was also relentless emphasis on the need for social and economic discipline.

When trainee teachers were thought to be getting insufficient "National Education" through infusion, the author was called upon to launch a separate interdisciplinary "Singapore Studies" module at the National Institute of Education. In 2003, the module description explained that this covered:

> ... issues of broad, contemporary relevance to Singapore's survival, health and growth as a nation and a global city-state. Inculcation of concepts essential for analysing related topics such as democracy, foreign relations, global economic challenges, and national identity.[23]

Inevitably, scholars taught the material in an open and critical way. Other modules — such as one on Multicultural Studies — tackled "national" issues in a more comparative framework, eventually supplanting Singapore as an "Essential Module" on the Bachelor of Arts (Education) degree.[24] At NUS, meanwhile, a range of "Singapore Studies" modules was made available not only by History Department modules being open to other disciplines, but also through the "Scholars Programme". The latter offered both traditional modules on building the "nation", and also modules by external lecturers who offered different perspectives on Singapore.

The mode by which students received the "Singapore Story" was thus constantly being refined and the modules involved were increasingly diverse. There was no clear evolution, but a jostling of old and new. Hence, at NUS, by the early 21st century, you could study more traditional courses on the nation-state, or Kwa Chong Guan's module on Singapore's emergence as a global city-state over 700 years. The perspective you got depended very much on your choice of individual module. At NIE and NTU, by contrast, a smaller number of courses each tended to include multiple approaches. Hence, my own suite of Singapore courses at NIE blended "people's history" (further discussed below), "alternative paths" (post-war politicians with alternative views to the PAP), heritage and the 700-year approach with more traditional topics. Later on, Nanyang Technological University (NTU) students were also offered a module in a History Minor, at least one version of which offered a very wide range of approaches and themes.[25] With NTU's launch of a new History Major in its Humanities and Social Studies School from 2012, such choices could be expected to increase.[26] Overall, a much greater variety of "frames" were, and are, being used to teach Singapore's history as time marches on.

Despite some small mention in history texts of pre-war events, and the increasing use of "National Education" themes in more imaginative ways at university level, the emphasis in school texts nevertheless remained on the origins and formation of the modern nation and state, particularly from the war years onwards.

History in schools thus paid relatively little attention to the long duration, the "Straits Settlement Story" and the longer Malayan trajectory in the island's history. The latter became truncated to 1961–1965. Instead of coming out of increasing interpenetration of the two areas, the "Malaysia" idea was now portrayed as if sprung on an unsuspecting Singapore public by Malaya's premier, Tunku Abdul Rahman, in May 1961. Hence its history, from inception to formation of Malaysia on 16 September 1963, becomes a brief aberration. The idea comes just in time to save a PAP leadership terrified its left wing might otherwise defeat it, and demand separate independence. Malaysia plays the function of flushing that left wing out into the new Barisan Sosialis party, and of defeating them in the merger referendum of September 1962. Malaysia is then inaugurated in September 1963, but quickly undermined by Malay "ultras" from the mainland whose reckless campaigning in Singapore sparks racial riots in July and September 1964.

The breakdown of this brief marriage of convenience, and separation of 9 August 1965, is dealt with elsewhere, by scholars such as Tan Tai Yong and Albert Lau. The subsequent presentation of the period almost as an interruption of the development of Singapore and a sense of its identity from "suffering together" in the war onwards, is of course contrary to the PAP's own plans at the time.[27] Lee Kuan Yew had sought merger because he — along with most major Singapore politicians — genuinely thought that it was the only viable route to independence. With Lee and Lim Chin Siong as exceptions that prove the rule, most senior PAP leaders had been born in Malaya, and had family there.

Notwithstanding this "Malayan" reality, the emphasis in National Education was on the "Malaysia" period as an exceptional time. It also portrayed it as another of the many threats that allowed the PAP to prove its abilities, and which forced Singaporeans to buckle down to national survival against the odds under PAP leadership. The longer-term significance of Malayan trajectories in Singapore history — before and after merger and separation — is for the most part ignored.

What emerged from the 1990s was thus rather more complex than the PAP had first envisaged. There was indeed a "Singapore Story", and "National Education", with the detail in that being filled out, and increasing attention given to what one book dubbed *Lee's Lieutenants*: the generation who faithfully and successfully served the PAP-state in its early decades.[28] But in reality, there was also a vibrant debate about "200 years versus 700", and increasing experimentation at university level with teaching different aspects of Singapore history, with courses approaching Singapore history from perspectives as varied as media and cultural history on the one hand, and left-wing attempts at revisionism on the other. There was, therefore, both a restrictive vision at school level, which downplayed the long duration and "Straits" and "Malayan" frameworks, and yet a competing range of alternative framings at university and research tiers.

These major alternative frames are perhaps the most obvious, but others — both existing and potential — also present themselves. What I want to do now is to briefly survey some additional ways in which we can radically reframe Singapore history.

The Really Long Duration

We have already seen tension between the 700- and 200-year approaches to Singapore's history. But while Kwa, Heng, Miksic and others propose a "long duration", there is a still longer perspective. For even the 700-year approach still sticks to a conception of history as solely about people, institutions, and social forces. Yet we can also think of Singapore's past as about "place", even as the "biography" of a place. Hence, Peter Ackroyd's *London: The Biography* (London: Vintage, 2001) touches on Neolithic origins, and has chapters on waste and light. Norman Davies recasts his history of Britain as *The Isles* (London: Macmillan, 1999), and begins after the last Ice Age.

Ackroyd's approach might suggest a "biography" of place that covered similar themes for Singapore, and Davies' a chronology stretching at least to first human habitation. The approach can be pushed even further. We could reframe history as that of the physical mass that now makes up what we call Singapore, and the things that have happened to this mass, and on it. At its extreme, this suggests a geological timescale.

This approach can reach back to discuss the very origins of Singapore's separate and distinct existence. Some 200–300 million years ago, in the Triassic period, "the land we now call Singapore" was a rock mass that was joined to the Asian mainland. This rock mass was in turn located up to 3,000 miles east of its current location. The Sajahat Formation of rocks, whose jagged mass juts out to sea from Pulau Tekong, dates from this period.[29] If we scratch the surface of the land, and tap Singapore's subterranean and geological history, we are forced to adopt a framework of thousands of miles, millions of years, and of shifting tectonic plates. We are also forced to see Singapore not as separate, but as a local manifestation of larger patterns.

Even if we restrict our history merely to the planet's surface and its flora and fauna, "the place we now call Singapore" needs to be placed in a very wide frame, and considered as an integral part of the wider region in which it is situated. Singapore is too narrow a framing device for this. So too is Malaysia. One wider area may be "Sundaland". A mere million years ago, the islands of "Sundaland" were connected to each other, and to mainland Asia. "Singapore" was one part of a mostly continuous land mass. As sea levels changed during the Pleistocene period, this connection periodically disappeared, eventually leading to the current isolation of the islands. Stephen Oppenheimer describes this process succinctly:

> At the height of the last Ice Age around 18,000–20,000 years ago, Southeast Asia formed a continent twice the size of India, and included what we now call Indo-China, Malaysia, and Indonesia. The South China Sea, the Gulf of Thailand and the Java Sea, which were then all dry, formed the connecting parts of the continent. Geologically, this half-sunken continent is termed the Sunda shelf, or Sundaland.[30]

Oppenheimer's wider claims, that this flooding caused an exodus of Austronesian peoples, that carried Southeast Asian influence to many other civilisations, is contentious. But his genetic research tallies with other scientists. Indeed, it has merged into a contestation of the old idea that Austronesian languages and cultures spread from the Taiwan region into Southeast Asia. Hence, Pedro Soares *et al.* argue, in the journal *Molecular Biology and Evolution*, that:

> Modern humans have been living in Island Southeast Asia (ISEA) for at least 50,000 years ... The attention of archaeologists and geneticists has usually been focused on the last 6,000 years — in particular, on a proposed Neolithic dispersal from China and Taiwan. Here we use complete mitochondrial DNA (mtDNA) genome sequencing to spotlight ... that haplogroup E, an important component of mtDNA diversity in the region, evolved in situ over the last 35,000 years and expanded

dramatically throughout ISEA around the beginning of the Holocene, at the time when the ancient continent of Sundaland was being broken into the present-day archipelago by rising sea-levels. It reached Taiwan … within the last 8,000 years. This suggests that global warming and sea-level rises at the end of the Ice Age, 15,000–7,000 years ago, were the main forces shaping modern human diversity in the region.[31]

Thus, what is now maritime Southeast Asia — taking in Malaysia, the entire of Indonesia, Borneo, and coincidentally "the land now called Singapore", originated as one geographic unit.[32] Moreover, the very identity of "island" or "maritime Southeast Asia", as an area of diverse but interconnected groups with intense maritime linkages, is rooted in a last major global warming. In the very widest sense, "histories" of Singapore ought to include a map of Sundaland, and discussion of the formation of the unique blend of genes, geology, geography and climate which gave rise to this one tiny fragment of the wider regional system.

The term "Sundaland" is still used by scholars, for the biogeographical region that is the legacy of that landmass. Biogeographically speaking, there is no distinction between one side of the Singapore Strait and the other. Both belong to a region characterised by a diversity of freshwater habitats including hill streams, lowland floodplains, and peat swamps. Indeed, until very, very recent times, the terrain on both sides of the Straits was very similar, with its mangroves, creeks and then jungle inland. Even an event as apparently "modern" as the campaign for and Fall of Singapore (8–15 February 1942) is inexplicable without understanding that the Singapore Strait united as much as divided "Singapore" from Johor. The broken terrain of creek and jungle, and easily crossed Strait, made it easy for the Japanese to obtain surprise and local superiority.[33] Nearly four decades earlier, in 1904, people on the island could still talk of going "to Singapore". Jurong pepper farmer Yao Ah Soh had to get up at 4.30 a.m. to go "to Singapore" to sell fowl, only returning at 2 p.m. For people like him, "Singapore Settlement" was still distinct, and his life distinctly rural, like that of the Malayan peninsula.[34]

Until very recently, then, "Singapore" suggested the maritime settlement around the Singapore River as much, if not more than, the island as a whole. This is how the Malays of the Melaka Sultanate and its Johor-Riau successors viewed Singapore across several centuries, as one river/sea settlement amongst the many in the broader Straits area that was their domain.[35] In short, one way of framing Singapore is by its geology, geography, and the wider setting they are embedded in.

People's Histories

> *I am a tailor and have a tailor's shop at Sago Street, Chop Wong It. ... I have a*
> *partner in the chop. I live with my wife at No: 1-4 Upper Chin Chew Street ... a*
> *lodging house above a Chinese doctor's shop. The corpse that the coroner viewed ... is*
> *that of my wife, named Choo See, aged 31 years. We have been married for 10*
> *years. There were no children. I procured my wife from Perak, where she was in a*
> *brothel ... On Tuesday she told me that she had lost $400 dollars at Johore at the*
> *gambling table. She pawned all her jewellery to the value of $330 ... I told her to*
> *take comfort and that when I had the money I would redeem the jewellery ... [upon*
> *returning from work] ... I observed that her hands and mouth were smeared with*
> *chandu. Her skin was not quite cold, but she was quite dead.*[36]

While we could reframe Singapore's history to geological timescales, from the late 1980s, some historians have sought to do the opposite, and focus down on individuals, such as Yao Ah Soh and his wife Choo See, and their personal, intimate experiences. In short, they began to experiment with something else that Turnbull's account gives relatively short shrift: "people's history", otherwise termed "history from below" and overlapping the history of the "everyday".

Singapore history, and university-level history courses, have long included "pioneer" Asians, immigrants-made-good and businessmen who also became community leaders. Turnbull's histories include such figures.[37] But there has also been a trend from the late 1980s towards giving "everyday" life and ordinary people more of a place, and even a "voice" of their own. That is, there has been a trend towards "history from below", which goes beyond mere description and statistics, to try and recapture the voice, perspective, and agency, of ordinary rickshaw pullers, prostitutes, opium addicts, and of the populace in general. Instead of the canvas showing a portrait of the ruler, or group portrait of their court, it now teems with as much life as a Hogarth sketch, or as Rembrandt's "Night Watch", crowded with people from all walks of life.

There have been at least three major forces behind this trend, namely a "Warren" school of Singapore history, the rise of oral history, and the general increase in "history from below" internationally.

The most prominent influence has come from James Francis Warren. Warren is an Australian-based American scholar who has written books on pirates, and two major works of "collective biography". The latter are *Rickshaw Coolie: A People's History of Singapore, 1880–1940* (Singapore: Oxford University Press, 1986), and *Ah Ku and Karayuki-san: Prostitution in Singapore 1870–1940* (Singapore: Oxford University Press, 1993). Warren's work gives a more direct voice to ordinary people even than Lee Poh Ping in her *Chinese Society in Nineteenth Century Singapore* (Singapore: Oxford University Press, 1978), or Brenda Yeoh in her *Contesting Space in Colonial Singapore* (Singapore: Singapore University Press, 2003). Though the latter works are interested in ordinary people, they lack the depth with which Warren recreates the world "from below", and his intensive search for their actual words. Indeed, for Brenda Yeoh, they are interesting specifically in relation to government housing and environmental policy, rather than for their own sake.

Warren's two main works in this area sprang from a desire shared by a number of scholars to reinsert the missing objects of colonial policy, or even better to write what some of them termed "people's history", history "from the underside", and "history from below". Peter Rimmer and Lisa Allen, in their *The Underside of Malaysian History* (Singapore: Singapore University Press, 1990), described their motivating questions as: "how do we write an authentic history of individuals and groups who have left few, if any, records; and how do we bring out the everyday lives of the people?"[38] Given that many of immigrants were illiterate, this posed enormous challenges.

Warren came across one answer to this question serendipitously, when he discovered the un-catalogued coroners records for Singapore, and was allowed to work on them. He describes his methodology as "prosopographical", in the sense of using recurring records — in this case about death — as fragments from which to construct "collective biographies" of groups of people. It is rather like trying to make a single mosaic of "rickshaw pullers and their life" from shards from thousands of different mosaics. On the other hand, through interweaving of coroners records, court records, reports, newspaper records and the occasional snippet of oral history, Warren is able to let "ordinary" people speak for themselves (albeit through statements to authorities).

In this, Warren was influenced by American scholars' work on the everyday. But his approach also echoes the work of third-generation *Annales* historians such as Emmanual Le Roy Ladurie, who in his microhistory, *Montaillou*, tried to reconstruct the daily life of 13th-century Alpine villagers through inquisition records. The strengths are the same, the vivid invocation of people's thoughts and passions and experience of gender, power religion, agricultural practice, and the everyday, often extracted by reading "against the grain" (that is, for things incidental to what the interrogator or official was seeking). The weaknesses are also the same, that court records originate in extraordinary circumstances, and by their nature (especially coroners' records) may sift out life's winners (the rickshaw puller made good) in favour of its losers (Ladurie's 30th-century Cathars, tried as heretics, or the tuberculosis-ridden puller who overdoses on opium). However much you seek agency and balance through court records, you are liable to find an inordinate share of misery. If you traced the lives of Europeans in Singapore through the coroners record, you might conclude that rather a high percentage committed suicide following financial troubles.[39]

Warren has not only given us books that we can use (in Ladurie's redolent phrase) to "breath life" into the everyday, but has also supervised students after his own image. Notable examples include Stephen Dobbs and Loh Kah Seng, both of whom broaden the approach to include a heavier reliance on oral history: something all the more necessary as the Singapore National Archives (who now hold the coroners records) have imposed tighter conditions on their use.[40] To a degree, reliance on oral history also sidesteps the criticism of microhistorians such as Ladurie and Carlo Ginzburg, and of Warren's collective biography, that the records they relied on were mediated. They were court records obtained under threat of court intervention in people's lives.

Stephen Dobbs penned *The Singapore River: A Social History 1819–2002* (Singapore: Singapore University Press, 2003), which brings to life the world of the boatmen who frequented the Singapore River, before their relocation. Loh Kah Seng, meanwhile, has explored "people's history" from the Great Depression, through the post-war Singapore left, to ordinary Singaporeans responding to British military withdrawal in the 1970s.

Quite separately from these developments, Cambridge-trained Chua Ai Lin (initially with Mark Emmanuel) began to teach a course on "Popular Culture in History" at NUS. Chua had also introduced, by 2010, an advanced "Approaches to Singapore" course that included heritage, social memory such as that of clubs, and oral history.[41]

"History from Below" had also made an appearance at the National Institute of Education by this time. Between 2001 and 2006, together with Kevin Blackburn, I integrated many of these approaches into courses taught to trainee teachers there. Students were asked to do their own oral history project on a place, event, or on the immigrant origins of their family. This acted as a training in oral history, before they considered issues such as the nature of prostitution, and the significance of opium (which furnished 40–60 per cent of Singapore's pre-1914 revenue) on local society. Hence, 2004 questions for the first-year History course "Themes in Singapore History" included: "How far and in what ways is it true to say that Singapore's prosperity and growth have been reliant on the harsh exploitation of immigrants and underclasses?", and "To what extent do you agree with James Francis Warren's assessment of the impact of prostitution on prostitutes' lives?".

Thus, at NIE, "people's history" was integrated into modules, along with oral history, heritage (Chinatown), and the 700-year perspective, along with more traditional study of the war, and the post-war origins of the modern state. Since 2006, successor courses at NIE, if anything, seem to incorporate slightly less "people's history", though they still range over pre-1819, heritage, and "alternative" political views of the MCP and left: no mean feat for a single module.[42]

Where issues such as "people's history" had to be crammed, with other approaches, into just one module, one trick was to use them as a window into vital issues such as immigration, the nature of the colonial state, and the transition of Singapore from almost a "Wild East" Chinese immigrant boomtown of the 1870s–1890s, to a modern cosmopolis of the 1920s. Hence, for instance, the pervasive use of opium by pullers and in brothels reflected the colonial state's emphasis on free trade and *laissez faire*, meaning low revenues and low levels of state interference. That led to a degree of indirect rule (hence farming out revenue "farms", that is, the right to sell specific substances and services). So too the state's emphasis on open borders and immigration was vital to economic growth, and to providing tens of thousands with economic opportunities, but the cost was terrible housing, poor services, and for many, harsh toil and early death. "People's history" presented alongside imperial and state history could thus be "mainstreamed". Hence, Warren's works can be used alongside Edwin Lee's work on the colonial state, and Carl Trocki's on the central place of opium in early state formation, and on building relationships between Chinese elites and the colonial state.[43]

In short, "people's history, especially as "collective history", can intersect the Rankean "national history", in the sense of events broadly shared by a community, and therefore constitutive of a shared or imagined commonality. Likewise, the history of collective memory need not be something disconnected from "national" history. Kevin Blackburn and Karl Hack's *War Memory and the Making of Modern Malaysia and Singapore* uses differing memories of the Second World War, from the political to the everyday — to show how the various levels — individual, community (Malay, Indian, Chinese, European, and Eurasian), and state interact. This allows the construction of unifying, state-sponsored narrative about the war and its significance to be tested alongside community and individual experiences. "People's" history does not have to be marginalised and oppositional to a mainstream.

Nevertheless, a certain type of "people's history" — one formulated in direct opposition to the "Singapore Story", has enjoyed a startling rise in the first few years of the 21st century. As I noted above, by 2010, the NIE course on Singapore history appeared to have little on "history from below" in the sense of "ordinary" people, but did tackle the 1940s–1950s from the perspective of "Political Alternatives? — Malayan Communist Party, Trade Unions and Student Movement".[44] This might be termed the left-wing, radical, or "alternative paths" approach to framing Singapore's history.

Alternative Paths

the British and Lee Kuan Yew conspired and collaborated to crush the opposition before the 1963 General Elections. The whole aim of this merger was to crush the opposition. … In examining their past records, they are standing on a pedestal that is leaking with worms and vermin.

> — Ex committee member of Barisan Sosialis, and ex-detainee (1963–1982) Dr. Lim Hock Siew, speaking at the launch of *The Fajar Generation* in 2009[45]

Operation Spectrum is an open wound … a little black hole in history.

> — Playwright Alfian Sa'at in a speech at The Legends Hotel at Fort Canning, 26 June 2010, referring to the arrest and detention of 22 mainly Catholic social workers, lawyers and activists in 1987, accused of being Marxist conspirators[46]

There was no Marxist conspiracy. I was never the leader of the alleged Marxist group … Victims have kept silent for too long … Before the assault I firmly stood my ground, refusing to be intimidated. After the assault I succumbed and allowed them to make me into a docile puppet, writing and signing long tracts of self-incriminating lies and half-facts. … let us not forget the hundreds of other ISA detainees who have suffered much much more without the chance of seeking redress, especially those who have gone to their grave in a blanket of silence. We who are still alive owe them the duty to seek out the truth and accordingly proclaim their contribution to the true history of Singapore. … We must fight for the abolishment of the ISA. … It is time for us to stand up for our human rights.

> — Ex-detainee from Operation Spectrum Vincent Cheng, to an SDP crowd at Hong Lim Park in Singapore, 26 September 2010[47]

The perceived need for a history of "alternative paths" stems from the very dominance of the "Singapore Story", with its emphasis on the PAP saving the island from communist, chauvinists, naïve liberals and others whose dreams — it is suggested — could have led to disaster. In this story, there was only one safe way: that of the multiracial, technocratic, PAP. So strong is the pull of the "Singapore Story", that even those whose stance is critical, such as social scientist Yao Souchou in *Singapore: the State and the Culture of Excess*, have tended to focus more on the state itself than on alternatives Hence, in an attempt to explain how protest has been inhibited, Yao ends up focusing mostly on the state. His conclusions end up being about how intelligent leadership, colonial and postcolonial, calibrated coercion, opting for the least harmful control (such as press licensing rather than arresting journalists).[48]

In this context, alternative models for Singapore have tended to wilt in the face of increasing PAP control of the press, and development of a model of "communitarian" society,[49] and of disciplined, state-led, foreign-investment-driven, development. These left little space, in the 1970s to 1980s, for public discussion of alternatives.

As a consequence, it has sometimes seemed as if no one could escape being framed by the "Singapore Story". One could be for the "Singapore Story" (and writing down of left opponents as simple communists and fellow travellers). Or, as with Carl Trocki and other critics, one could be for modifying it on the grounds that it exaggerates threats, dismisses real alternatives, and downplays the contributions of non-PAP actors to post-war history. Even Carl Trocki and Michael Barr's *Paths Not Taken: Politial Pluralism in Postwar Singapore*, which explicitly gives voice to groups such as trade unionists and the MCP, ultimately balks at totally rejecting the "Singapore Story". It claims that it "complements it" by adding the stories of "unrecognised contributors to the construction of Singapore".[50]

Hence, one either subscribes to the "Singapore Story" (which Hong Lysa and Huang Jianli further dissect in their *The Scripting of a National History*),[51] or argues that the PAP's opponents were not mere communists, fellow travellers and dupes, but genuine left wingers and liberals whose alternatives were victims of collateral damage in the PAP's struggles against communism and communalism. In short, critics imply the PAP used a sledgehammer to crack a nut, continued using the sledgehammer long after the remaining nutshell had been pulverised, and in the process destroyed liberal and other alternatives. In their eyes, the PAP threw out the baby with the bath water, and so was left with a shackled and timid civil society (ever afraid of transgressing uncodified "out of bounds" markers, and of the possibility of detention without trial), a state-owned and chastened press, and in general an authoritarian environment.

Hence, the title of Michael Barr and Carl Trocki's *Paths Not Taken: Political Pluralism in Postwar Singapore* (Singapore: NUS Press, 2008). This resulted from a project which aimed to uncover alternatives, in the sense of alternatives at the time and alternative interpretations of history since. *Paths Not Taken* includes chapters on the liberal vision of the first Chief Minister David Marshall (Chief Minister 1955–1956) on ex-detainees such as trade unionist Michael Fernandez, and on youth, Catholic activists and civil society up to the 1980s.

David Marshall's liberal vision — inspired by the lawyer's respect for the sanctity of the individual tagged on to the Labour Front's commitment to social justice — here provides one of the most tantalising "alternatives". It raises the question of whether the PAP's communitarian approach (placing community above individual freedoms and rights) and technocratic and disciplinary slant was the only way. Was there an alternative to removing trial by jury, and so allowing Singapore courts to decide for themselves — and within the "rule of law" — whether people were guilty of defamation or contempt of court without the balance of a non-judicial jury?[52] Was communitarianism indispensable, or could the rights and freedom of the individual have been accorded greater emphasis? David Marshall's belief in the need to protect and advance the individual is used to suggest an alternative vision of civil society, governance, and trial by jury.

This sort of "alternative paths" approach does not necessarily imply "people's history", but the two do overlap. It has been fuelled by the growth of oral history due to the ending of the Cold War around 1989–1991, and the slight easing of the state's stance on criticism from the 1990s.[53] These factors have encouraged ex-detainees, and members of the left in general, to be slightly more willing to talk in public rather than risk taking their stories with them to the grave, as Lim Chin Siong did in 1996. Vincent Cheng voiced their feelings in the September 2010 speech cited above, when he said, "The first step towards redress is for victims to open their mouth or to pick up their pen".

These changes have coalesced into what might be termed a new wave of history about Singapore, which focuses on alternative voices and "paths" for the period from the 1930s to 1960s, and especially for the 1950s–1960s. In one sense, this is a delayed version of what had already happened in Malaysia, where the signing of a final peace agreement with the Communist Party of Malaya in December 1989 saw some ex-insurgents return, and a significant number write memoirs. While the most notable of those was communist party Secretary-General Chin Peng, they also included the memoirs of Singapore's Fong Chong Pik (Fang Chuang Pi), who Lee Kuan Yew had dubbed the communist's "Plen" (plenipotentiary) in Singapore for the 1960s. Fong had fled to Riau in 1963, and then to the jungles to fight, before dying in southern Thailand in 2004.[54]

There is therefore an exercise in "recovery" of history which spans everything from liberals in civil society, to card-carrying communists, including those with blood on their hands. It is emphatically not just about recovering the voices of "revolutionaries", though the recovery of voices of the left wing is a major component. This recovery does, however, contest the framing of the Singapore left wing as merely "communists" and therefore dangerous individuals who had to be defeated even if that meant not playing by "Queensberry" rules.

This left wing covered a very broad range of people, and at one time encompassed most of those in the PAP. *Men in White: Untold Stories of the PAP* (2010) — the product of three *Straits Times* journalists and more than 300 interviews — shows how even Fabian Socialists such as Maurice Baker could flirt with Marxism while students. Baker is shown reminiscing about reading both *The Communist Manifesto* and *Daily Worker*.[55] The environment of post-war London, where many future PAP leaders studied, and of the communist victory in China in 1949, encouraged people across the left to ask questions. How far would constitutional measures suffice to ensure decolonisation? How far would direct union and street action be required to win *Merdeka* and secure people's rights? For some, there was also the question of whether the gun would also be necessary. In this context, people such as Chinese-educated Jek Yuen Thong and English-educated trade unionist C.V. Devan Nair might start out communist, and gradually elide with the non-communist, "right" wing of the PAP; while others might move in the contrary direction. This was the fluid, fervid, effervescent world of the left.

In 1956, Singapore's Special Branch estimated there were not more than 25 MCP members in Singapore, with about 1,500 Anti-British League (ABL) mass executives, and another 1,500 not fully integrated into the latter. Membership of the ABL itself did not indicate MCP membership, since in the anti-colonial atmosphere of the 1950s, being anti-British, hence anti-colonial, seemed natural to many in Chinese-language schools. This relatively modest MCP level was before waves of arrests in 1956–1957 devastated the party, and the at times barely functional MCP Singapore Town Committee. Communists in this order of numbers, inchoately connected through a clumsy cell structure, and intermittently funnelled instructions from leaders in Malaya and Indonesia, were in a weak position to "control" a mass party such as the Barisan was from its foundation in mid-1961.

On the other hand, they did have key MCP cadres such as Chan Sun Wing inside the PAP, and later in the Barisan Sosialis (to which he defected in 1961). The MCP was also used to cooperating with a range of politicians including Lee Kuan Yew himself (hence having members within the PAP from 1954, and Lee meeting Fang as the "Plen" several times). Furthermore, prestige attached to the communists for their wartime resistance to Japan, for post-war political and union struggles against the British, and for communism's role in liberation movements around the world. In the context of worldwide anti-colonial struggle, this meant that they could influence, if not set, the tone of Barisan Sosialis policy from its formation in mid-1961, and could compete to win over members of the "progressive" left to actual party membership.

Despite their tendency to talk of "communists", Special Branch sometimes saw the likes of Lim Chin Siong as also "under strong communist influence" rather than as members. The language employed by British and federal representatives was elastic, reflecting the reality that Lim and many others had a Marxist frame of reference, and shared with communists the willingness to act as part of united fronts and to resort to direct action if constitutional means failed.[56] British Commissioner for Southeast Asia Lord Selkirk believed, in 1961–1962, that Lim would not necessarily incline towards the Soviet Union and China if he won power, and might keep to constitutional means in the meanwhile. For a while in 1961–1962, Selkirk was therefore reluctant to sanction arrests of Lim and his associates, arrests sought first by UMNO representatives within Singapore's Internal Security Council, and in late 1962 by PAP representatives too.[57]

The Barisan was, then, a "progressive" left party in its own eyes which — like the early PAP — overlapped communism at its extremes. Its journal *The Plebeian* and many members conceived of themselves as part of a worldwide, anti-colonial, "progressive" trend which included communists.[58] The Barisan tried to position itself as the party that truly represented the working classes (notably the Chinese working classes) in opposition to the now overwhelmingly bourgeois (and mainly English-educated) topmost leadership of the PAP, and jostled to control the labour movement.[59]

This label of "progressive" left — which identified people with world-wide anti-colonialism, socialism, and campaigns in places such as Algeria — was arguably the key one for many. The way merger with a highly conservative Malayan Federation seemed to be foisted on them from 1961–1963, and subsequently the mass arrests under Operation Cold Store of February 1963, further radicalised the Barisan. In other words, Operation Cold Store was possibly as much the cause of Barisan's radicalisation and willingness to consider extra parliamentary methods — such as protests and strikes — as the consequence. From their viewpoint, events from Cold Store to 1966 gradually confirmed there was little or no scope for them to pursue their aims through meaningful parliamentary politics. Hence, their final Barisan withdrawal from Parliament in 1966 to take to street protest, which then led to further arrests.

The way the "progressive" left wing shaded into communism, and the fact that Singapore has never ended the conflict with the MCP, have made it difficult for people to talk openly about their views of communism. Hence, for instance, Michael Fernandez and Loh Kah Seng have written an intriguing chapter on post-war unionism, which nevertheless fails to grapple with the issues of unionists' actual relationships to communists, and communism.[60] This means that an ironic result of the PAP's refusal to make a final peace with the MCP, is possibly that the PAP and public are denied full information on the real extent of many people's communist sympathies and connections.

An additional result of the struggle for survival in the 1950s–1960s was that it endowed the PAP and the Singapore state with a set of discourses, or ways of thinking about, whether or not people were "communist" or "subversive". Given the fluidity of the left wing, and yet equally real danger of entryism and subversion of Singapore parties, the PAP needed ways of classifying some people as beyond the pale. How could they do this?

The case of Lim Chin Siong is instructive. For *Men in White*, Lee Kuan Yew revealed that the Internal Security Department had records that Lim Chin Siong "met the Plen three times", once in 1961. Lee continues, "These revelations showed that even though Lim denied he was a communist, he did make contact with the communist underground and that he collaborated with pro-communist PAP assemblymen in a bid to topple the PAP government in 1961." In fact, this does not prove that Lim was doing any more than Lee himself, meeting the Plen in order to be aware of and take advantage of MCP policy.[61] The more interesting claims come from Chan Wun Sing, the ex-PAP and Barisan member who became a full MCP member in the late 1960s. He claims that Lim was close to becoming a party member when his contact disappeared. Lee concludes from such evidence that Lim was not only in contact with, but also "taking orders" from the MCP. Again, given that Lee himself met the Plen, and that Lim Chin Siong also made sure he met Lord Selkirk, Britain's regional Commissioner, in mid-1961, this is a non-sequitur. The most that can be said from this is that Lim saw himself as a member of the "progressive" left wing, inspired by events in China and willing to work alongside communists, and that though he may or may not have considered joining the party formally, he almost certainly did not. However, the discussion in *Men in White* is perhaps more instructive on how the PAP categorised people, and so framed Cold War history. This suggests a gap between people's subjective classification of themselves, and the PAP view of their "objective" status.

People on the left seem able to conceive of themselves as progressive, Marxist, or Anti-British without being necessarily "communist". Lee Kuan Yew by comparison classifies as a communist anyone "who took orders from either the communist party or its affiliates". Though apparently tight as a definition, he then states in *Men in White* that Lim was "taking orders", though the only overt evidence for this is that Lim met the Plen. If that is the level of proof required, the distinction becomes potentially meaningless and dangerous. Proximity and meetings do not constitute "taking orders".

Former PAP Organising Secretary and Home Affairs Minister Ong Pang Boon, meanwhile, also appears to start with a tight definition of a communist, as "one who swore allegiance to MCP and was a card-carrying member of the party or its communist organizations". That is very clear. But when it comes to Lim, we find a far more elastic approach. Hence, *Men in White* states that Ong accepted that Lim might not be a card-carrying member, "but by his actions and speeches in the 1950s, he sounded like a communist and he supported communist objectives".[62] The latter suggests a more communist-style approach to categorisation. That is, following Marx, communists distinguish between people's subjective position (what they think they are) and their objective position (how they act, and its practical effect). Hence, it may be that neither Lim's — nor by extension other people's — formal party position, nor their subjective beliefs, are in themselves the deciding factors in whether a person is labelled "communist". Rather, the questions are whether they have any proximity, which can be interpreted as "taking orders", and if their actions are deemed to have objectively "supported communist objectives".

On the PAP side, faced with MCP entryism, such tough criteria possibly seemed justified in the 1950s to 1960s. People were not going to simply admit to membership of an illegal organisation, which was still waging guerrilla warfare in Malaya. On the other side, however, it meant that a progressive left-wing politician or unionist could all too easily be categorised "communist". This then made them vulnerable to detention without trial. Lim Chin Siong himself went to his grave denying he was ever a communist, and the evidence — thus far — proves only that he maintained contact with communists, and shared much of their worldview.

Our main interest here is not whether Lim could be classified a communist, but the way the PAP and Singapore state classified people, and thus "framed" this period of history. This shaping of the PAP by the 1950s–1960s struggle extended beyond mere attitudes: it rewrote the very DNA of the party. Hence, it became, in 1958, a cadre party like the MCP, in which the Central Executive Committee (CEC) selected cadres, who helped to select the CEC. Its very structure was dictated by the need to defeat entryism, or a left-wing mass membership "capturing" the party. Even so, the party was severely damaged by desertions when the Barisan Sosialis was formed in 1961.

The cadre system, and the use of loose criteria to label people "subversive" then outlived the period of significant communist entryism into the PAP.[63] This survival may in turn go some way to explaining the arrest of Catholic social activists in May 1987 as "Marxists", regardless of their claimed, subjective position. Their use of social action to influence society and labour conditions had been, to PAP eyes, Marxist (class-based and extra-parliamentary) subversion, as well as "subversive" of the state's ability to manage society and economics. These tendencies survived the end of the Cold War in 1989–1991. While Malaysia and Thailand signed peace terms with the remaining communist insurgents in 1989, Singapore did not.

This Cold War echo continues to "frame" the PAP understanding of recent history. This can be seen in *Men in White* (2009). This was written by a team of journalists seconded from the government-controlled *Straits Times*, giving it quasi-official status. This book falls into a number of traditions. First, that of journalists claiming to present all sides of the story, while adopting PAP categorisation, ranging back to Lee's press secretary Alex Josey, through Dennis Bloodworth, to this present-day creation. Such works include interviews with or about "opposition", but tend to paraphrase these or frame them as respondents to the main PAP story. Second, therefore, it belongs to the tradition of allowing PAP opposition to speak but mainly in relation to the PAP story rather than of their own plans, ideals and visions for Singapore. This second tradition is cemented by PAP guardianship of sources. The authors are given privileged access to official sources, and both these and the oral histories used are not made publicly available, or only selectively so after publication of the quasi-official version. Combined with the lack of any regular, and regularised, release of state papers, this means that fully balanced, academic source analysis and construction of alternative interpretations is rendered impossible. Thus, *Men in White* undoubtedly gives greater insight into the right-wing PAP's enemies, but mediates their testimony mostly as paraphrase, and "frames" it as part of a story of PAP "Heroes" overcoming people who followed communist orders and communalist instincts.

This issue of Cold War framing is vital not just to individual reputations, but also to how significant events are viewed, such as Operation Cold Store of February 1963. Initially, the British Commissioner for Singapore, Lord Selkirk, had been sceptical of the case for arrests. The British move towards accepting detentions came in 1962, and more for political than security reasons. The Malayans demanded arrests in Singapore before the planned merger, and the Brunei revolt of December 1962 provided the pretext for these. In February 1963, the PAP leadership then ensured that over a hundred of the left — more than Kuala Lumpur or Britain initially thought justified — were detained in Operation Cold Store. Perhaps the most glaring omission of *Men in White* is any serious analysis of the events immediately surrounding Operation Cold Store, or any space for alternative voices on Operation Spectrum: the arrest of 16 "Marxist" social activists (later widened to 22) in 1987.[64] There is, therefore, a real clash between the PAP presentation of merger as a necessary move opposed by opportunists following MCP orders, and the Barisan interpretation of merger as an opportunistic move by the PAP right wing, in order to crush the left. There is also a fundamental difference over whether the people arrested from 1961–1966 were "communist" and subversive, or (for some at least) progressive left-wingers willing to use strikes and protests as well as Parliament. The point here is not whether one side or the other is wrong, but that these represent very different ways of "framing" key events.

To be fair, there were other dividing lines than communist/non-communist. Lee Kuan Yew had a radical conception of the supremacy of Parliament, one which did not allow for challenge of its decisions and right to govern whether by union action or other non-parliamentary sources of power.

Over time, increasing numbers of people have started to challenge the PAP framing of the Cold War period. By around 1999 to 2001, a range of such people — veterans of mid-century politics, ex-detainees, academics seeking a more varied view of the past — was beginning a process of recovering suppressed and self-censored voices.

Two of the earliest such alternative readings concerned Lim Chin Siong — PAP co-founder, who in 1961 became Lee's enemy when he left the PAP to help found the breakaway Barisan Sosialis Party and oppose the specific form of merger the PAP were pushing for.[65] These two works included a chapter on Lim Chin Siong, and the book *Comet in Our Sky*, in which ex-detainees and colleagues such as Tan Jing Quee joined academics to try and give a glimpse of Lim's life and beliefs.[66]

What the proponents of this compensatory history have in common is that they all suggest that within the overall PAP-driven framework, there should be a greater range of "Makers and Keepers of Singapore History", and a greater range of "voices". "Makers and Keepers of Singapore History" was the title of a journal special edition in 2007, a 2008 workshop, and a 2010 book.[67] This "new wave" of history gathered support from a range of young Singaporean schoolteachers — doctoral candidates, schoolteachers and from the arts and university world — who launched an online journal in 2007: *S/pores* (http://s-pores.com).[68] In reality, this "new wave", including contributors to *S/pores* had much broader interests than merely the left wing, embracing amongst other things culture, the arts and popular history. From the beginning, however, *S/pores* gave a great deal of its space to oral history of the left and ex-detainees, and commentaries on these. It included accounts, for instance, of the 1954 trial of University of Malaya socialists over an article on "Aggression in Asia" in their journal *Fajar*.

S/pore's focus reflected a flowering of forums and publications on and by the left. Its coverage of the *Fajar* trial, for instance, was followed in 2010 by Poh Soo Kai, Tan Jing Quee and Koh Kay Yew publishing *The Fajar Generation: The University Socialist Club of Malaya and the Politics of Postwar Malaya and Singapore* (Petaling Jaya: SIRD). In *The Fajar Generation*, ex-detainees such as Poh Soo Kai and Dr. Lim Hock Siew directly challenge PAP interpretations of them as communist, and suggest their own rationale for opposing merger in 1961–1962, and their own progressive socialist mentality. The book also portrays the essentially socialist and anti-colonial radicalism of the University of Malaya Socialist Club of 1953–1972. Tan Jing Quee *et al*.'s *The May 13 Generation* does the same job for the Chinese Middle School Students, explaining how a generation of Chinese-educated students saw themselves as bearing intellectual, social, cultural and political responsibilities: which just happened to find expression in a range of "progressive", "anti-British" and leftist activities. They were as passionately "anti-Yellow Culture" (denoting degraded media including the pornographic) as anti-British. We too easily forget now how such young men were amongst the most highly educated vanguard of a Chinese-speaking generation whose education had been vitiated by war and the Japanese Occupation: what NTU sociologist Kwok Kian Woon has called the "otherness" of their past.[69] They felt a burden of responsibility to lead as intellectuals and activists, and what we have in English thus far is merely the tip of a vast Chinese-language iceberg of their publications and memories.[70]

As of writing in 2010 to early 2012, further memoirs (in Chinese) were being prepared. So too were additional English-language books: on Lim Chin Siong (a biography by Kevin Tan); and on, *The University of Malaya Socialist Club and the Contest for Malaya* (edited by Loh Kah Seng, Edgar Liao, Lim Cheng Tju and Seng Guo Qian).

Some scholars have questioned whether this trend might go too far, and "romanticise" even violent subversives. Ong Wei Chong, then a Research Fellow at the Rajaratnam School of International Studies, pointed out that the MCP did wage guerrilla warfare from 1948–1989, and set off explosive devices even in 1970s Singapore. The threat of violence was by no means imaginary. In reality, however, many if not most of the broad left whose stories are being told were not espousing actual violence. In addition, the Malaysian case shows that any such tendency towards romanticising violence is soon more than countered by the memories of those who suffered it. A stream of memoirs of insurgents, from two books on Chin Peng in 2003–2004 onwards — there set off equally robust responses from veterans and Malay politicians.[71]

This oral history and memoir work sometimes does, in brief moments, escape the gravitational pull of the "Singapore Story", to offer glimpses of non-PAP actors, ideas and motivations on their own terms, in their own voices. Hence Fong Chong Pik's memoirs (Fang Chuang Pi) convey how passionately he believed in the 1950s–1960s that only the communists might effectively oppose and reform "the darkness of colonial society". They also convey the sense in which young Chinese-educated students felt themselves to be intellectuals with a responsibility to lead society, in the tradition of Chinese student radicalism of the previous half century.[72]

These "alternative histories" are also seen by some as a potential path to political healing, an idea expressed in a 26 February 2006 "Detention-Healing-Writing Forum" in Singapore. At this, ex-detainees described the torment of detention with no known date of release or trial, and the healing power of writing and discussing their experiences. Michael Fernandez, for instance, both claimed he had been a genuine unionist trying to help the Singapore Harbour Union — "the rice-bowl of 11,000 workers and their families" — before his arrest in 1964, and that he wrote on toilet paper in detention, as he was denied writing paper. For him, writing, having his own voice, was and is vital. Considering that the longest detentions (Dr. Lim Hock Siew and Chia Thye Poh) ran to two decades or more, and were only terminated with conditions, the significance of such work is obvious.

But the Ministry of Home Affairs declined the theme of political healing through writing, restating its opinion (in a letter to the *Straits Times* of 8 March 2006) that men such as Michael Fernandez were "communists", who if unchecked would have threatened Singapore's stability.[73] Since then, some political videos have been banned, and in 2010, the National Library of Singapore insisted that ex-detainee Vincent Cheng be removed from the list of speakers for a public forum on history organised by the NUS History Society. Vincent Cheng was one of the 22 — including lawyers and Catholic social activists — arrested for an alleged "Marxist" conspiracy in 1987. The government had accused him of "carrying out Tan Wah Piow's instructions to build up a mass-based united front of grassroots organizations in Singapore to oppose the government, by violent means, if necessary".[74] The alleged mastermind, Tan Wah Piow, continued to deny there was any such thing, or that he supported communism, and to insist that he merely corresponded with people about how to seek change for Singapore through democratic means. More to the point, he and others argued that using the Internal Security Act when there was no imminent security threat, rather than the courts, denied basic justice. It removed people's opportunity to defend their actions as within the law.[75]

In addition, Goh Chok Tong later told interviewers that "Some were conscious of what they were doing. Many [of the others] had their own ideas of what was good for Singapore but they were not fully aware that they were being manipulated by other people". Author Michael Barr was informed by one ex-detainee that he had been urged to admit he was "an unconscious conspirator". Together, such evidence suggests that the approach of labelling some opponents "objective" subversives or communists — the Cold War mode — was at play again.[76] In this sort of Orwellian context, a person's subjective identity and aims were not necessarily a defence.[77]

Clearly, there were still limits to Government toleration, especially where the possibility of ex-detainees discussing detention itself, or denying the basis of their detention, arose. But even the act of holding such a meeting was unprecedented. From its formation in 1966, the Singapore Ex-Political Detainees' Association had acted as a control on what ex-detainees could do. That ex-detainees would address a public meeting of more than 200 in 2006 was evidence of the state's increased willingness to tolerate discussion at the margins.[78] In addition, the internet was making policing of information increasingly difficult. You can ban an individual from making an article or film, but once it is already on the internet, it is almost impossible to prevent its circulation. Martyn See's video of ex-detainee Lim Hock Siew speaking was banned in 2009, but only after more than 40,000 people had seen it, and it had gone viral.[79]

As of 2011, the recent wave of "alternative" history was, therefore, tolerated rather than endorsed by the state. It is variously a set of "reclamation" activities for lost voices and previously suppressed or self-censored accounts, a project to recapture the "dynamic and idealistic culture of political contestation and pluralism" of the 1940s–1960s,[80] a restoration of reputations and "societal memories", a cry for the recognition of the harshness if not "injustice" of detention and for the removal of impediments to liberal democracy, and an attitude of alertness versus perceived "Singapore Story" distortions of history. I say alertness because *Men in White* was reviewed soon after its 2009 publication, both in a public forum and on *S/pores*. These reviews claimed that the book downplayed crucial episodes (Operation Cold Store), ignored alternative views (the Barisan's own reasons for opposing merger at the time), stereotyped the party's triumphant right wing as heroic men of principle, and its opposition as weakly following communist orders, and generally framed events in the traditional "Singapore Story". While accepting the book as a riveting

read which did give additional coverage to PAP opponents, they nevertheless tried to out what they saw as its narrative devices, biases, and
omissions.[81] Indeed, if anything, the criticism failed to acknowledge that
Men in White probably went as far as could be expected — in the context
of its time and authors — to acknowledge the left-wing contributions to
Singapore history, including: providing the initial mass base for the PAP;
putting crucial pressure on the British to accelerate concessions; and by
its example and competition forcing the right wing to try and "outleft the
left" in social and housing programmes in dedication and selflessness.[82]

It seems as if a kind of stalemate has come about, in which "alternative" views of recent political history dominate non-state sites on the
internet, and seep into the state-dominated media in a limited and ambi-
valent way,[83] while the government keeps a tighter lid on state papers,*
insists its framing of the Cold War period is the only valid one, and with-
holds adequate documentation for re-examination. In some ways, this
situation works to the government's advantage. It focuses debate onto the
radical left and ex-detainees per se, and away from other "alternative
paths" and issues such as those of liberalism, the rights of the individual,
the case for reform or abolition of the Internal Security Act, the scope of
civil society, and the relative distribution of benefits in society.[84] It presents Singapore's post-war history — and by implication present — as
a choice between bad communism and communalism on the one hand,
and good technocractic PAP rule on the other, rather than as a myriad
of ideas, experiments and options of all kinds. That deflects attention
from the new wave historians' much broader agenda of putting all areas
of life (culture as much as politics) and all levels of society (from the impoverished to the politician) back into the picture. As such, this issue of
how to frame just a few crucial decades of Singapore's history remains
highly contested, and highly relevant to contemporary politics, society,
and security.

Conclusion: The Postmodern Condition and the History of Singapore

This chapter does not claim to be comprehensive, but rather to locate
Mary Turnbull's work as one of many different actual and possible

---

*Singapore does not release departmental papers on a 25- or 30-year rule as in
Australia and Britain respectively, let alone have the kinds of "Freedom of Information" regulations enjoyed there and in the United States.

"framings" of Singapore history. There are other frames which have had to be omitted. For instance, Singapore not as a coherent place in itself, but rather as a kind of nexus for different networks and flows: rather like the point on a Venn diagram where all circles overlap. This is an approach hinted at by Catherine Paix's work on Singapore-China interactions, and Mark Frost's work on "Nanyang" networks.[85] Alternatively, Philip Holden has talked about the way gender, and emplotment, are used to shape narratives about Singapore.[86]

What I have tried to show is not, therefore, the totality of ways in which the island's history could be framed, but rather a challenging selection of them, and through that selection the "postmodern" condition of Singapore's history. That is, we have a plethora of voices, framings and perspectives, sometimes even for a single main event. It is almost impossible to combine all these in a single work, or module. In analysis, the first question needs perhaps to be how the account has been framed, and how else it could have been framed. In writing and teaching, the problem is how to offer a coherent course or suite of courses, while also making students engage with a range of these framing devices. Mary Turnbull defended to the end the need for a fairly traditional, chronologically structured account of Singapore's history, and as a result, left one of the most reliable, and cited, accounts of Singapore. But Mary herself, along with many other historians of the island, actually adopted different frames for different works. So what would a "postmodern" history course or text look like?

The world of heritage and museums may offer some clues. Hence, for instance, the number of museums has multiplied in Singapore from the 1990s onwards, with the two Asian Civilisations Museum locations giving, on the one hand, a broad and long duration view of Asian cultures which form the foundation of Singapore, and on the other of their blending in Singapore in Peranakan culture in the 19th to 20th centuries.

The increasing diversity of museums in itself suggests a postmodern condition, in which any one text or institution can only hope to capture part of the story. The National Museum of Singapore tried additional tactics when it reopened in December 2006, with a new "Singapore History Gallery". This featured two pathways (connected at regular intervals): an "events path" of central events and well-known national figures; and a "Personal Path" of varying voices: both knitted together using artefacts, some oral history, and commentary from an audio guide. In one sense, this retains the strong narrative thread that Turnbull felt readers needed as a spine. On the other, it enables us to see history as the combination of distinct cultures, groups, and projects coming together, and even forming history as the dialectic: the clash of their opposing aims and narratives. The sheer variety of choices on which numbered artefacts to press for audio-commentary on, and how far to pursue that commentary, also gives the visitor some opportunity to shape how they experience the gallery. No two visits need be exactly the same.

Weaving diaries and oral history interviews alongside artefacts also allows an element of "history from the underside" to creep in.[87] Finally, the inclusion of some of history's "losers", such as a Fong Swee Suan interview, hints at further approach, which is made good use of until the post-1965 period. That is the museum not as a narrator or instructor, but as an "argument" or discussion place, where different voices and perspectives might be deliberately juxtaposed.[88] Furthermore, the same approach is reflected in the follow-up book, that is Mark Frost and Yu-Me Balasingamchow's *Singapore: A Biography* (Singapore: Editions Didier Millet for the National Museum of Singapore, 2009). That book's narrative reflects the new emphasis on a full 700 years of history (including the period 1611–1819), and also interweaves images of artefacts and interviews into a multi-vocal narration.

All this contrasts quite sharply with the previous history of the museum. Its ancestry can be back to the Raffles Library and Museum set up in 1849, with the museum given separate existence in 1887. That had been a museum in the imperial mould, collecting a wider range of natural history as well as human history from the Malayan region and beyond, including a large whale skeleton that graced the museum into the postwar period. Latterly natural history had been split off, and the museum given a nationalist twist as the Singapore History Museum (1993–2003). That version had featured galleries for paintings and other types of display, but its main history gallery had featured "The Dioramas: A Visual History of Singapore". Using models, these 20 or so vignettes started with "Ruins of Ancient Settlement on Fort Canning Hill, 1823 [excavation scene]", worked through 19th-century growth and life, and finished with the first post-independence meeting of Parliament, on 8 December 1965. After three year's redevelopment (2003–2006), the Museum reopened in 2006 as the National Museum of Singapore, with the new multimedia history gallery being just the most dramatic of several, including others on life stories, food and film.[89]

What I am suggesting is that museums in Singapore, in their diversification and new approaches, are a metaphor for the "postmodernisation" of Singapore's history, with innumerable ways of "framing" it. History teaching at university level has likewise tried to accommodate some of this new diversity of framings, whether by single courses which embody different approaches at NIE and NTU, or by a variety of distinct nation-building, "Global City", "Cultural" and other courses at NUS. Whether or not this condition could be reflected in a new text on Singapore history is a moot question. Could a single narrative thread be combined with boxed pages giving "alternatives", "voices from the underside" and more?[90] Should a text "out" its framing devices — Sundaland, central Southeast Asian, Straits, Malayan, Singaporean and others — and discuss alternatives? Should the "Singapore Story", like that in the Hong Kong Museum of History, commence with galleries on "Natural Environment", the "Prehistoric" period and "The Dynasties" (for Singapore, meaning the Melaka Sultanate and EIC), featuring life-sized models?[91] How can a balance be struck between the Rankean history of things that bind and create a state and nation, and a sense of place, diversity and contestation? At the least, being aware of the possibility of framing "Singapore" history in vastly different ways liberates. The question is no longer "Do you understand the 'Singapore Story'", but rather "Which 'Singapore Story'?", or "How can we accommodate different ways of framing Singapore's past?".

Notes

1. C.M. Turnbull, *A History of Singapore* (Singapore: Oxford University Press, 1989), Preface, pp. vii–viii, xii.

2. K.G. Tregonning, *A History of Modern Malaysia and Singapore* (Singapore: Eastern Universities Press, 1972). See discussion of how these works meshed with the state-sponsored story in Derek Heng Thiam Soon, "From Political Rhetoric to National History: Bi-Culturalism and Hybridisation in the Constitution of Singapore's Historical Narrative", in *Reframing Singapore*, ed. Derek Heng and Syed Muhd. Khairudin Aljunied, pp. 24–5.

3. Kwa Chong Guan, "Singapura as a Central Place in Malay History and Identity", in *Singapore from Temasek to the 21st Century: Reiventing the Global City*, ed. Karl Hack and Jean-Louis Margolin, with Karine Delaye (Singapore: NUS Press, 2010), pp. 133–54.

4. Turnbull, *A History of Singapore*, p. xii.

5. There were also a handful of Chinese when Raffles arrived in 1819.

6. Personal copies of NIE exam papers from 2000–2005, and course descriptions from NIE, NTU and NUS.

7. USE2304, Singapore Studies, "Singapore: The Making of a Nation", at http://www.usp.nus.edu.sg/soc_eco_pol/use2304/index.html. This did lack

significant pre-1819 components, but included lectures on the nature of history, "Ethnicity and Multiracialism" and "Nation under Globalization" at the other.

8. See especially Karl Hack and Jean-Louis Margolin, "Singapore: Reinventing the Global City", in *Singapore from Temasek to the 21st Century*, ed. Hack and Margolin, with Delaye, pp. 3–36.

9. Author's notes and programme from "Rethinking Singapore History by C.M. Turnbull, Kwa Chong Guan and Hong Lysa", Asian Research Institute Seminar, National University of Singapore, 7 February 2006.

10. Turnbull, *A History of Modern Singapore*, pp. xi–xii.

11. C.M. Turnbull, "Penang's Changing Role in the Straits Settlements, 1826–1946", in *Penang and its Region: the Story of an Entrepôt*, ed. Yeoh Seng Guan, Loh Wei Leng, Khoo Salma Nasution, and Neil Khor (Singapore: NUS Press, 2009).

12. Turnbull, *The Straits Settlements*, p. 3.

13. Wang Gungwu and Anthony Reid discussed this at a workshop on "Southeast Asian History: Styles, Directions and Drivers", Asia Research Institute and Department of History, NUS, 25 September 2002. See also Karl Hack, "The Malayan Trajectory in Singapore's History", in *Singapore from Temasek to the 21st Century*, ed. Hack and Margolin, with Delaye (Singapore: NUS Press, 2010), pp. 243–91.

14. Ernest Koh Wee Song, "Ignoring 'History from Below': A People's History in the Historiography of Singapore", *History Compass* 5/1 (2007): 11–25. Also available as Chapter 1 of his University of Murdoch thesis, "Singapore Stories — Language and Class in Singapore: An Investigation into the Implications of English Literacy as a Life Chance among the Ethnic Chinese of Singapore from 1945 to 1980," University of Western Australia, 2007, at http://theses.library.uwa.edu.au/adt-WU2007.0196/public/02whole.pdf [accessed November 2010].

15. You could claim that de facto the Straits Settlement ended in 1942 with the Japanese Occupation, but it was only formally ended in April 1946, with the formation of the Colony of Singapore and the Malayan Union. The scale is what matters here, not the precise basis of calculation and resulting number.

16. The museum — which ultimately traces its ancestry back to the Raffles Library and Museum set up in 1849 and given separate existence as a museum in 1887 — reopened in December 2006 with a name change from the Singapore History Museum (1993–2003) to the National Museum of Singapore, with the new multimedia history gallery being just the most dramatic of several including others on life stories, food and film. *National Museum of Singapore Guide* (Singapore: Editions Millet, 2007).

17. Lee Kuan Yew announced that he would retire as Minister Mentor (and Goh Chok Tong that he would retire as Senior Minister) on 14 May 2011, following PAP losses in the general elections of 7 May 2011. The opposition

Workers Party had won one Single Member Constituency, and one five-member Group Representation Constituency (Aljunied), which together with two out of three Non Constituency MPs (selected from the highest polling losers) gave them eight out of 90 members of the new Parliament. The PAP voted had fallen to just over 60%, with its margin in several constituencies now slender. The critical point, however, was probably the perception that the electorate (especially younger votes) had become notably more critical of disciplining and warnings about opposition more associated with the PAP "old guard", and more demanding of a responsive style of governance and politics.

18. This section on the "Singapore Story" is taken from Karl Hack and Jean-Louis Margolin, "Singapore: Reinventing the Global City", in *Singapore from Temasek to the 21st Century*, ed. Hack and Margolin, with Delaye, p. 6.

19. Hong Lysa and Huang Juanli, *The Scripting of a National History: Singapore and Its Pasts* (Singapore: NUS Press, 2008).

20. While helping to fill in important moments in the "Singapore Story" such as merger and separation, these books nevertheless have their origins in painstaking academic approaches. See works by NUS historians Tan Tai Yong, *Creating 'Greater Malaysia': Decolonization and the Politics of Merger* (Singapore: ISEAS, 2008); and Albert Lau, *A Moment of Anguish: Singapore in Malaysia and the Politics of Disengagement* (Singapore: Times Academic Press, 2008). They tend to use western archives (especially British) intensively, and draw on Singapore perspectives. Partly due to a perceived difficulty in accessing relevant Malaysian archives, the latter's perspectives tend to be less well represented.

21. *The History of Singapore*, Discovery Channel, shown in Singapore on 4 December, repeated 5, 12, 19 December 2005; related Singapore Heritage Society-Asia Research Institute Forum of 13 December 2005; and Zakir Hussain, "Singapore's Past Rehashed", *Straits Times*, 12 December 2005.

22. See Hack, "The Malayan Trajectory"; C.J.W-L Wee, "The Vanquished: Lim Chin Siong and a Progressivist National Narrative", in *Lee's Lieutenants: Singapore's Old Guard*, ed. Lam Peng Er and Kevin Tan (New South Wales: Allen & Unwin, 1999), pp. 169–90; and Tan Jing Quee and K.S. Jomo, *Comet in Our Sky: Lim Chin Siong in History* (Kuala Lumpur: INSAN, 2001).

23. Personal notes, but as of 2010 still online at http://www.nie.edu.sg/itt_hb/web/babsc03/em.html; and http://www3.ntu.edu.sg/OAS2/nanyangbulletin/nb0607/nyb_design_finaldraft2/P3-09NIE/NTU-P3-09NIE.html.

24. This refers to the "Essential Module" for students studying a Bachelor of Arts and intending to teach Arts subjects. Science trainees were offered a different module.

25. HH203 History of Singapore. The course lecturer and content can change, but under Loh Kah Seng, it took a critical look at the 200- versus 700-year and Singapore Story debates, and covered politics, opium, urban change

and people's history. The School of Humanities and Social Sciences History Minor commenced 2006–2007. Previously NIE history modules were available to NTU students.

26. As of 2011, NTU was committed to beginning a History Major programme from 2012 or soon after, having started offering minors in Academic Year 2006/7. The emphasis was intended to be less Asia-centric, and more on Asia in global and transnational perspective. *Straits Times*, 18 November 2011, p. A6.

27. For a full study of this theme, see Karl Hack and Kevin Blackburn, *War Memory and the Making of Modern Malaysia and Singapore* (Singapore: NUS Press, 2012).

28. The book referred to is Lam Peng Er and Kevin Tan's path-breaking edited work, *Lee's Lieutenants: Singapore's Old Guard* (New South Wales: Allen & Unwin, 1999), which also started the process of resurfacing academic study of the "losers" such as Lim Chin Siong (see C.J.W.-L. Wee's article in the same). Thereafter, of course, many of this generation have had biographies published, or issued their own memoirs (notably in a procession of books issued by the Institute of Southeast Asian Studies under the directorship of K. Kesavapany). These tell the story on their own terms. See, for instance, Irene Ng, *The Singapore Lion: A Biography of S. Rajaratnam* (Singapore: ISEAS, 2010), Kwa Chong Guan, ed., *S. Rajaratnam on Singapore: From Ideas to Reality* (Singapore: World Scientific, 2007), and S.R. Nathan's *An Unexpected Journey: Path to the Presidency* (Singapore: Editions Dider Millet, 2011).

29. "Digging Deeper", *Straits Times*, 6 April 2009, p. B4.

30. Stephen Oppenheimer, *Eden in the East: The Drowned Continent of Southeast Asia* (London: Weidenfeld and Nicolson, 1998), p. 10.

31. Pedro Soares, Jean Alain Trejaut, Jun-Hun Loo *et al.*, "Climate Change and Postglacial Human Dispersals in Southeast Asia", *Molecular Biology and Evolution* 25, 6 (2008): 1209–18.

32. For similar conclusions based on "Quatamary stratigraphy, sea-level history and detailed bathymetry", see M.I. Bird, W.C. Pang and K. Lambeck, "The Age and Origins of the Straits of Singapore", *Palaeogeography, Palaeoclimatology, Palaeoecology* 241, 3–4 (2006): 531–8.

33. Karl Hack and Kevin Blackburn, *Did Singapore Have to Fall? Churchill and the Impregnable* Fortress (London: Routledge, 2004), pp. 12–3, 79–81.

34. Singapore National Archives: Coroners Records, 15 February 1904, on the death of Siamese woman Lim Ah Hiap, wife of Planter and Christian Yao Ah Son of 9¾ Mile Jurong Road. He returned to find his wife's throat cut and her face gashed by his own *parang*.

35. See Kwa Chong Guan, "Singapura as a Central Place in Malay History and Identity", in *Singapore from Temasek to the 21st Century*, ed. Hack and Margolin, with Delaye, pp. 133–54.

36. Singapore National Archives: Coroners Records, 19 January 1905, on death of a Macao female named Choo See at No. 1-A Upper Chin Chew Street on 19 January. Despite the gambling, witnesses described the deceased as "a good, quiet woman". Common causes of death at this time included accidents around the docks, boats and ships.

37. See, for example, Turnbull, *A History of Modern Singapore 1819–2005*, pp. 116ff for Lim Boon Keng, and pp. 155ff for prominent Arab families.

38. Peter Rimmer, Lenore Manderson and Colin Barlow, "The Underside of Malaysian History", in *The Underside of Malaysian History: Pullers, Prostitutes, Plantation Workers...*, ed. Peter Rimmer and Lisa Allen (Singapore: Singapore University Press, 1990), p. 3. History from below suggests not just history *of* underclasses, but *from their perspective*. See Karl Hack, "Sex and Empire", in Open University, *A326 Empire: 1492–1975*, Block 4 (Milton Keynes: Open University, 2009), pp. 271–311.

39. See the entry on Ladurie in Marnie Hughes-Warrington, *Fifty Key Thinkers in History* (London: Routledge, 2000), pp. 194–201; and his *Montaillou* (London: Penguin edition, 2002).

40. The Singapore National Archives notionally can release papers after 25 years, but in fact, the process seems somewhat arbitrary, with no presumption of automatic release bar papers screened for security and other reasons, as in other advanced countries, let alone any Freedom of Information rules. See Loh Kah Seng and Liew Kai Khiun, *The Makers and Keepers of Singapore History* (Singapore: Singapore Heritage Society and Ethos Books, 2011). This collection of papers originated in a 10 November 2008 Workshop of the same name at Singapore's Asian Research Institute, with some papers appearing in a special edition of *Tangent* 6, 2 (2007).

41. Chua Ai Lin and Mark Emmanuel introduced a course on the Cultural History of Singapore at the National University of Singapore, though by the time this book was completed, the latter had left NUS.

42. See AAH 103, "Singapore: the Making of a Global City". This appears to drop oral history and people's history, but includes pre-1819, a heritage, and approaches some of the traditional post-war topics from an "alternatives" perspective, for example: "Political Alternatives? — The Malayan Communist Party, Trade Unions and Student Movement". It also gives scope for using any of the different approaches via student topic choice for a term paper. In addition, Kwa Chong Guan *et al.*'s *Singapore: A 700-Year History* shares pride of place on the reading list with Turnbull, Carl Trocki (*Singapore: Wealth, Power and the Culture of Control* [London: Routledge, 2006]), Edwin Lee (*Singapore: The Unexpected Nation* [Singapore: ISEAS, 2008]), and Ernest Chew and Edwin Lee, eds. (*A History of Singapore* [Singapore: Oxford University Press, 1991]).

43. Carl Trocki, *Opium and Empire: Chinese Society in Colonial Singapore, 1800–1910* (Ithaca, NY: Cornell University Press, 1990), and *Opium, Empire and the*

Global Political Economy: A Study of the Asian Opium Trade, 1750–1950 (London: Routledge, 1999).

44. Course outline for AAH103, "The Making of a Global City", at http://www. hsse.nie.edu.sg/courseList/BA/aah103.htm [accessed 11 November 2011].

45. The quotation is taken from a video made by Martyn See, who had previous videos banned. I accessed and used this only outside of Singapore. The video contains a simple evocation, in the gentle tones of a now elderly man, of the psychological horror of unlimited detention without trial, and of pressure techniques such as prolonged solitary isolation. This is more powerful coming from a man who accepted continued detention rather than compromise socialist principles. In his words, "A life without convictions, without idealism, is a mere meaningless existence". That claim hits at the heart of the PAP's contention, that the threat to society and development is such that more abstract individual rights and natural justice may be tempered, albeit within the "rule of law". Martyn See has taken down the video, but it was freely available at http://vimeo.com/13319568 [accessed 10 November 2010], and other sites.

46. Taken from an online account of the launch of Teo Soh Lung's *The Blue Gate*, at http://theonlinecitizen.com/2010/06/an-open-wound/ [accessed 10 November 2010]. See also Fong Hoe Fang, ed., *That We May Dream Again* (Singapore: Ethos Books, 2009), and Tan Jing Quee, Teo Soh Lung and Koh Kay Yew, *Our Thoughts are Free: Poems and Prose on Exile* (Singapore: Ethos Books, 2009).

47. The speech could be viewed online at several sites, which were used to check the text as given at http://www.yoursdp.org/index.php/news/singapore/ 4182-text-of-vincent-chengs-speech-at-sdps-rally [accessed 13 January 2011]. He claimed "slaps" and a "knock-out punch" to the abdomen. The issue of what interrogation methods (and limits) were inherited from the British period remains to be fully documented.

48. Yao Suchou, *Singapore: The State and the Culture of Excess* (London: Routledge, 2005) comes to this conclusion using a social science battery of approaches on issues such as the caning of Michael Fay, judicial decisions on fellatio, and the war on terror. See his *Singapore: Wealth, Power and the Culture of Control* (London: Routledge, 2006). For the Barisan perspective on merger, see also Karl Hack, "The Malayan Trajectory in Singapore's History", in *Singapore from Temasek to the 21st Century*, ed. Hack and Margolin, with Delaye, pp. 264–80. For a view of how PAP control relied on "bureaucratic proxy democracy" as well as calibrated coercion, see Karl Hack, "Remaking Singapore, 1990–2004: From Disciplinarian Development to Bureaucratic Proxy Democracy", in *Singapore from Temasek to the 21st Century*, ed. Hack and Margolin, with Delaye, pp. 345–83.

49. The still classic study of communitarianism is Chua Beng Huat's *Communitarian Ideology and Democracy in Singapore* (London: Routledge, 1995). As a

sociologist, Chua has since looked instead at how identity is constituted in a partly depoliticised society. Hence, discussions of, for instance, food hybridisation and cultural producers, focus on the underside of success, allow him to see how Singaporeans challenge official views, and constitute their identities semi-autonomously in ways that contradict, for instance, state stress on the innate separateness of Chinese, Malay and Indian realms. See his *Life is Not Complete without Shopping: Consumption Culture in Singapore* (Singapore: Singapore University Press, 2003), pp. vii–viii, *passim*.

50. Barr and Trocki, *Paths Not Taken*, pp. 1–2. How far this was the editors' preferred position, and how far merely an expedient position when publishing a book for use in Singapore, remains a moot question.

51. Hong and Huang, *The Scripting of a National History* is the best study of this process, including both mainstream state efforts, and the treatment of "Chinese heroes" such as Sun Yat Sen (at the Sun Yat Sen Memorial Hall) and Aw Boon Haw. It also reprints Hong's "The Lee Kuan Yew Story as Singapore's History" from the *Journal of Southeast Asian Studies* 33, 3 (October 2002): 545–57.

52. Kevin Tan, *Marshall of Singapore: A Biography* (Singapore: ISEAS, 2008) is the latest work; Chan Heng Chee, *A Sensation of Independence: A Political Biography* (Singapore, 1984) is the classic version; and for the flavour of the man, see also Melanie Chew, *Leaders of Singapore* (Singapore: Resource Press, 1996), pp. 69–82. The PAP view of Marshall tends towards arguing that — though he played a role — his recklessness over-stimulated events and his subsequent opposition to merger and formation of the Workers' Party was opportunistic if not dangerous. Chan Heng Chee gives a more generous view of his role in the early years of nationalism.

53. For a discussion of the scope and limits of this, see Karl Hack, "Remaking Singapore 1990–2004: From Disciplinarian Development to Bureaucratic Proxy Democracy", in *Singapore from Temasek to the 21st Century*, ed. Hack and Margolin, with Delaye, pp. 345–83.

54. *Fong Chong Pik: The Memoirs of a Malayan Communist Revolutionary* (Petaling Jaya: SIRD, 2008). C.C. Chin and Karl Hack, eds., *Dialogues with Chin Peng: New Light on the Malayan Communist Party* (Singapore: Singapore University Press, 2004); and Chin Peng is told to Ian Ward and Norma Miraflor, *Alias Chin Peng: My Side of History* (Singapore: Media Masters, 2003). More recent memoirs are discussed in Blackburn and Hack, *War Memory and the Making of Modern Malaysia and Singapore*.

55. Sonny Yap, Richard Lim and Long Weng Lam, *Men in White: The Untold Story of Singapore's Ruling Political Party* (Singapore: Straits Times Press, 2009), p. 16. Typical of the slightly over-hyped style, Baker is described as having read "the entire Manifesto". The Penguin version is 120 pages of easily digested propaganda. It is hardly *Das Kapital*.

56. Ooi, *The Reluctant Politician*, p. 140ff.

57. T.N. Harper, "Lim Chin Siong — The Man and His Moment", in *Comet in our Sky: Lim Chin Siong in History*, ed. Tan Jing Quee and K.S. Jomo (Kuala Lumpur: INSAN, 2001), pp. 3–55.

58. The "progressive" theme emerges from the *Plebeian*, the journal of the *Barisan Sosialis*, from its first issues in 1962 until Operation Cold Store arrests in February 1963 shifted its focus towards the line of Beijing and direct action. Copies are held in NUS Library and the National Library of Singapore. The feeling by many of members that they and communists shared many aims is expressed in Poh Soo Kai, "Detention in Operation Cold Store: A Study in Imperialism", in *The Fajar Generation: The University of Socialist Club and the Politics of Postwar Malaya and Singapore*, ed. Poh Soo Kai, Koh Kay Yew and Tan Jing Quee, p. 156.

59. See NRA: A816/19/321/43, "Subversion and Counter Subversion in Singapore", RL Harry Commissioner to RG Casey Ministry of Foreign Affairs, 27 July 1956; and Poh Soo Kai, Koh Kay Yew and Tan Jing Quee, eds., *The Fajar Generation: The University of Socialist Club and the Politics of Postwar Malaya and Singapore* (Petaling Jaya: SIRD, 2009).

60. Michael Fernandez and Loh Kah Seng, "The Left-Wing and Trade Unions in Singapore", in *Paths not Taken*, ed. Barr and Trocki, pp. 206–27.

61. Sonny Yap, Richard Lim and Long Weng Lam, *Men in White: The Untold Story of Singapore's Ruling Political Party* (Singapore: Straits Times Press, 2009), p. ix.

62. *Men in White*, pp. 321–3.

63. *Men in White*, p. 337 also claims that "the legacy of the left has left an indelible imprint on the psyche of the PAP pioneers. Indeed the lessons ... from the climacteric clash ... have been internalised in its institutional memory ... That perhaps explains the unyielding reflexes ... which characterise its no-holds-barred approach towards the opposition to this day".

64. A.J. Stockwell, *Malaysia*, discusses this on pp. lxiii–lxiv, stating baldly that "Lee, too, manipulated detention for political, not simply security, reasons". Academics have uniformly interpreted Selkirk as determined to play by the rules in 1961–1962. See, for example, S. Ball, "Selkirk in Singapore", *Twentieth Century History* 10, 2 (1999): 162–91. For a left-wing view that liberally quotes British archives, see Po Soo Kai, "Detention in Operation Cold Store: A Study in Imperialism", in *The Fajar Generation*, ed. Poh, Tan and Koh, pp. 155–221. This is one area where the "Singapore Story" interpretation fits the documentary trail less well than that of the left wing, which is that detentions were for political as much as security reasons.

65. The Barisan viewpoint, based on their press statements and the *Plebeain*, is presented in Hack, "The Malayan Trajectory in Singapore's History".

66. C.J.W.-L. Wee made a brave first attempt in "The Vanquished: Lim Chin Siong and a Progressivist National Narrative", in *Lee's Lieutenants: Singapore's Old Guard*, ed. Lam Png Er and Kevin Y.L. Tan (New South Wales: Allen

& Unwin, 1999), pp. 169–90. This was followed by Tan Jing Quee and K.S. Jomo, eds., *Comet in our Sky: Lim Chin Siong in History* (Kuala Lumpur: INSAN, 2000). As of writing, a biography was being written by Kevin Tan.

67. This trend to increase the number of individuals and organisations acknowledged as having made positive contributions to Singapore need not be anti-PAP. One notable example is Lam Peng Er and Kevin Tan, eds., *Lee's Lieutenants: Singapore's Old Guard* (New South Wales: Allen & Unwin, 1999). Loh Kah Seng and Liew Kai Khiun, *The Makers and Keepers of Singapore History* (Singapore: Singapore Heritage Society and Ethos Books, 2011).

68. *S/pores: New Directions in Singapore Studies*, at http://s-pores.com/ [accessed 22 July 2009]. Issue 2, 1 (February 2009) was a special edition on the leftist Dr. M.K. Rajakumar, including articles by historians (Hong Lysa and Mark Ravinder Frost) as well as people with experience of the left, such as ex-Barisan Sosialis leader and detainee Poh Soo Kai, and Tan Jing Quee. The first four editions concentrated on the 1950s.

69. Tan Jing Quee, Tan Kok Chang and Hong Lysa, eds., *The May 13 Generation: The Chinese Middle Schools Student Movement and Singapore Politics in the 1950s* (Petaling Jaya: SIRD, 2011). The editors thus combine an academic (Hong Lysa) and ex-detainees, one of whom (Tan Jing Quee) died on 14 June 2011. See "Tan Jing Quee (1939–2011), "Setting New Directions in Singapore Studies", *S/Pores*, online journal, at http://s-pores.com/2011/06/tan-jing-quee/ [accessed 5 October 2011]. Kwok's comment is in the Foreword to the same, p. x. Launched at the same time was a translation of MCP member He Jin's realist Chinese-language novel, *Ju Lang*, about the May 13 incident and the school student movement, as *The Mighty Wave* (Petaling Jaya: SIRD, 2011), translated by Tan Jing Quee, Loh Miaw and Hong Lysa. He Jin is the pen-name for Lim Kim Chuan (Lin Jin Quan).

70. For a taste of the range of just the left-leaning works — including issues such as the "new woman" and styles such as socialist realist short stories — see for instance Hong Lysa, "'Facts' from Fiction: The Histories in He Jin's Short Stories", in He Jin, *The Mighty Wave*, pp. 311–38.

71. These issues are discussed in Blackburn and Hack, *War Memory and the Making of Modern Malaysia and Singapore* (Singapore: NUS Press, 2012). The debate over memory work was sparked by the launch of the Fajar generation book. It involved Hong Lysa and Ong Wei Chong in RSIS Commentaries 113, 117 and 118 of September 2010, at http://www.rsis.edu.sg/publications/commentaries.html.

72. See also Poh Soo Kai, Koh Kay Yew and Tan Jing Quee, eds., *The Fajar Generation: The University of Socialist Club and the Politics of Postwar Malaya and Singapore* (Petaling Jaya: SIRD, 2009). There is a book in English on Lim, namely Tan Jing Quee and K.S. Jomo, *Comet in Our Sky: Lim Chin Siong in History* (Kuala Lumpur: INSAN, 2001), but the volume of his memoirs containing speeches is only available in Chinese. Consequently, there is the

feeling of never seeing through Lim's eyes. Even those speeches we have in translation — for instance in *The Plebeian* — lack punch in English. But there is also a swelling stream of oral history and memoirs emerging, including Fong Chong Pik [Fang Chuang Pi, dubbed "the Plen" by Lee Kuan Yew], *Fong Chong Pik: The Memoirs of a Malayan Communist Revolutionary* (Petaling Jaya: SIRD, 2008), especially pp. 74–8; and the work of C.C. Chin and others.

73. *Straits Times*, 8 March 2006. For the forum, see *S-Pores* at http://s-pores.com/2009/10/detention-transcript/ and Kevin Blackburn, "Ex-Political Detainee Forum of 2006", *Oral History Association of Australia Journal* 29 (2007), at http://s-pores.com/2009/10/blackburn/. As of late 2010, Fernandez was still denying that he ever plotted versus the government or to use violence, and suggesting he might sue the government.

74. Vincent Cheng versus Ministry of Home Affairs, Judgement of K.C. Lai J., 31 January 1990, citing the "allegations of fact" against Cheng, at http://www.ipsofactoj.com/archive/1990/Part01/arc1990(1)-003.htm [accessed 12 November 2010.

75. See Tan Wah Piow, *Let the People Judge: Confessions of the Most Wanted Person in Singapore* (Kuala Lumpur: INSAN, 1987), and the government side as summarised in *Men in White*, pp. 435–44. The latter highlights Tan's two brothers being "associated" with the MCP in the 1960s. The story overlaps Law Society questioning of legislation, social activism, and Tan's off the stage presence as an exile in London.

76. Michael Barr, "Singapore's Catholic Social Activists: Alleged Marxist Conspirators", in *Paths not Taken*, ed. Barr and Trocki, pp. 243–4, suggests Government targets were primarily: (1) a fear of the future potential of Liberation Theology, even though the activists did not espouse its revolutionary elements; and (2) the activists' ability to operate across social boundaries (students, workers, church) to protest government policy and contest discourses such as those on work conditions, graduate mothers policies, etc.

77. For Goh Chok Tong's comment, see *Men in White*, p. 439. For the detainee and Tharman, see Michael Barr, "Singapore's Catholic Social Activists: Alleged Marxist Conspirators", in *Paths not Taken*, ed. Barr and Trocki, pp. 218–47. Some sources suggest many of the "conspirators" did not know one another.

78. Other ex-detainees have also been penning memoirs, for instance, those detained in the alleged "Marxist" conspiracy of 1987. See Teo Soh Lung, *Beyond The Blue Gate: Recollections of a Political Prisoner* (Kuala Lumpur: SIRD, 2010). She was detained in 1987, and 1988–1990 following a recantation and assertion of innocence. At the launch in Singapore at Fort Canning Park, 26 June 2010, she likened the detainees to rape victims. See also http://www.singapore-window.org/tfhmemo.htm [accessed 10 November 2010] for Tang Fong Har's memories of detention from 1987.

79. Martyn See's http://singaporerebel.blogspot.com/2010/07/martyn-see-complies-with-mdas-order-but.html [accessed 12 November 2010].

80. Carl Trocki and Michael Barr, "Introduction".

81. *S/Pores* No. 7, August 2010, is a special edition on *Men in White*, including: Hong Lysa, "The Forever Missing Handshake", Tan Tarn How, "What a Book! What a Launch! What a Story!", whose title parodies the *Straits Times'* lauding of what is effectively its own book, and who claims the *Straits Times* lapses into "mere public relations"; Chua Beng Huat, "Forum [16 January 2010 at the National Library of Singapore] on Men in Black or White: History as Media Event in Singapore". See: http://s-pores.com/category/7-men-in-white/.

82. *Men in White*, pp. 335–7.

83. See Clarissa Oon, "In Search of the Other Singapore Story", *Straits Times*, 14 August 2010. This framed the "flurry of books on Singapore's left-wing movement" as a response to the "Singapore Story" and National Education. Nevertheless, it cites K. Kesavapany (who as ISEAS Director is commissioning books and oral histories on the left) as saying these "must not be to reinterpret history", and notes the banning of a Martyn See video of a speech by ex-detainee Lim Hock Siew, as contrary to public interest. Anyone reading this piece will, ironically, have sufficient information to trace viral copies on the internet and view them without downloading or possessing them. What is prevented is therefore not the video per se, but rather fully informed public discussion of the need for, and administration of, the ISA, and so issues of law, justice, habeas corpus, freedom of speech and more. In other words, democratic discussion of Singapore's laws and their de facto operation. See Martyn See's comments at http://singaporerebel.blogspot.com/2010/07/martyn-see-complies-with-mdas-order-but.html [accessed November 2010].

84. These themes of individual rights above mere communitarianism, and of natural justice as something more than mere "rule of law", feature in J.B. Jeyeratnam's career and speeches to Parliament, as published in *Make it Right for Singapore: Speeches in Parliament 1997–1999* (Singapore: Jeya Publishers, 2000).

85. Mark Ravinder Frost, "Emporium in Imperio: Nanyang Networks and the Straits Chinese in Singapore, 1819–1914", *Journal of Southeast Asian Studies* 36, 1 (2005): 29–66.

86. Philip Holden, "From People's Party to Men in White", *S-Pores* 7, at http://s-pores.com/2010/08/frompap-to-miw/ [accessed 11 November 2010]. Catherine Paix, "Singapore as a Central Place between the West, Asia and China: From the 19th to 21st centuries", in *Singapore from Temasek to the 21st Century*, ed. Hack and Margolin, with Delaye, pp. 210–42.

86. "Casting Singapore's History in the Longue Durée", in *Singapore from Temasek to the 21st Century*, ed. Hack and Margolin, with Delaye, pp. 55–75.

87. Personal visits, participation as an interviewee and in roundtable discussions for drafts in 2005. See also *National Museum of Singapore Guide* (Singapore: Editions Dider Millet, 2007). I am also indebted in several ways to the Director, Lee Chor Lin, and key staff, notably Iskandar Mydin.

88. This was an original idea for the British Commonwealth and Empire museum, formerly in Bristol and now awaiting new premises in London. In the end, they opted for the less controversial approach of straightforward unilinear storylining of places and periods.

89. For 2003–2006, the museum operated from its temporary "Riverside" premises along the Singapore River. The dioramas provided a good mix of elite and people's history in a narrative thread, being: "Ruins of Ancient Singapore"; "Singapore, 1818 Rivers and Waterways"; "Arrival of Sir Stamford Raffles 29 January 1819"; "Chinese Junk Trading Season 1820s"; "Bugis Trading Season 1830s"; "A Gambier Plantation, 1840s"; "Commercial Square, 1850s"; "Construction of Government House by Convict Labour, 1860s"; "A Chinese Clan, 1870s"; "Telok Ayer Street, 1880s"; "Serangoon Road 1890s"; "A Cooli Room 1900s"; "Female Immigration 1920s"; "Opening of Naval Base 1938"; "Japanese Victory Parade 1942"; "Japanese Creening [*sook ching*] 18–22 February 1942"; "City Day Celebrations 22 September 1951"; "Communist Inspired Riot 12 May 1955"; "Referendum for Merger with Malaysia, 1962"; "Meeting of First Parliament 8 December 1965". The script for the last noted the discussion of "creating a national identity, by building a strong economy ..." etc., and the empty seats for the opposition, which had boycotted the first session. Source: personal visits and *The Dioramas: A Visual History of Singapore* (Singapore: National Heritage Board, Singapore History Museum, booklet with no date). During its latter years, the museum added a permanent exhibition — "Singapore 700 Years" — using excavated artefacts.

90. A good example of the flexibility of this approach is Norman Davies, *Europe: A History* (Oxford: Oxford University Press, 1996), which commences: "In the beginning there was no Europe ..." before proceeding from Ice Age and Environment, across the centuries to multiple appendices. But it is 1,365 pages long.

91. The Sarawak Museum also begins its walk-through storyline with the prehistoric period, using a "Niah Cave" grotto. Personal visits, and see *Hong Kong Museum of History* (Hong Kong Museum of History, 2006 edition). The museum of Macao takes yet another approach, beginning with a corridor along which there are major western achievements on one side (writing, transport, religion, etc.), and their Chinese counterparts on the other. Hence, they frame their history as that of the meeting place of cultures.

3

Mary Turnbull's History Textbook for the Singapore Nation

Kevin Blackburn

In 1977, Mary Turnbull wrote the first general history textbook for the new Singapore nation that did not view its history as a small part of the history of Malaya. Previously, history textbooks used throughout Singapore and Malaysia catered to a common history taught for the two countries. In contrast, her general history, called *A History of Singapore, 1819–1975*, traced the development of Singapore, not as part of Malaya, but as a distinct nation with its own history separate from that of Malaya.[1] She was ahead of the Ministry of Education of Singapore's own textbook on Singapore history. This official government textbook did not appear until the new subject of Singapore history was introduced in schools during 1984. The Ministry of Education's two-volume work, called *Social and Economic History of Modern Singapore*, drew extensively on the chronology and themes that Turnbull had developed. This chapter traces how history was taught in Singapore schools before the publication of Turnbull's general history, then proceeds to evaluate the influence of Turnbull's Singapore history textbook over the education system of Singapore and the generations of school students who have drawn upon it to formulate their ideas about Singapore and its past.

The "Malayanisation" of the History Curriculum in Singapore

Turnbull was not the first historian to attempt to write a history of Singapore, but her history was the first conceived as a history textbook for the newly emerging Singapore nation-state. As Singapore moved towards self-government in 1956, the journalist and historian Harold Frank Pearson attempted to write a similar general history called *A History of Singapore.*[2] After Singapore was granted self-government in 1959, Pearson revised and updated his work, turning it into *Singapore: A Popular History, 1819–1960.* According to its publisher, Eastern Universities Press, the book was meant "for the student reader".[3] Pearson's history did not see Singapore as an emerging separate nation-state. In his 1961 history of Singapore, Pearson wrote of how he believed he was tracing the history of Singapore as "a vast international city and port" not that of a possible new nation.[4] He concluded in 1961 with the words: "It lies now with this new generation to ensure that Singapore becomes one of the great city states which have left their mark on the history of the world."[5] Albert Lau in his historiographical review of the writing of Singapore history observed that at the time, Pearson's work "failed to inspire further works on Singapore's general history", and that "by 1963, Singapore was reunited with the Malayan mainland in a larger Malaysia and the immediate rationale for a separate history faded".[6]

It was not surprising that Pearson's general history of Singapore meant "for the student reader" was not followed up, as it was out of tune with the Singapore history curriculum. The syllabus at the time was conceived in terms of an emerging Malayan nationalism in which the pasts of Singapore and Malaya were indissoluble.[7] After the 1957 declaration of independence of Malaya, Malayan nationalism came to the fore in ideas asserting the Malay, Chinese, and Indian races of Malaya and Singapore shared a common identity as Malayans with a loyalty to the country they lived in.[8] Future political merger between Malaya and Singapore into a form of federation was seen as overwhelmingly likely. The idea of Singapore being an independent nation-state was thought improbable.[9] The framework of the history curriculum in Singapore was laid down at this time, and would not substantially change until the early 1980s.[10] Independence for Malaya and coming self-government for Singapore meant replacement of a history curriculum that emphasised the rise of the British Empire with one that was more in accord with Malayan nationalism.[11] In 1957, Kennedy Gordon Tregonning, then a lecturer in History at the University of Malaya, changed the way the study of history in Singapore and Malayan schools was taught when he helped overhaul the old history curriculum based on the history of the British Empire. He published his own textbook for the new syllabus, *World History for Malayans: From Earliest Times to 1511*. Tregonning wanted to provide a textbook "to meet the requirements of the University of Cambridge Overseas Higher School Certificate and of the entrance examination and first-year studies at the University of Malaya".[12] Edwin Lee, a Singapore historian, reflecting in 2002 on the history syllabus he studied before entering the University of Malaya in 1959, recalled that Tregonning's textbook had a significant influence on the way he and other students saw their history. He recollected that Tregonning "was very aware of the social service historians perform", and that he "tailored his work for Malayans".[13]

Tregonning's 1957 textbook for Malayans surveyed the ancient civilisations of Greece, India, China, Rome, and Islam, then moved on to the development of the early modern world. There was also focus on the early kingdoms of Southeast Asia, such as Funan, Srivijaya and Majapahit. The rationale for learning such a broad sweep of civilisations was that "Malayans, who have been influenced by contacts with different peoples from all over the world, have a particular need for a broad knowledge of the history of both the East and the West".[14] The history of the ancient and early modern world was told with reference to Southeast Asia, and in particular Malaya. The textbook concluded at the Portuguese capture of the Melaka Sultanate in 1511.

Tregonning added his own perspective to his textbook. He did not see Malaya as just absorbing the influences of other civilisations like a sponge but already having existing cultural, social, and political institutions which adapted external influences. Tregonning said that in the book, he "attacked this attitude" that "everything of worth on this peninsula came from outside".[15] His history textbook urged its readers to "look at our story from the inside, not the outside".[16] He rejected the idea that the Malayan Peninsula had been thoroughly Indianised, arguing: "We must remember, and give full credit to, the indigenous culture of the Malay that took and adapted these foreign pressures, and produced something quite characteristic — something Malayan."[17] He gave examples, such as the word and political office of the *Temenggong* long preceding the influence of Indian elements in Malaya. The fall of the Melaka Sultanate to the Portuguese in 1511 was not seen by him as due to the superior power of the Europeans but because of internal decline which meant

"Malacca's internal disunity was fatal for its defence". He wrote: "Malays fought well, but Malacca fell because many Chinese, Javanese, and Indians in the town were either apathetic or on the side of the Portuguese. They had lost any sense of loyalty to the government and abstained from the fighting."[18]

Tregonning called for history textbooks written in ways "to give due weight to indigenous elements in the history of Malaya".[19] In doing so, he reflected the Malayan nationalism of the time. He criticised the existing history textbooks for Malaya and Southeast Asia: "Nearly all the authors have been Europeans brought up in the late 19th and early 20th century historical attitude of surveying the world through Europo-centric eyes. The predominant theme to them in Asian history (or African) is European expansion into that continent, the European in Asia, not Asia itself."[20] He affirmed: "In nearly all the books on Malayan history at our disposal — those by Winstedt, Dartford, Morrison and Hall in particular — the 16th, 17th and 18th centuries are divided neatly into two; the 16th century is dominated by the Portuguese — pages and pages about them at Malacca — and the 17th and 18th by the Dutch."[21] Tregonning suggested: "As far as the 16th and 17th centuries are concerned, it is the Achinese period in Malayan history, not the Portuguese, while the 18th is essentially the Bugis century. Both the Portuguese and the Dutch are minor partners, and play a minor part in the wars and developments of Malaya in this period."[22]

Tregonning's ideas found resonance among the history teachers of Malaya and Singapore who were had imbibed the ideas of Malayan nationalism. In August 1958, Tregonning organised a Conference of Senior History teachers of Malaya and Singapore at the University of Malaya in Singapore during which "delegate after delegate expressed great concern over the absence of suitable textbooks to meet the requirements of the new syllabus on Malayan History".[23] One teacher in the Malayan Education Service who would dominate history textbook writing for the next 20 years in Malaya and Singapore, Joginder Singh Jessy, was inspired by the conference to write the first edition of his long used textbook, *History of Malaya (1400–1959)* in 1961. Jessy's history carried on where Tregonning's finished, bringing the history of Malaya and the world up until Malayan independence. Following Tregonning's ideas, Jessy claimed: "I have tried my best to present the facts that I have considered important from a Malayan's point of view".[24]

Jessy was thoroughly inculcated with nationalist ideas. He was 33 when he graduated with First Class Honours from the University of

Malaya's History Department in 1958. Jessy was much older than his classmates, and only two years younger than Tregonning. His full-length honours thesis or academic exercise was on the Indian National Army (INA) during the Japanese Occupation, which was set up to help liberate India from the British with the backing of the Japanese Imperial Army. Jessy as a former member of the INA knew a lot about his subject. Tregonning regarded him as a "lifetime friend", who with other history students graduating to become history teachers carried on the work of the "Malayanisation" of the study of history in the schools.[25] Tregonning later recalled how "we effected a change in school syllabi" in which the "old British-based books vanished. In the classrooms across the land we helped nurture the consciousness of an emerging nation."[26] Tregonning claimed that before this change in 1957 and 1958, "school textbooks of relevance to the students' own environment scarcely existed".[27]

However, this political environment soon changed, and Tregonning's and Jessy's history syllabus and textbooks became less relevant to the students who were using them. The dramatic separation of Singapore from Malaysia in 1965 was slow in making its impact felt on the history curricula of the two countries, which remained identical.[28] A decade after their separation, they still shared the same curriculum for history and the same history textbooks. Tregonning's and Jessy's textbooks were revised in 1968 and used in both countries until the beginning of the 1980s.[29] Little was changed except dropping references about seeing history through Malayan eyes, as the heyday of Malayan nationalism had passed.

For Singapore, the shortcomings of a history curriculum that originated in ideas about Malayan nationalism were evident. Singapore history was taught simply as a brief appendage of the history of Malaya in the fourth year of secondary school. The first two years of secondary school still covered a wide panorama of the ancient civilisations of the world from the West, Middle East, and the East, including the early kingdoms of Southeast Asia. This colourful survey of world history ended at the completion of Secondary 2, as Tregonning had done, with the fall of the Melaka Sultanate in 1511. In Secondary 3 and 4, modern world history was covered with a section on the history of Malaya at the very end. Singapore figured hardly at all. Even worse for Singapore students wanting to know the history of their country, history was a compulsory subject at only Secondary 1 and 2. Only those choosing the arts stream studied history in Secondary 3 and 4 for their 'O' Level certificate. Therefore, only a small number of students learnt anything about their own country. The great mass of students only studied the ancient civilisations of the world. In the 1970s, history textbooks used in Singapore schools teaching this old curriculum that served up a smorgasbord of ancient civilisations had an odd response to the question, "Why study history?" Gone were references to a Malayan identity. They were replaced with the response that "history is the study of ourselves. In spite of the many differences in colour, race, religion and ways of life, the peoples of the world all belong to one family. We call this family mankind. By studying history, we come to understand mankind."[30]

These sentiments about why history should be studied were out of touch with an emerging view that Singapore history should be the main subject of study so that it fostered a Singapore identity. The new ideas were best articulated in Tregonning's own History Department after he had left in 1967. Just as Tregonning had helped transform the study of history in the schools during 1957–1958, so too another historian from the same History Department, Mary Turnbull, was aiming to transform the study of history among Singapore students by writing a history that appealed to a growing awareness of a new sense of identity.

Turnbull and Singaporean Nationhood

When writing her general history of Singapore, Turnbull was acutely aware of the emerging consciousness that Singapore as a new nation had a distinctive history. Speaking at the time of the publication of her general history, she observed in early 1978 that in the late 1960s and early 1970s when she was writing the book, "we were beginning to look at Singapore for the first time as a separate place".[31] Oxford University Press of Kuala Lumpur, sensing a developing market, approached her to write a general history of Singapore. In the early 1970s, both the University of Singapore and Nanyang University in Singapore began introducing first-year introductory courses on Singapore history, albeit still linked to Malaysian history.[32] Thus, thousands of university students needed a basic textbook. Turnbull in a 1978 interview about her book articulated the need for it in independent Singapore: "Up to the time Singapore became independent, histories of Singapore have been written as part of Malaya or Malaysia — Singapore was not taken alone." The result of this was, according to her, histories in which "there was a tendency to ignore whole sections of Singapore's development, resulting in a loss of continuity".[33] In 2006, when working on the third edition of her Singapore history book to take it up to 2005, Turnbull remembered much of this rationale from the late 1960s and early 1970s for writing the first edition:

> At that time in 1965, then, Singapore's experience was unique, and it needed, I felt, someone to have a look at how unique it was. What made it different from elsewhere? Up till that time it had always been thought of as just part of something else — the Straits Settlements, a colony of the British Empire, or latterly the Federation of Malaysia — but now it was an entity on its own, and so it really needed to look at what it was distinguished it from elsewhere. With this in mind then, I embarked on writing the history of Singapore, and this was published in 1977, nearly thirty years ago.[34]

Turnbull recollected how she was influenced by the nation-building impulse that she felt around her at the University of Singapore. When all the faculties of the university were asked what they could do for nation-building, she responded on how vital history was to such a task at a time when many young Singaporeans, according to her, were saying "Singapore has no history. History starts now." Turnbull saw her general history in context of Singapore being in a position where it "needed to forge a sense of nationhood where nothing had existed before", and that "an awareness of the past is an essential element in deciding what one is as a nation." At the time, she believed "Singaporeans ought to really look at their roots as a nation as well as individuals" as both needed "to know where they were coming from".[35]

In her 1978 interview on the rationale for her book, Turnbull elaborated on the areas of Singapore's history that she felt had not been adequately covered because a narrative of the history of Singapore as a separate entity had not been written until her general history. Many of these areas would be picked up and developed by curriculum specialists in Singapore's Ministry of Education for the first history textbook on Singapore in the schools, the two-volume set, *Social and Economic History of Modern Singapore*. Turnbull listed these areas that produced "a loss of continuity" in the narrative of the history of Singapore: "For example, Raffles was extremely important to the history of Singapore, but only a tiny portion of his career was in Singapore. Previous histories tended to relate his whole life and career." She added that in previous histories that covered Singapore and Malaya, "There was also a tendency to deal heavily with colonial issues which had very little to do with Singapore except indirectly. And the long period from 1870 to the Second World War has scarcely been touched by historians. I have tried to give full weight to this neglected period, not dealing just with superficial changes but also changes within communities like the Malays, the Chinese and their relationship with China."[36] Turnbull also noted in 1978 that the war history of Singapore also left out the experiences of the people of Singapore: "Wartime histories have tended to deal with the whole campaign of Malaya, and not from the Singapore angle." She added: "On the Japanese Occupation most of what are available are accounts by and of Europeans. I have tried to deal with Singaporeans who were here and the extent to which the Japanese period changed the attitudes of Singaporeans in Singapore."[37]

Turnbull was conscious that in writing a general history of Singapore for the Singapore nation she had to bring out the experiences of the ordinary people of Singapore, not just those of their colonial masters. She was aware that her writing would be judged "first of all in its attitude towards colonialism".[38] It was something that she vividly remembered in 2006 when reviewing how she wrote her general history of Singapore in the late 1960s and early 1970s:

> Any history book that started with Raffles in 1819 and only went up to the first decade of independence was bound to be a history almost entirely of colonial times. A history of colonial times need not necessarily, or desirably, be a history of what is going on in government house, or colonialism. But nevertheless at that time there was a great deal of material on colonial activities, the activities of the Western expatriate community for instance. And one was therefore conscious in writing this of how you were dealing with a small minority. Then behind that there was the vast majority of Singaporeans about which there was not really so much material as we had.[39]

Turnbull also included in her general history another period that had been left out of accounts of the history of Singapore. In 1978, she emphasised that "three-quarters of the book concerns the postwar period, based partly from personal involvement and partly on observations from the sidelines" while in "the rest of the book I have tried to represent from a Singapore angle, giving full weight to the periods in Singapore's history that have been previously neglected by historians".[40] The time covering her stay in Singapore and Malaysia from 1952 to 1971 coincided with the major political struggles prior to Singapore's independence in 1965 and the first decade of nation-building up until 1975. She had witnessed these tumultuous events first hand. Turnbull recalled that "those 19 years I spent in Singapore and Kuala Lumpur were the most exciting years to be in the two countries".[41] The turmoil of the 1950s and 1960s clearly left an indelible impression on her. She described the period almost 50 years later in 2006 as "a time of very considerable danger".[42] In this period, she was first a colonial civil servant, then after 1955, a lecturer in the History Department at the University of Malaya, moving to the History Department at the Kuala Lumpur campus of the University of Malaya from 1960 to 1963, then returning to the Singapore University History Department, before finally leaving to go to Hong Kong University in 1971. In 1978, Turnbull said that her book had the didactic purpose of telling the young Singaporeans about this chaotic period:

> Singapore's physical growth is impressive. The general affluence and rate at which people live is a great contrast to 10 years ago but we do not get the political excitement of those days…
>
> The dangers of affluence and a generation always accustomed to success — and therefore one that doesn't appreciate how things were not so long ago — are eminent. Therefore it is good that a history of those times should be written. The leadership is sometimes too critical of the apathy of the younger generation, and yet it is very reticent about what things were like in their younger days.
>
> I hope this book will make them open up and become more vocal about the past. People don't want to be reminded of the past, but the snag is you'd forget how far you've come.[43]

Turnbull's Influence on the Singapore History School Curriculum

Singapore's political leaders began echoing Turnbull's call for more prominence to be given to the history of Singapore in the education of a younger generation that did not know of the struggles of the 1950s and 1960s. In March 1979, the publication of the government's official report on education by Goh Keng Swee, the Deputy Prime Minister, put on the national agenda sweeping reforms for the education system. The main reform of the report was to have a common standardised education system in English instead of education being taught in Chinese, Tamil, and Malay, as well as English. The languages of the different ethnic communities however were planned to be taught intensively as "Mother Tongues" to encourage bilingualism. The objective was to bring the education system in line with the government's goal of nation-building.[44] The Goh Keng Swee Report did not recommend the introduction of the history of

Singapore in the curriculum but it did open up a debate about the content of education in Singapore schools and this highlighted areas that were not aligned with nation-building. Out of this debate, the concern to teach the history of Singapore in schools began to be articulated. In parliament, there were a few requests that the history of Singapore's path to independence be taught from the Second World War to the 1970s. On 28 March 1979, Ng Kah Ting, the ruling People's Action Party (PAP) member for Punggol, suggested a course in Singapore history would aid nation-building:

> ... students can acquaint themselves with the struggles in Singapore's history, viz., the Japanese Occupation (1942–45), the Battle for Merger (1961–63), Merger with the Federation of Malaysia (1963), Singapore's secession from the Federation (1965), Struggle for Nation Building and thereafter ... All these should be made compulsory learning as part of the school curricula. This comes under the topic of nation building. It may be pointed out that there is a subject on this but as I can see it from my own experience, the area covered during this period is very limited and grossly insufficient to make the student understand the very important chapter in the history of Singapore. As I said, this is important in respect of nation building. Therefore, the time has come for the Government to recognise this need and give it serious attention.[45]

The first major public call by a senior member of the PAP government for Singapore history to be taught in schools came from Goh Chok Tong, second assistant secretary of the PAP and Minister for Trade and Industry, on 27 January 1980, when he was opening the PAP's 25th Anniversary exhibition in his electorate in Marine Parade. He declared "the history of Singapore in the last 25 years should be written and then taught in schools". Goh asserted: "Young Singaporeans need to learn the whys and wherefores of Singapore, the struggles for independence and against the Communists, the building of a modern state, the society that was formed and the nation that was built." He argued that "this was not to glorify the PAP" as he "did not think the party needed glorification because its achievements had spoken for it".[46]

Goh's call for Singapore history to be taught in schools was picked up by the main English-language daily, the *Straits Times*, in its editorial which said that "his suggestion reflects a growing awareness" that the younger generation of Singaporeans should be taught the nation's history in school. The newspaper observed, "At present some mention in passing is made at the Secondary 3 and 4 levels as part of the history stream for arts students. But the bulk of the syllabus focuses on developments up to the 1950s". The editor urged action: "The Education Ministry would have to make the first move in initiating plans to introduce it into the curriculum to arrange for suitable textbooks and to prepare teachers to teach it."[47]

The demand for changes in the Singapore history curriculum reflected similar feedback from many history teachers, and this prompted the Ministry of Education in 1980 to review the curriculum.[48] History teachers in both the English and Chinese schools, which shared a common curriculum, had long complained that the bewildering array of world civilisations studied produced confused students. They argued that "at Sec 1 and 2 levels, History deals with a great multitude of facts and ideas which are difficult for students to remember" and "many of the ideas and concepts involve high-level abstractions or are beyond the limited experience and state of maturity of the pupils". The lessons were "crammed with endless uninteresting and unimportant details" with the result that "the majority of pupils find the lessons extremely dull, and many even dislike the subject intensely".[49] Introducing Singapore history seemed to be the solution in making history more relevant and interesting. This case was even stronger after the publication of Turnbull's general history, which had won praise from the *Straits Times*, for making history more interesting, with its young reviewer concluding: "I wish my history books in school and on campus had been as readable as this one."[50]

Inside the PAP government, Fong Sip Chee, Minister of State for Culture, in particular, lobbied Tay Eng Soon, the Minister of State for Education for the introduction of Singapore's history into the education system that was being transformed as a result of the Goh Keng Swee Report.[51] Fong had a keen interest in Singapore's political history, writing in 1980 a history of the PAP's role during the 1950s and 1960s called the *The PAP — The Pioneering Years*.[52] On 16 July 1981, Fong publicly announced when opening the Singapore Historical Pictures Exhibition, organised by the Chinese newspaper the *Sin Chew Jit Poh*, that Tay had informed him that "Singapore's history in the 1900s will soon be part of the history secondary school curriculum".[53]

On 21 August 1982, Tay formally announced that from 1984 the history of Singapore would be introduced in schools at Secondary 1 and 2 levels, replacing the study of the array of ancient civilisations taught since Tregonning was involved in overhauling the history curriculum in 1957 and 1958. Tay placed the introduction of the study of Singapore's own history, as Turnbull had done, in terms of the youth of the country developing a Singaporean identity by studying their own past. He said, "We need to know our past so that we can know ourselves and our historical roots better." He went on to argue, "A knowledge of our historical past would certainly give us a better perspective of the present and a direction for the future." Tay confirmed that "the new syllabus would show how our forefathers who were poor immigrants from China, India and neighbouring countries sank their stakes in a young port and trading centre and built it up, literally, from nothing."[54] The *Straits Times* in its editorial the following day was jubilant that from 1984, Singapore students "will be able to study the social and economic history of their own country — from the time of Raffles in 1819 to independence in 1965 — instead of world history". The editor remarked: "Introducing local history to schools as a subject on its own seems so sensible and logical that it begs the question why it was not done much earlier."[55]

The Ministry of Education's history curriculum specialists used Turnbull's general history as a guide in writing the new textbooks for Secondary 1 and 2. When preparing the new syllabus, in the words of one of the members of the project team, "many of us referred to Mary Turnbull as one of the main references".[56] There was also an expectation, as the *Straits Times* advised, that "the History Department of the University of Singapore can be called upon to offer its resources and manpower."[57] The input of the University of Singapore's History Department was thus sought. The historians who acted as consultants included Wang Gungwu, then in 1982 a visiting professor from the Australian National University, as well as historians of Singapore history, Edwin Lee and Ernest Chew.[58] Wang cautioned about removing too much world history when writing the history of Singapore, arguing that Singapore was "not an island unto itself, but as part of a larger more complex world." He said he believed "it is a mistake to see Singapore's history in terms of the physical island".[59] Turnbull herself, not being in the Department, but now Professor and Head of Hong Kong University's History Department, was not a consultant on the project. However, her influence appears significant, as one of the key consultants from the History Department, Edwin Lee, regarded her 1977 book as being at that time "the one and only general history, and an excellent one at that".[60]

The extent of the use of Turnbull's general history of Singapore in the preparation of the new history syllabus was evident in the advice that the Ministry of Education history curriculum specialists gave to the school teachers in the material they prepared to go with the two-volume textbook, *Social and Economic History of Modern Singapore*. At the end of many topics dealt with in the syllabus on Singapore's history, teachers were advised in the Ministry of Education's teacher's guides to consult Turnbull's *A History of Singapore, 1819–1975* for further information and as a source of any additional reading for the students. The advice for the first section on Raffles' founding of modern Singapore as a trading port in 1819 set the tone that became a familiar one as teachers moved through the syllabus instructing their students on the history of Singapore. The treatment of Raffles by the school textbook was similar to that found in Turnbull's general history. Raffles was not depicted as a lone founding father of Singapore but due credit was given to William Farquhar, the first Resident of Singapore, as well as the Chinese, Malay, and Indian pioneers who built the town, such as Tan Che Sang, the wealthy Chinese merchant who arrived in Singapore in 1819 and owned many buildings of the town. The Ministry of Education's guide for teachers instructed, when referring to Turnbull's general history: "This book is useful as a general reference book for the whole History course."[61]

The Ministry of Education's treatment of colonialism showed the strong influence of Turnbull's framework by mainly breaking the period up into phases of immigration of the different Malay, Chinese, Indian, and other communities.[62] The history of the colonial period was looked at, not only through the eyes of the occupants of Government House, but also the ordinary labourers and ethnic communities' leaders and business-men. Emphasising this approach, the secondary history textbook claimed in its introduction that it "deals with the origins of our multi-racial and multi-cultural society, and gradual transition of an immigrant society to one that is locally oriented and possesses a sense of identity with this country. It portrays the hard work and enterprise of our forefathers and their contribution to the progress and prosperity of Singapore."[63] Turn-bull in her writing also had been very conscious that the story of the migration of the diverse group of people to Singapore was one of her book's major themes when dealing with colonialism. She was so aware of this in her 1977 book, she wrote, "It is difficult to see that any 'standard' history of Singapore can be written for some time to come, since the diversity of cultural background and experience is so great that no foreigner or Singaporean of any one community can speak for the society as a whole."[64] From the first chapter of her general history, Turnbull stressed Singapore as "a cosmopolitan town".[65] In each chapter on the colonial period, she traced the events of the different communities, high-lighting the pioneers of each ethnic group but also detailing the lives of the ordinary people.

Turnbull's writing demonstrated a refreshing historical empathy with the young, poor, and illiterate immigrants. She described how they "were used to working long hours or gruelling labour, to living frugally", and "coming from such a background were ideal pioneers in facing the hardships, dangers, and deprivations of a new life".[66] Turnbull called her book "a sympathetic personal interpretation" of the Singapore past, and this was most evident when she dealt with the immigrant experience.[67] The activities in the students' workbooks of the Ministry of Education that went with the new textbooks pursued this theme of historical empathy with the downtrodden immigrants that Turnbull had developed in her history of the colonial period. In the school workbooks developed by the Ministry of Education, there was an emphasis on identifying with the immigrants who were the forefathers of young Singaporeans. One activity asked the students to assume the role of letter-writers in the 1830s writing letters for these immigrants who did not know how to write. The workbook placed the pupils in a situation in which "one day an uneducated labour who had just arrived in Singapore asked you to write a letter for him to send to his family in his homeland describing his life and work in Singapore."[68] Turnbull's description of the life of the ordinary people of Singapore provided the basis from which students could gather their material for the letter from the labourer to his family in his homeland. Her book was one of the key references which was readily available to the pupils.

The Ministry of Education workbook went further and told the students how learning about the experience of the young immigrants was learning about themselves. Turnbull had also emphasised in interviews on her general history this aspect of the value of studying history. The workbook requested that the students "find a very old relative who came from a foreign country a long time ago" and "talk to this relative and then write a short report based on the story he tells you". The pupils were also instructed: "trace your family history as far back as possible in order to find out who your ancestors were, what they were like, what interesting events happened in their lifetime".[69] The teacher's guide emphasised that one of the key objectives of teaching studying the history of Singapore this way was "to enable pupils to appreciate the pioneering efforts of our forefathers, whose hard work, thrift, enterprise and skills have contributed towards the transformation of a tiny fishing village on our island to a prosperous city-state".[70]

The Singapore history syllabus also followed Turnbull's approach to the period of the Japanese Occupation, which she had claimed tended to focus too much on the experience of the imprisonment of the Europeans by the Japanese and not enough on the trials and tribulations of the local people. Turnbull dealt at considerable length with the experiences of the different ethnic groups. She explained in detail the process that led to the Japanese massacre of the Chinese during the *sook ching* operations. She gave an extensive and balanced account of why the surrendered Indian soldiers and the local Indian community formed the Indian National Army with Japanese cooperation to achieve the aim of liberating India from the British. Unlike many accounts of the Japanese Occupation given by other British textbook writers on Malaya and Singapore, she was more able to see the period through the eyes of the local people. She devoted a significant section of her chapter on the Japanese Occupation on how the ordinary people of Singapore coped in finding enough food to eat and dealt with a currency that was rapidly losing its value as the war dragged on. Turnbull went to the trouble of using historical sources for the Japanese Occupation that many historians focusing on the experience of the Europeans had overlooked, such as Chinese, Indian, Malay, Eurasian, and even Japanese accounts of the period.[71]

The Ministry of Education's textbook reproduced the perspectives of Turnbull's chapter on the Japanese Occupation, which saw the period through the views of the local population, using historical sources that they had produced rather than British sources. As with the syllabus' treatment of the migrant experience, it went further, using Turnbull's chapter as its basis. Again the history of Singapore syllabus encouraged the use of oral history as a way of seeing history through the eyes of the ordinary people. The workbook asked the students: "Find out from your grandparents, or granduncles or grandaunts, (or other old people) about their experiences, that is, what they met with or lived through during the Japanese Occupation." The pupils were then "encouraged to tell the class about their experiences".[72] The teacher's guide instructed history teachers: "Please encourage your pupils to ask their grandparents and other old relatives and any other old people about their experiences during the Japanese invasion. Such oral history should prove very interesting and will help pupils know what war is like." The guide outlined the purpose of these activities in conjunction with the themes of the chapter on the Japanese Occupation: "By reading this chapter you will have some idea of how hard life was for your relatives and other Singaporeans who had to live under Japanese rule."[73] Turnbull's chapter on the Japanese Occupation, with its themes covering the experiences of ordinary people of the different ethnic groups rather than only the European elite, provided the basis for this encouragement of the use of empathy in historical understanding by the Ministry of Education curriculum specialists.

The history of Singapore syllabus also focused on the period of the 1950s and 1960s, which Turnbull in her 1978 interview had said she had taken care to describe in detail for the younger generation of Singaporeans who had not lived through these times. Reflecting on the 1950s and 1960s, when revising her history in 2006, Turnbull again quite unashamedly endorsed the PAP government's strong arm tactics during this period in curbing civil and democratic rights to tackle what it saw as attempts by the Communists to take over the country through political violence and the PAP's fight against the communalists seeking to divide the country and create racial antipathy and riots. She recalled: "I was in Singapore in the 1950s and 1960s and understood the risks and dangers of wistful liberal feeling. A lot of people got hurt. A lot of people spent time in prison. Half an hour of anarchy is worse than a century of tyranny. It was a time of considerable danger." She added, "A remarkable transformation has taken place. An economic miracle has taken place and political stability that was never thought possible." In 2006, she described her favourable view of Lee Kuan Yew's interpretation of the events of the 1950s and 1960s in his 1998 memoirs: "Reading those memoirs took me back as if it was happening. It was a true representation of those times. I could quite see it the way it was."[74] Not surprisingly, it did not go unnoticed in Singapore that Turnbull was an admirer of Lee Kuan Yew and the PAP for, in her view, bringing order out of chaos. The review of her book in the *Straits Times* in 1978 noted that when she wrote about the 1950s and 1960s: "What stands out in this period is her underlying admiration for Lee Kuan Yew's successful handling of Singapore. Yet this does not come across blatantly — Turnbull maintains perspective in evaluation and a detached tone in narration."[75]

The Ministry of Education's textbook when dealing with 1950s and 1960s tended to follow this approach as well.[76] However, many of the details of political debates and contests of the period were simplified or left out due to their complexity being thought too much for the Secondary 2 students to cope with. Recognising this, the teacher's guide advised at one point on the reasons for the separation of Singapore from Malaysia in 1965: "What the authors have presented is only a very brief and simplified account of what were really very complex issues."[77] It was left up to the teachers to fill in many of the details. The source that was readily available to the teachers to enable them to do this was, of course, Turnbull's general history and its chapters on the 1950s and 1960s. They were structured, like all her chapters, as easy to read chronological narratives of Singapore's past. This made them valuable for history teachers covering the new syllabus. For many of the younger history teachers, they still had copies of Turnbull's book from their days studying Singapore history at the National University of Singapore's History Department, where it was a required textbook.[78] The Ministry of Education's own textbook only covered political events up to Singapore's independence in 1965. It dealt with the first decade of independence in terms of recording national development and the nation's progress thematically according to topics such as industrialisation, housing, and healthcare. Once again, Turnbull's easy-to-read and informative narrative chapters aided the history teacher. Her account of the first decade of independence was also sympathetic to the PAP government. She told her readers that by the end of the 1960s, "the bulk of the population accepted PAP leadership" and "Singaporeans showed little concern over growing PAP power in the immediate post-independence years."[79]

Turnbull's general history of Singapore quickly became in the 1980s and 1990s, more than the source for the structure and content of the Ministry of Education's own history textbook, but also a teaching aid as teachers sought to look for material that added to that in the official textbook.[80] Demand for the book among the younger generations in Singapore being trained in history at the National University of Singapore and teachers in the schools, as well as school students, became so strong that Oxford University Press asked Turnbull to revise and update the book. This second edition was published in 1989, with very little done to it apart from carrying the narrative up to 1988.

However, the reliance upon Turnbull's lone general history of Singapore started to fade among history school teachers in late 1990s. The amount of history being written on Singapore had considerably increased since the early 1980s, and much of this was readily available to school teachers.[81] Oxford University Press in Kuala Lumpur and Singapore ceased to be profitable and closed as a publisher, so imprints of Turnbull's handy volume for teachers no longer appeared in Singapore schools. When the history curriculum was revised in 1994, the impact of the expansion of new writings on Singapore's history that could be used by teachers was evident when the new guide for teachers only suggested using Turnbull's history for the relationship between Raffles, Farquhar, and Crawfurd, where there had been little research compared to other topics, such as immigration, the Japanese Occupation, and the political struggles of the 1950s and 1960s.[82] For many topics of the history syllabus listed in the 1994 teacher's guide to the history of Singapore, Turnbull's book was not recommended for the students to read as there had been an increase in other writings that were thought were better pitched at the level of the students. Turnbull was only regarded as optional reading for the teachers, not the students.

In the 1999 and 2007 revisions of the Singapore history curriculum made by the Ministry of Education, the wealth of material published on Singapore history since Turnbull's history had appeared in 1977 was even clearer. A common feature in the revised textbooks was the presence of extracts from Turnbull juxtaposed with the several views of other historians and material from primary sources.[83] Pupils were then asked to draw their own conclusions from the variety of secondary and primary historical sources presented to them. This was very different from the time Singapore history was first introduced in 1984 when there was a dearth of historical material suitable for the pupils and Turnbull was almost the only source that was easy to use in the classroom.

* * *

TURNBULL'S HISTORY OF THE MODERN SINGAPORE NATION helped transform history teaching in Singapore schools. Her 1977 general history was a model for the drawing up of the Ministry of Education's textbooks. It demonstrated to many Singaporeans that Singapore history could be written into a fascinating narrative that was suitable for teaching the younger generation. Her book contributed to producing a new history syllabus that was more in tune with the new Singapore nation than the Tregonning-inspired history syllabus which had its origins in a Malayan view of world history. When the new syllabus was introduced in 1984, it built upon Turnbull's work and devised activities that furthered her approach to writing history. The heyday of the use of her general history by teachers and their pupils lasted until well into the late 1990s when other written historical material became more easily available for teachers and pupils to use. Turnbull's work in this new context of the plethora of sources on Singapore history for the classroom still demonstrates its relevance, but now this is as the interpretation of one historian among several and as one source among many for the younger generation learning about the history of the Singapore nation.

Notes

1. C.M. Turnbull, *A History of Singapore: 1819–1975* (Kuala Lumpur: Oxford University Press, 1977).
2. Harold Frank Pearson, *A History of Singapore* (London: University of London Press, 1956).
3. *Straits Times*, 21 November 1961.
4. Harold Frank Pearson, *Singapore: A Popular History, 1819–1960* (Singapore: Eastern Universities Press, 1961), pp. v–vi.
5. Pearson, *Singapore: A Popular History, 1819–1960*, p. 158.
6. Albert Lau, "The National Past and the Writing of the History of Singapore", in *Imagining Singapore*, ed. Ban Kah Choon, Anne Pakir, and Tong Chee Kiong (Singapore: Times Academic Press, 1992), p. 49.
7. See Teaching of History in Malayan Schools, File Number SF 66/52, Microfilm Number ME 3904; A History of Malaya for Children, File Number SF 62/53, Microfilm Number ME 3909; and Archives of the Singapore Ministry of Education held in its Heritage Centre.
8. See Cheah Boon Kheng, *Malaysia: The Making of a Nation* (Singapore: Institute of Southeast Asian Studies, 2002), pp. 9–13.
9. Tan Tai Yong, *Creating 'Greater Malaysia': Decolonization and the Politics of Merger* (Singapore: Institute of Southeast Asian Studies, 2008), pp. 30–59.
10. See Textbooks and Syllabus Committee — History in S'pore Schools, File Number SF 2174/56 Microfilm Numbers ME 3874 and ME 3875 (Archives of the Singapore Ministry of Education held in its Heritage Centre).
11. Malayanization of Textbooks, File Number SF 3443/59, Microfilm Number ME 3782 (Archives of the Singapore Ministry of Education held in its Heritage Centre).
12. Kennedy Gordon Tregonning, *World History for Malayans: From Earliest Times to 1511* (London: University of London Press, 1957), p. v.
13. Edwin Lee's address from Southeast Asian History: Styles, Direction and Drivers, organised by the Asia Research Institute and Department of History, National University of Singapore, 25 September 2002.
14. E.H. Dance and G.P. Dartford, *Malayan and World History Book 1* (Hong Kong: Longmans, 1959), Preface.
15. Kennedy Gordon Tregonning, "New Approach to Malayan History: Not All Cultures in Malayan History are Foreign", *Straits Times*, 21 November 1958, p. 8.
16. Ibid.
17. Tregonning, "New Approach to Malayan History: Not All Cultures in Malayan History are Foreign", *Straits Times*, 21 November 1958.
18. Ibid.
19. Ibid.
20. Tregonning, "New Approach to Malayan History: Look at Our Story from the Inside, Not from Outside", *Straits Times*, 24 November 1958.

21. Ibid.

22. Ibid.

23. Joginder Singh Jessy, *History of Malaya (1400–1959)* (Penang: United Publications, 1961), p. v. See also History Conference — August 1958, File Number SF 1883/58, Microfilm Number ME 4305 (Archives of the Singapore Ministry of Education held in its Heritage Centre).

24. Jessy, *History of Malaya*, p. v.

25. Malayanization of Textbooks, File Number SF 3443/59, Microfilm Number ME 3782 (Archives of the Singapore Ministry of Education held in its Heritage Centre).

26. Kennedy Gordon Tregonning, *Home Port Singapore: An Australian Historian's Experience: Australians in Asia Series No. 4* (Brisbane: Griffith University, Division of Asian and International Studies, Centre for the Study of Australia-Asia Relations, 1989), p. 12.

27. Tregonning, *Home Port Singapore*, p. 11.

28. Gilbert Khoo, *A History of South-east Asia since 1500* (Kuala Lumpur: Oxford University Press, 1974), 2nd revised edition, Preface.

29. Joginder Singh Jessy, *Malaya in World History Book Three* (Penang: Darulaman Publications, 1968), 2nd revised edition, reprinted in 1974; and Kennedy Gordon Tregonning, *World History for Malayans: From Earliest Times to 1511* (London: University of London Press, 1968), 2nd revised edition.

30. N. Rajendra and V. Rajendra, *New Secondary Histories Book One* (Singapore and Kuala Lumpur: Longman, 1976), p. 1.

31. Interviewed in Nancy Byramji, "Remember the Past so You'll Know Just How Far You Have Come", *Sunday Times* (Singapore), 19 March 1978, p. 16.

32. University of Singapore 1971–1972 Arts Social Sciences pp. 19–20, in University of Singapore Courses and Curricula (National University of Singapore Library); and Nanyang University Faculty of Arts Handbook 1977–78, p. 55, in Nanyang Universty Courses and Curricula (National University of Singapore Library).

33. "Remember the Past so You'll Know Just How Far You Have Come", *Sunday Times*, 19 March 1978.

34. Constance Mary Turnbull, "Rethinking Singapore History Thirty Years On", at Roundtable on Rethinking Singapore History, National University of Singapore, 7 February 2006.

35. Turnbull, "Rethinking Singapore History Thirty Years On".

36. "Remember the Past so You'll Know Just How Far You Have Come", *Sunday Times*, 19 March 1978.

37. Ibid.

38. Turnbull, "Rethinking Singapore History Thirty Years On".

39. Ibid.

40. "Remember the Past so You'll Know Just How Far You Have Come", *Sunday Times*, 19 March 1978.

41. Ibid.
42. Turnbull, "Rethinking Singapore History Thirty Years On".
43. "Remember the Past so You'll Know Just How Far You Have Come", *Sunday Times*, 19 March 1978.
44. Goh Keng Swee and the Education Team, *Report on the Ministry of Education 1978* (Singapore: Singapore Government, 1979).
45. Ng Kah Ting, *Parliamentary Debates Singapore*, 28 March 1979, Vol. 39, No. 2, columns 123–4.
46. *Straits Times*, 28 January 1980.
47. *Straits Times*, 29 January 1980.
48. Chai Chong Yii, Senior Minister of State for Education, *Parliamentary Debates Singapore*, 18 March 1980, Vol. 39, No. 13, column 1093.
49. Ministry of Education, Singapore, Workshop on The Teaching of History in Chinese Secondary Schools: Final Report, 23 October 1974 (National Institute of Education Educational Resources Library).
50. Pakir Singh, "This History Book Will Live Happily in Homes", *Sunday Times* (Singapore), 19 March 1978, p. 16.
51. *Straits Times*, 18 July 1981.
52. Fong Sip Chee, *The PAP Story — Pioneering Years* (Singapore: Times, 1980).
53. *Straits Times*, 17 July 1981.
54. *Sunday Times* (Singapore), 22 August 1982.
55. *Straits Times*, 23 August 1982.
56. Personal communication with Fang Swee Im, formerly of the Curriculum Development Institute of Singapore, 23 December 2009.
57. *Straits Times*, 29 January 1980.
58. *Straits Times*, 23 January and 10 October 1982; and Curriculum Development Institute of Singapore, *Social and Economic History of Singapore 1* (Singapore: Longman, 1984) p. i. There is some discussion of the Ministry of Education's preliminary consultations during 1980 with Yong Mun Cheong and Cheng Sok Hwa of the History Department in Jacinta Tan Poh Joo, Teaching of History in Singapore Schools (1959–1980) (Academic Exercise, National University of Singapore, 1983).
59. *Straits Times*, 23 January 1982.
60. Edwin Lee, "The Historiography of Singapore", in *Singapore Studies: Critical Surveys of the Humanities and Social Sciences*, ed. Besant K. Kapur (Singapore: Singapore University Press, 1986), p. 10.
61. Curriculum Development Institute of Singapore, *Social and Economic History of Modern Singapore, Teacher's Guide 1* (Singapore: Longman, 1984), p. 3.
62. Turnbull, "Rethinking Singapore History Thirty Years On".
63. Curriculum Development Institute of Singapore, *Social and Economic History of Modern Singapore 1* (Singapore: Longman, 1984), p. iii.
64. Turnbull, *A History of Singapore: 1819–1975*, pp. xiv–xv.
65. Ibid., p. 14.

66. Ibid., p. 53.
67. Ibid., p. xv.
68. Curriculum Development Institute of Singapore, *Social and Economic History of Modern Singapore, Workbook 1* (Singapore: Longman, 1984), p. 37.
69. *Social and Economic History of Modern Singapore, Workbook 1*, p. 51.
70. *Social and Economic History of Modern Singapore, Teacher's Guide 1*, p. iv.
71. See Turnbull, *A History of Singapore: 1819–1975*, p. 219.
72. Curriculum Development Institute of Singapore, *Social and Economic History of Modern Singapore, Workbook 2* (Singapore: Longman, 1985), p. 89.
73. Curriculum Development Institute of Singapore, *Social and Economic History of Modern Singapore, Teacher's Guide 2* (Singapore: Longman, 1985), pp. 38–9.
74. Turnbull, "Rethinking Singapore History Thirty Years On".
75. Singh, "This History Book Will Live Happily in Homes", *Sunday Times*, 19 March 1978.
76. Curriculum Development Institute of Singapore, *Social and Economic History of Modern Singapore 2* (Singapore: Longman, 1985), pp. 219–32.
77. Curriculum Development Institute of Singapore, *Social and Economic History of Modern Singapore, Teacher's Guide 2* (Singapore: Longman, 1985), p. 53.
78. Oral history interview with S.N. Chelva Rajah, history teacher since 1979 and involved in history curriculum review with the Ministry of Education, on 17 February 2010.
79. Turnbull, *A History of Singapore: 1819–1975*, p. 320.
80. Oral history interview with S.N. Chelva Rajah.
81. Ibid.
82. Curriculum Development Institute of Singapore, *History of Modern Singapore* (Singapore: Longman, 1994), pp. 40–1.
83. Curriculum Planning and Development Division, *Understanding Our Past, Singapore: From Colony to Nation, Teacher's Resource* (Singapore: Federal, 1999), p. 40; and Curriculum Planning and Development Division, *Singapore: From Settlement to Nation, Pre-1819 to 1971* (Singapore: EPB, 2007), pp. 16–7.

4

The Limitations of Monolingual History

P.J. Thum

Introduction

THE HISTORIOGRAPHY OF SINGAPORE IS DOMINATED BY an elitist English-language nationalist narrative. It is an important perspective and central to Singaporean decolonisation, but it can neither explain the nature of indigenous and vernacular Singaporean nationalism, nor the profound displacements taking place below the elite level which made these mass movements possible. Its inadequacy is a direct result of the narrow and partial view of politics to which it is committed by virtue of its language. It is limited to equating the scope of politics with the aggregation of activities and ideas of both the colonial authorities and the Anglophone elites who were directly involved in operating governmental institutions. English-language sources are by definition unable to access the norms, values and idioms inherent in the vernacular.[1]

Similarly, the historian who is unable to access different languages is placed at a severe disadvantage in accessing this history of a multi-lingual state such as Singapore. Professor Mary Turnbull's work is illustrative of this deficit. A British civil servant turned academic, Turnbull was unable to speak or read Chinese, Malay or Tamil with any fluency. Her *A History of Singapore* (later *A History of Modern Singapore, 1819–2005*) relies entirely on English-language sources. In her bibliography, she lists official records from the UK, USA, India and Singapore, personal papers, nine English-language newspapers, and an extensive list of books and articles. Every single item is in English.

Turnbull's work is by no means the most egregious example of a neglect of non-English sources. Nor does she indulge in the culturalism and soft bigotry of works such as Dennis' Bloodworth's *The Tiger and the Trojan Horse* or John Drysdale's *Singapore: Struggle for Success*.[2] However, as the progenitor of a modern Singapore-centred historiography, many of the inadequacies of her work were subsequently repeated in later historiography. In addition, the remarkable longevity of her work means that it remains the definitive text for Singapore history, thus continuing to influence new histories which repeat many of her misconceptions.

A brief analysis of Turnbull's work will demonstrate how a reliance on English-language sources paints an incomplete picture of Singapore history. A study that focuses on Chinese perspectives in the post-war period, and in particular the years leading up to independence, is instructive. This period represents the apogee of the Chinese language political influence in Singapore. The great breadth and diversity of Chinese reporting and commentary during this time is fertile ground for the historian seeking to access the Chinese sphere and is thus easiest to illustrate.[3] However, with deeper and more careful study, undoubtedly many other examples from across Singapore's modern history can be illustrated.

Using three issues which were very close to Chinese hearts — education, labour rights, and merger with the Federation of Malaya — one is able to discern how an inadequate or partial reporting of facts, a lack of adequate context, and other general cultural barriers prevent the historian from creating a complete view of the situation.

Education Policy

A sense of frustration among the Chinese-educated was palpable during the post-war period. Turnbull touches on the systemic government discrimination which characterised the Chinese middle school education when she noted that

> For the traditional Chinese, the most alarming aspect of colonial policy was its threat to Chinese-medium education. The Singapore Chinese were concerned about a new education policy launched in the Federation in 1952, which concentrated on English and Malay schooling. They feared that the authorities were also bent on burying Chinese education in Singapore: in devoting the greater part of finances to the English-language medium schools, it appeared that the colonial government was content to see Chinese education atrophy and die.[4]

Turnbull describes the poor state of Chinese school facilities, the low pay of most teachers, and the struggles of the schools to make ends meet.[5]

However, Turnbull blames the schools themselves for much of this situation. Turnbull states that "Chinese schools showed no desire to integrate with any unified system and continued to be run by independent management committees."[6] She further elaborated this reluctance by noting how the Chinese schools rejected a deal offered by the colonial government in 1954. The government offered $3.5 million in additional grants, in exchange for increased oversight in the form of a supervisory board that would allocate grants and supervise discipline, curriculum and textbooks, with the Governor having the final say. Governor Sir John Nicoll assured the schools that the government had no intention of destroying Chinese culture. On the contrary, they believed Chinese culture had many important contributions to make to the future of Singapore.[7] Yet the Chinese community overwhelmingly rejected the proposals. Turnbull records that "The Chinese Chamber of Commerce protested that the board should be appointed and run entirely by Chinese, and the new offer failed to satisfy the student population ... Students protested against the government having any say in the content and method of teaching."[8] In other words, Chinese wanted the money without giving up any significant control. Turnbull concludes that their selfish intransigence led them to reject an unreasonable, equitable deal that would allow them to survive.

What is notably absent from descriptions of this situation in government documents, newspapers and other English-language sources is the background to this seemingly short-sighted decision by the Chinese community to reject the deal.

In 1946, the Singapore colony government introduced a Ten-Year Plan for Education, a policy aimed at the creation of a comprehensive education plan for Singapore. It awarded grants to vernacular schools, although at much reduced levels compared with government-run English schools. Ostensibly giving all schools equal status, in reality it "encouraged the natural withering away" of vernacular schools, to be replaced by English schools.[9] Government officials even attempted to withdraw grants from Chinese schools entirely in 1951, but backed down in the face of enormous protests.[10] In 1952, Chinese primary schools in the Federation of Malaya accepted the New Salary Aid Scheme, which traded increased aid for increased government control.[11] They were given assurances that Chinese education would be protected, and that Chinese culture had an important part to play in Malaya. Two years later, this was forgotten. In October 1954, faced with a projected $200 million deficit, the Federation Legislative Council tabled a White Paper which proposed slashing government expenditure. Among the measures proposed was a freeze on building and funding new "National Schools", which taught primarily in English and Malay and were designed to create a "Malayan" educational system. Instead, it proposed forcing all vernacular schools to introduce the concept as "National streams" within the schools. These "National streams" would feature multiracial classes teaching in English, and would be gradually expanded while grants to vernacular education would be simultaneously frozen.[12] The eventual result was that vernacular schools would eventually be taken over completely by the better funded "National Streams", thus converting them into de facto "National Schools".[13] The Chinese primary schools, having accepted the 1952 New Salary Aid Scheme, were powerless to resist. Singapore Chinese schools watched from across the causeway in horror. If the Federation's "education policy of eliminating vernacular schools" was implemented in Singapore, the *Sin Chew Jit Poh* editorialised, "the future of Chinese schools would be unthinkable".[14] This prediction was prescient: by the end of 1961, the vast majority of Chinese schools would bow to government policy and agree to stop teaching in Chinese. A small minority would opt to become entirely private schools, forgoing government aid, to keep teaching in Chinese; but Chinese education would disappear from the mainstream of Federation education.

This news coming days just before Nicoll's speech and was foremost in Chinese minds as they listened to his proposals. His promises were regarded with great suspicion. Apart from the issue of control, the total amount of grants was minuscule in comparison with English schools — just a twentieth on a per student basis. A consensus emerged in the Singapore Chinese community that control over Chinese schools could not be surrendered for such a token sum. The supervisory board, depending on how it was constituted, could permanently transfer control of Chinese schools to the government and set up Singapore's Chinese schools for the same fate as the Federation. While there was a general agreement that other conditions for increased aid could be considered, there was tremendous disagreement over what sort of conditions were acceptable.

In the meantime, opposition to the government's proposals solidified. 1,600 Chinese school teachers signed a joint petition for unconditional increased aid. Chinese student groups wrote letters opposing any conditional aid. Tan Wee Keng, President of the English Teachers (Chinese Schools) Association, wrote in to the NYSP criticising the government for their attempt to use a small sum of money as a bait to induce the Chinese to surrender their right of control over Chinese schools, which they had established with their own blood, sweat, tears, and toil. "The fact is this," he wrote, "Opposition or no opposition, the government in its benevolent and dictatorial form of government, is bent on controlling the Chinese schools ... This will eventually result in the Chinese schools being bound hand and foot and trampled under the feet of the British education authorities in Malaya to be dealt with in any desired manner."[15] A survey of a cross-section of principals also found them against the conditional aid.[16] During his Teachers' Day address on 21 October, Tan See Hou, Chairman of the Chinese School Teachers' Association, reminded everyone what happened in the Federation after they accepted the government's salary scheme. After a long meeting on 23 October, the Chinese Schools' Management and Staff Association decided to oppose the proposals as well.[17]

The Singapore Chinese Chamber of Commerce (SCCC), the traditional lead of the Chinese community and whose constituent bodies ran many of the schools in question, called a meeting of all Chinese public bodies to discuss potential counter-proposals to the government's new policy on Chinese schools. However, before the meeting could take place, the SCCC authorised its Vice-President, Yap Pheng Geck, to meet with the Governor and present a 10-point counter-proposal. The chief counter-proposal was for the statutory body's members being appointed by the Chinese educational community, not the government. The SCCC's unilateral action caused unhappiness among many Chinese bodies, including many SCCC member bodies, who did not agree with all the points in the counter-proposal.[18]

At the meeting, the Governor rejected the SCCC's proposals and decided to withdraw all offers of aid, even the original $3.5 million. Instead, Chinese schools could apply for full financial aid under the same terms as aided English and Tamil schools, i.e., in exchange for full control.[19] This, many argued, proved that the government did not care about the Chinese schools' financial difficulties, as it had claimed. Rather, its only reason for the aid was to induce the schools to accept greater government control.[20] In response to a question from the *Nanyang Siang Pau*, the Director of Education admitted that no uniform standard of control existed for the aided English and Tamil schools, nor was any being considered.[21] Some blamed the SCCC for destroying the Chinese schools' chances for aid by not respecting public opinion and waiting for the general public meeting to discuss the government's proposals.[22] The SCCC subsequently decided that, in light of the governor's decision, it would not call the general meeting and would proceed no further on the matter.[23]

Throughout the period, a vast, furious debate took place in Chinese newspapers on the issue, on both the front pages in the form of editorials and commentary, and on the back pages in the form of letters from the public. The depth of feeling over the issue is clear, as is the numerous divisions in the Chinese community surrounding the issue. Yet this sense is completely missing from official documents and *Straits Times'* reporting on the issue. Comparisons with the Federation's policies are cursory and quickly dismissed, and the SCCC's position is taken to be representative of the Chinese community as a whole. The depth and complexity of the debate within the Chinese community are completely absent.

Student Activism

Chinese students were one of the largest groups involved in anti-colonial protests. Their motivations have been consistently credited to communist manipulation. Turnbull makes the claim (without attribution) that their anger and frustration about the systemic bias against the Chinese-educated made them ripe for manipulation:

> The frustration of intelligent and ambitious Chinese school students combined with intense pride in communist achievements in China to feed pro-Chinese and anti-colonial feeling. Chinese middle school graduates were not qualified to gain access to the English-medium University of Malaya or to English-speaking universities overseas. Nor were there any openings for the vernacular-educated in government and quasi-government organisations in Singapore ... These youths and their teachers had good reason to be bitter against the colonial government. They admired the Beijing regime and eagerly absorbed contraband books and communist propaganda from Chinese.[24]

Building on this, she repeatedly describes (again without attribution) student activism as being due to the Malayan Communist Party and that it issued orders to the Singapore Chinese Middle School Students Union.[25]

Yet the same activism among the English-educated is credited to the impact of the Second World War:

> The overnight collapse of a seemingly unshakeable colonial regime in 1942 and the ingenuity required to survive the hard years that followed provided the nursery that bred a crop of remarkable political leaders among the English-educated middle class, who had formerly accepted without question the colonial society and their own semi-privileged position within it.[26]

If the war produced strongly anti-colonial leaders among those who were already semi-privileged by the colonial system, surely it would produce even stronger and more radical anti-colonialism amongst those who were discriminated against.

Exploration of Chinese sources will find that episodes of student activism can be explained solely on their own terms. For example, Turnbull mentions the organisation of "class boycotts that resulted in police raiding the school" as an introduction to future political and trade union leaders Lim Chin Siong and Fong Swee Suan, but does not elaborate.

A brief perusal of the Chinese newspapers' reporting of the incident reveals a simple explanation. Before 1949, if a Singapore student desired to qualify for higher education in China, they had to sit for an external common junior middle III examination conducted by the Kuomintang government. With the Communist Party's victory, however, admission to universities in the new People's Republic of China was banned. The replacement examination which the Singapore government wanted to impose served no equivalent purpose. It would not qualify students for senior middle I, or entry into the government service, or admission into the University of Malaya. It was utterly pointless, and yet the government insisted all students of Chinese schools had to take it.

The students' graduation committee (an existing committee already formed to organise student graduation activities), which had Chen Say Jame as Chairman, Lim as Secretary and Fong as a member, launched a protest. They went around to the other Chinese schools to solicit support, penned pamphlets, and made speeches condemning British colonialism, calling for fair and equal treatment for Chinese schools.

The Special Branch responded with force, raiding the schools and detaining several of the student leaders, including Chen and Lim, for interrogation. This outraged the student body. On the day of the examination, 80 out of the 108 students turned in blank sheets in protest. They were all promptly expelled for taking part in subversive activities. Their educational futures ruined, Chen, Lim, and Fong all ended up working menial jobs, and became thoroughly set against a repressive and unreasonable colonial government.

One of the most important instances of student activism was the unrest surrounding the introduction of the National Service Ordinance. Turnbull wrote:

> The government's decision to enrol 2,500 youths for part-time national service provoked mass student protest demonstrations in May 1954. Police broke up the demonstrations, and many students were arrested. This stirred up further demonstrations to demand their release, and nearly all students refused to register for national service. [27]

This broadly reflects the reporting in the *Straits Times*, which supported the National Service Ordinance, blamed the riots on the students, and absolved the police and the government of blame. In the Chinese newspapers, however, a different story was told.

In December 1953, the National Service Ordinance was passed. It provided for the registration of all male British subjects and Federal citizens between the ages of 18 and 20 for part-time military training. It was announced that a tenth of the total 25,000 eligible would be called up.

Turnbull records that the announcement "provoked mass student demonstrations in May 1954. Police broke up the demonstrations, and many students were arrested. This stirred up further demonstrations to demand their release, and nearly all students refused to register for national service".

Nothing could be further from the truth. The Ordinance was supported by the Chinese press, who recalled the heroic defence of Singapore by volunteers in 1942.[28] They even argued that non-citizens should be given the opportunity to serve, in exchange for citizenship rights at the end of their service.[29] Community leaders also praised the ordinance. Tan Lark Sye called on the Chinese community to "fulfil our glorious task of defending our country", an appeal echoed by Ko Teck Kin, the Singapore Chinese Chamber of Commerce President.[30]

However, yet again the precedent set in the Federation cast a shadow. The implementation of National Service there had been very flawed. Some overage students had been forced to miss examinations or leave school as a result of a call-up. Others had returned to school after National Service but then had been put into a higher standard due to their age and been unable to catch up.[31] The Chinese-educated were particularly susceptible as the Chinese educational system was a year longer than the English system. More overage students were enrolled due to the practice of retaining failing students, rather than expelling them, and because poorer students would drop out and re-enrol later depending on family fortunes.

The government also badly bungled its communications and registration process. The term "National Service" was mistranslated as *minzhong fuwu*, 民众服务, literally "servitude by the masses", a term with demeaning connotations implying the mass of the people acting as indentured servants of the elite. A better translation for national would have been 国民, 人民, or 公民, meaning "people" or "countrymen", and 服役, implying "selfless service", which taken together means the duty or responsibility of the people or citizens to serve their fellow countrymen.[32] No documents were sent to young men to explain the purpose of national service or the registration process. Instead, the government relied on private media to get the message out.[33]

In spite of this, registration proceeded smoothly and uneventfully in the first few days. Young men of all ethnicities arrived to register themselves.[34] Two weeks into the five-week-long registration period, on 21 April, the government without warning sent a team into Chung Cheng High School — the biggest of Singapore's Chinese middle schools — to facilitate the process. The team set up a temporary registration office in the staff room, before going from class to class to distribute registration forms, interrupting lessons. Teachers who refused to halt their lessons were forced to leave the classroom. Unsurprisingly, the students were outraged and not in the least convinced to register to serve a state which acted in such an authoritarian and heavy-handed manner.[35] This was repeated on 23 April at Chinese High School.

A *Nanfang Evening Post* reporter, talking to students as they left the school, found them angry and upset at their treatment. Before that day, they had received no documents or information about National Service, nor had anyone taken time to explain it to them. Misinformation and rumours had filled this gap. Many students, and even their parents, believed that they would be sent into the Malayan jungle to fight the Emergency for the British.[36]

The same day, the *NYSP* reported that the Malayan Associated Chinese Chambers of Commerce had assumed responsibility of investigating the survivors and families of those who had been forced to work by the Japanese to work on the "Death Railway". Survivors had received no compensation apart from token sums from Chinese charities. For 12 years, the Malayan governments had neglected to investigate and pursue compensation claims, despite reports that British, American and Australian survivors of the "Death Railway" had all been duly compensated.

The article, coming in the midst of National Service registration, was a poignant reminder to all Malayans that they were being asked to fight for governments which would not stand up for them.[37]

Despite this, the vast majority of youths registered. By the original closing date of registration on 12 May, 24,425 youths (98% of the total eligible number) had registered for National Service.[38]

Most of the roughly 600 other students had signed a petition, sent by post to the Governor on 7 May. The petition specifically stated they supported National Service, but asked for exemptions for students who were still in school and that those with extenuating family circumstances would not be forced to leave school and abandon their families to serve National Service.

The Governor ignored them. On 11 May, with the deadline impending, a delegation sought a meeting with the Chief Secretary, William Goode. He granted a meeting at 3pm on 13 May with a small delegation and agreed to extend the registration deadline by ten days. The Secretary for Defence, Mr. Davies, pointed out that there was a provision in the Ordinance for students to apply for postponement of service, but only after they had registered.[39] However, again the precedent set in the Federation failed to give the students any comfort. The same provision had been in the Federation ordinance, but many students had their applications turned down.[40] Also, the Government announced that certain categories of students would automatically be granted postponement when they applied. These included students at the University of Malaya, pupils in Standard 8 and 9 of English schools, and in Senior Middle II and III in Chinese schools.

On 13 May, the delegation arrived at Government House, accompanied by over 900 anxious students who waited at nearby King Albert V Park. It was not a planned protest. Rather, many of the students had walked over from the Chinese inter-schools sports competition — just a 30-minute walk away at Jalan Besar Stadium via Serangoon Road and Bukit Timah Road — to await the outcome of the meeting.[41]

Under Singapore's Emergency Regulations, such a large gathering was technically illegal. Police Commissioner Nigel Morris, on his first day in office, had vowed to pre-emptively stamp out any threats to Singapore's social order by cracking down on potential riots.[42] This was his first opportunity to demonstrate his resolve. He sent in the Singapore Police Riot Squad, which had been formed in the aftermath of the Maria Hertogh riots in 1950 but had not yet seen action. According to eyewitness reports printed in Chinese and Malay newspapers, they charged into the unsuspecting crowd, smashing with batons and lashing out with fists and boots.[43] A reporter from the Malay newspaper *Warta* noted that the police had arrived already fully armoured and armed with rifles and batons, leaving no doubt to their intentions.[44] Some students defended themselves by throwing stones. 30 students were injured and 48 arrested.

The Chinese press, *Singapore Standard*, and *Utusan Melayu* all condemned the unprovoked and excessive force used by the police and demanded an official enquiry. The *Straits Times*, on the other hand, reported that the police had only been doing their job. Its 14 May editorial argued that "the police always appear to be a target for criticism — for doing either too much or too little."[45] It also reported that the students had been "opposing registration for National Service" or "opposing the National Service Ordinance". Its reporting drew an angry rebuke from the *Sin Chew Weekly*, which reminded it of the responsibility of the press to report the truth. The students had unequivocally stated their support for the Ordinance, but instead were asking for clarification on exemptions from National Service.[46]

The night after the clash, over 1,000 students gathered at Chung Cheng High School to decide what to do. They elected representatives, and decided to ask the SCCC, the traditional leaders of the Singapore Chinese community, to mediate.[47] At a press conference, the students stressed that they did not object to National Service and fully intended to register. All they wanted was written assurance from the Government that students would be allowed to postpone their National Service till their schooling had been completed. It also condemned "some sections of the press" for their "distortion of facts" and hoped that the press would report and comment impartially.[48]

Ignored again by the government, the students sent further petitions to the Governor. These petitions asked for a written assurance of postponement of service for all students while schooling, failing which students would accept the censure of the law and submit themselves en masse to jail. The first petition was returned to them unopened because "it was not submitted through the proper channels". They were not told what the proper channels were. They resubmitted the petition by registered mail. Two days later, the petition was returned to the students by Director of Education McLellan with the instruction that petitions from students should be submitted through the principal and management committee of their school. This was done. In the meantime, the students emphasised that all they wanted was a direct, honest, proper response from the Government to settle the issue. If the Government felt they were in the wrong, they would voluntarily submit themselves to jail.[49] The government never replied.

The SCCC later gave a guarantee to the students that their applications for postponements would be approved by the Government if the students registered properly, and all students would be readmitted to schools when the schools reopened. Satisfied, the students agreed to register. They were told to come to the SCCC building on 23 June to register. Unfortunately, the Government supplied only one registration officer, who was unable to process all 190 students. So the remaining students were not registered until 24 June.[50]

The next day, the government announced that it had not agreed to any conditions. The students felt betrayed by the SCCC.[51] Later, seven students were charged for the 13 May incident. They were not tried for rioting, but merely for obstructing the police. Convicted, they were sentenced to three months' rigorous imprisonment, the maximum penalty. The trial clearly established that the police had taken excessive action and the students had no intent to riot when they gathered at King Albert V Park.[52] It was a moral victory for the students. Again, over 700 students sat outside the court on the Padang to await the result. When it was announced, they quietly tidied up after themselves and left.[53]

In the meantime, the Government called up a number of students for National Service, including — despite the Government's earlier promise — 11 in Senior Middle II and III, whose applications for postponement were denied. Three refused to serve and were prosecuted.[54] The students' representatives angrily put out a statement quoting the Secretary for Defence's statements on 12 May and 18 June which explicitly promised exemption for Senior Middle II and III students. They condemned him for breaking his word. "The fact of today has clearly shown that we were not wrong in the past on insisting on written assurances from the government," they angrily declared.[55]

Thus, contrary to the erroneous *Straits Times* reporting and to statements by government officials in the Legislative Council, the students did not object to National Service, nor did they riot, nor were they unreasonable. Rather, they merely asked for the government to give in writing what it had verbally promised. The government's own actions, including sending in the riot squad and refusing to acknowledge the students, escalated the issue. In this case, misconceptions are created as much by omission as by misconception. The government's silence on this issue in its official record makes it seem that the students were occupying the school for no reason at all.

Labour

Labour activism was another major prong of the anti-colonial movement. As with Chinese education, much of this was rooted in working-class anger and frustration over systemic oppression and exploitation.

Throughout 1953 and 1954, Chinese newspapers were filled with details about working class anger. A recession had gripped Singapore since the end of the Korean War rubber boom. To cover its budget deficits, the Singapore government had steadily raised consumption taxes. Commodity prices had steadily risen while real wages remained stagnant.[56] In 1954, workers worked an average of 50.5 hours per week — almost 8.5 hours daily for six days — just a tick below the maximum allowed by law (nine hours a day, six days a week).[57]

A fundamental problem was the lack of effective representation for the workers. The Emergency Regulations had stifled union activity. Unionists lived in fear of being branded communists or fellow-travellers, meetings were harassed by Special Branch, and union leaders regularly hauled in for interrogation. Unions deemed untrustworthy were forced to disband.[58]

The colonial government and employers cooperated to render unions ineffective. With the full force of the law behind them, employers easily broke strikes by hiring new workers and imposing lock-outs at will, by intimidating union officials, by having workers arrested, and by transferring disputes to the Labour Department, which would rule in favour of employers.[59] Workers were pressured to join rival unions established by the employers.[60]

As a result, attempts by unions to negotiate for fairer wages and rights frequently failed. Employers used the legally required 14-day strike notice to hire replacement workers.[61] At best, the unions received insulting offers. In the rare event a strike succeeded, the government found a way to minimise its cost. After a long strike forced the City Council to finally implement an improved pay scale that had been delayed for over a year, the City Council promptly announced it would raise public utility tariffs to compensate for the $3 million rise in its wage bill.[62] This was despite the fact that the Council had had over a year to prepare for the implementation, as well as a $6 million budget surplus from the previous year.[63] It also proposed to eliminate cleansing and waste removal services on Sundays to avoid having to pay workers extra.[64]

The election of a pro-Labour government in 1955 gave many workers hope. It was in this context that the Hock Lee Bus strike occurred.

In February 1955, seeking better conditions of employment, 229 out of the 300 workers in the Hock Lee Amalgamated Bus Company formed a union and affiliated themselves to the Singapore Bus Workers' Union (SBWU). Their employer immediately attempted to head off this new union by firing the two organisers. On 24 February, the day the new union was formed, their employer then announced in the Chinese press the formation of a rival union in his company. Seeking to pre-empt the SBWU branch union, he accused them of being communist-led and preparing to stir up industrial unrest. He announced that he had hired 200 workers so far and was looking for 50 more to replace all the workers who had joined the SBWU branch union.[65] Unsurprisingly, when the new SBWU branch union was formed, its first act was to seek the reinstatement of their two organisers. Arbitrators ruled that one had to be reinstated. A company director offered him six months' pay to resign. The man refused.[66]

The SBWU branch union subsequently agreed to new terms of employment with the employer on 4 April. During this time, however, the employer was steadily hiring new employees on the condition they join his company union, paying them $2 a day to do nothing but wait until he had enough to replace all the SBWU branch members. Once he had enough workers, he reneged on the agreement. On 22 April, the workers responded with a strike notice. On 24 April, the employer sacked all 229 workers affiliated with the SBWU. Angry, the workers picketed the bus depot the next two days and blocked buses from leaving the depot. The employer called in the police, but the workers linked arms and passively resisted removal. On 27 April, clashes broke out between the strikers and police and 15 workers were injured, with some hospitalised.

To ease the situation, the Commissioner of Police advised the company to suspend services, and it did so. Existing legislation only permitted the Labour Front government to organise a Commission of Inquiry to determine the cause of the dispute.[67] This was appointed on 27 April. In the meantime, Chief Minister David Marshall and Minister for Labour Lim Yew Hock continued attempting to mediate the dispute.[68]

The Commission of Inquiry met on 5 May, and the SBWU and its branch union fully cooperated. Fong Swee Suan, General Secretary of SBWU, and the branch committee went before the Commission, which ruled in favour of the workers and ordered their reinstatement. However, as the workers prepared to return to work, they got wind that the employer would make them fill out forms, which he had never previously asked them to do, before permitting them to return to work. Uncertain of the implications of the forms, they contacted their legal advisor, Lee Kuan Yew.[69]

After a long telephone discussion between Lee, the Hock Lee Bus company lawyer and the company manager, it was agreed that no forms would be distributed and the workers would return to work at 5.15 a.m. to begin the morning shift. The company lawyer's parting words to the manager were to warn him not to do anything foolish. These words went unheeded. An hour later, when the workers appeared, they were presented with forms and asked to fill them out before they could return to work. Furious, they stormed out. Worse, when Lee later examined the forms, he realised that the forms only asked for information the company already possessed, such as names and badge numbers. It had been merely a psychological ploy by the company to reassert its dominance.[70]

The furious workers returned to the picket; and as word spread over the weekend (7–8 May), more people turned up. Attempts by the riot squad to clear the crowd failed, as they passively resisted and simply returned when carried away. On 10 May, the riot squad brought in water hoses. Pieces of the pavement were ripped up by the water and the flying stones injured the workers. Public support was firmly on the side of the strikers, although the Chinese newspapers appeal for calm.[71] The SBWU angrily condemned the police action. Pointing out that the police action had been entirely legal, it asked what kind of law could permit the employers to renege on contracts and workers agreements, permit the police to employ force to clear a strike, but offer workers no protection?[72] Chief Minister Marshall, when he went to talk to the strikers, was met with the same explanation. The workers knew their blockade was illegal — but was it fair that the employer could get away with his behaviour and continue making profits while depriving workers of their livelihoods? Marshall agreed it was logical, but the fact was the law did not support it.[73] His experience goes a long way towards explaining why, as Turnbull records, "ignoring the Governor's advice, Marshall refused to call in troops to restore law and order".[74] The problem to him and to the strikers was not the restoration of law and order, it was that law and order did not embody justice. To a man like Marshall, who believed that "the rights and liberties of the individuals, human justice, dignity, equality, and protection for the underprivileged took first priority", the restoration of law and order would have been unjust.[75]

With no legal recourse, the SBWU used their only remaining weapon and called a one-day general strike; the police responded by forming road blocks and massively increasing their presence in the city area. With

numbers massing on both sides, a combustible situation steadily degene-
rated into a riot on the night of 12 May.

Turnbull described the riot in this way:

> Lim Chin Siong and extremist leaders ignored constitutional methods
> and launched the student and labour movements into a joint direct
> militant campaign of obstruction and violence ... In May 1955 students
> joined workers in escalating a strike at the Hock Lee Bus Company
> into a violent demonstration, which led to a night of terror and death.
> Ignoring the Governor's advice, Marshall refused to call in troops to
> restore order, and the strike resulted in triumph for the Singapore Bus
> Workers' Union and its Singapore Factory and Shop Workers' Union
> allies.[76]

Turnbull's depiction of illegal and unconstrained violence reflects both
the *Straits Times'* coverage of the event as well as her own perspective. She
was undoubtedly influenced by the *Straits Times'* coverage, which emphasised the illegality of the strike and its violence, as well as its belief that it
was communist-inspired.

For example, the Chinese, Malay, and Indian Press all closely covered
the Commission of Inquiry, where evidence had been presented proving
how the Hock Lee Bus company owner had attempted to bully, bribe,
and coerce workers not to join the SBWU branch union, and had reneged
on the 4 April agreement. The *Straits Times*, by contrast, spared their
readers these details in favour of reporting how the Company's lawyer
asked the workers if they were being controlled from Beijing. By mere
suggestion, it created the impression in its readers that genuine trade
unionists were subversive elements of a vast communist conspiracy with
tentacles spreading out from Beijing.[77]

This impression found a welcoming audience in the minds of the
British, who could not comprehend the frustration and anger of the
working classes. In the Legislative Assembly, Lee Kuan Yew made this
point when he argued that the colonial authorities, unable to comprehend
the workers' bitterness and anger, had leapt to false conclusions and resorted to violence out of fear of the unknown. "It is a difficulty of people
from other countries of never understanding the Asian mind, and they
try to hide their embarrassment behind a sneer."[78] This, he suggested,
created a vicious circle. Violent reactions to repression were explained by
conspiracy theories, which led to more repression.

Chief Secretary William Goode unwittingly proved this point when
he accused the Chinese press of "failing to give any support to the side of

law and order" and acting irresponsibly.[79] The Chinese newspapers had consistently urged compromise and patience, sentiments that were accurately represented in the translations he could have read in the *Weekly Digest of Vernacular Press*. However, his interpretation of their editorials and commentary shows that anything less than full, unequivocal backing of the authorities and police was seen by the colonial authorities as undermining their authority.

This vast difference in values and perception was further underlined by Goode's description of the riot. His comments attribute only the best of intentions to the police, praised them for their courage and discipline, and personalised them with their English names.[80] In contrast, the workers were depersonalised and depicted as an amorphous, violent mob. No names of the arrested were given, nor of the student (Zhang Lun Quan) who was killed. Goode "grieve[d] for the loss of those two Police officers and journalist who were killed doing no more than their duty" but neglected to grieve for Zhang. The only shots fired the whole night were from police revolvers, but Goode refused to attribute the bullet that killed Zhang to them.

Goode further accused the workers and students of having been manipulated by the MCP into inciting violence. Yet this directly contradicted the MCP's policy aims for peaceful constitutional change. By their own admission, the violence made their goals more difficult to achieve. An editorial in the next issue of the MCP newspaper, the *Freedom Press*, made this point. While celebrating the triumph of the workers, it also warned that the way in which the success had been achieved would make future success more difficult. It urged the people to be less leftist in the future.[81] Special Branch evidence in fact suggests that the rapid escalation of the strike after the Commission of Inquiry caught the MCP unawares.[82]

This did not stop the *Straits Times* from continuing to write about the communist origins of the strike. This consistent misrepresentation of the truth drew angry attacks from Chinese newspapers and their readers. One bilingual reader who wrote to the *Nanyang Siang Pau* noted how the *Straits Times* consistently distorted facts and made exaggerated statements. The reader attributed the *Straits Times*' coverage to conspiracy. By ignoring important facts while selectively magnifying tiny details, it drew a compelling picture of conspiracy that would simultaneously incriminate workers and students, bring down an anti-colonial government, and turn public opinion in Britain against self-determination for Singapore. He suggested that the *Straits Times* was in fact trying to bring down the anti-colonial, pro-worker, Labour Front government. Malaya, he argued, needed an English press that was run by locals which could rival the British-run *Straits Times*, or its campaign to delay Malayan independence would run unimpeded.[83] Throughout this pre-independence period, many politicians from both sides of the Legislative Assembly, including most notably David Marshall, would express anger and frustration with the *Straits Times'* inaccuracy and irresponsibility.[84]

The vast difference between how the Hock Lee Bus strike was covered in the *Straits Times* as opposed to the vernacular press, as well as how officials spoke about the event, demonstrates the assumptions and ignorance that coloured the way different groups viewed the event. The British point of view, which could not comprehend the suffering and oppression of the workers, failed to distinguish between law and justice, and attributed organisation to the manipulation of a mysterious unknown foe, dictated they respond to the strike with increasing repression and force. Turnbull, herself part of the British establishment in 1955, sympathised with the British point of view. Her values colour her evaluation of the situation as a historian.

Language and Meaning

Translations inevitably lose some of the nuance and meaning of the original language. Apart from the government's own mistranslations of important concepts (such as National Service, detailed above), other English translations fail to do the Chinese terms justice. One example is the debate over the citizenship issue as part of merger with the Federation of Malaya. Turnbull states that "the Barisan Sosialis opposed the government's approach to merger, criticising in particular the restrictive citizenship restrictions."[85] However, the debate over citizenship restrictions in the Chinese newspapers throughout 1962 was not that they were restrictive, but that they were *less than* what Federation citizens were getting. The original proposals for merger distinguished between a "Federation National", which was what Singapore citizens would become, versus a "Federation Citizen", which was a category that excluded Singapore citizens.

Throughout the debate, Chinese newspapers carefully distinguished between terms such as the redefinition of resident (*jimin*, 籍民), nationality (*guomin*, 国民), and citizenship (*gongmin*, 公民) and the rights associated with each. *Gongmin* is a term which in Chinese traditionally referred to people in general. It followed naturally that when the term "civil rights" entered the Chinese lexicon, it was translated into *gongminquan* (公民权). However, the usage of *gongmin* in this case to refer to citizenship conflated the ideas of citizenship rights and civil rights, as both translated identically into *gongminquan*.[86] Thus, the original proposal implied that Singapore citizens would have fewer rights than Federation citizens. This gave the issue of citizenship rights a far greater significance to the Chinese than can be understood in English, as it appeared to the Chinese that their civil rights were being taken away. In this light, the depth of feeling amongst the Chinese community over what in English appears to be a legalistic difference between nationality and citizenship becomes very understandable.[87] This fear was solved with a simple change of terminology. Lee Kuan Yew obtained the Tunku's agreement that Singapore citizens would also be called Federation citizens. Nothing else was changed, including the restriction of Singapore citizens to vote solely in Singapore, but the furore died away.

Conclusion

The severe limitations of a purely English language historiography are thus evident. By remaining in a single language, one is subject to incomplete or inaccurate reporting of events. The context and background to the 13 May National Service incident or the Hock Lee bus riots were only obtainable in the vernacular press, while the reporting on the events themselves was subject to cultural or class bias. Even when events are reported accurately, other linguistic, class, or cultural barriers prevent an accurate depiction.

Naturally, Turnbull cannot be blamed for her own limitations. Indeed, she struggled against them. Amongst the possessions she left behind is a beginner's course in Chinese that she never was able to complete. Nor can she be blamed for being a product of her era and of the prevailing historical trends of her time. On the contrary, Turnbull advanced Singapore history far beyond what it had been before. In establishing the field and setting it on a professional academic footing, she established a very high bar for future historians to surpass.

What is regrettable is that, to the end, she continued to militate against alternative histories. In *A History of Modern Singapore, 1819–2005*, Turnbull masterfully traced the transformation of the free-minded and friendly European community of the early 19th century into the snobbish,

colour-conscious, and closed community of the 20th. Yet Turnbull regret-
fully was never able to see those faults in herself. On the contrary, in her
introduction to the third edition of *A History of Modern Singapore, 1819–
2005*, Turnbull dismissed historians who tried to reintegrate the histories
of those who ended up on the wrong side of Singapore's struggle for
independence, and those who lost out in the PAP's relentless pursuit of
stability and development.[88] Reiterating her belief in the importance of
law and order and her conviction that the ends of economic development
justified the means of repression, she argued that the "prosaic path of
eschewing ideology in favour of practical common sense" was the correct
one. Sadly, to the end, she still refused to countenance that "law and
order" and "practical common sense" were themselves linguistically, cul-
turally, and ideologically influenced concepts.

Notes

1. Ping Tjin Thum, "Chinese Newspapers in Singapore, 1945–1963 —
    Mediators of Elite and Popular Tastes in Culture and Politics", *Journal of
    the Malaysian Branch of the Royal Asiatic Society* 83, 1 (2010): 53–76.
2. Siew Min Sai and Jianli Huang, "The 'Chinese-Educated' Political Van-
    guards: Ong Pang Boon, Lee Khoon Choy and Jek Yueng Thong", in *Lee's
    Lieutenants*, ed. Lam Peng Er Lam and Kevin Y.L. Tan (Singapore: Allen &
    Unwin, 1999), pp. 132–6.
3. Thum, "Chinese Newspapers in Singapore, 1945–1963", pp. 55–60.
4. C.M. Turnbull, *A History of Modern Singapore, 1819–2005* (Singapore: NUS
    Press, 2009), p. 249.
5. Ibid.
6. Ibid.
7. Colony of Singapore, Proceedings of the Second Legislative Council, 3rd
    Session, 1953 (Singapore: Government Printing Office, 1955), p. B299;
    Nanyang Siang Pao (henceforth *NYSP*), 21 October 1953; *Sin Chew Jit Poh*
    (henceforth *SCJP*), 21 October 1953; *Chung Shing Jit Poh* (henceforth *CSJP*),
    21 October 1953; *Nanfang Evening Post* (henceforth *NEP*), 21 October 1953.
8. Turnbull, *A History of Modern Singapore, 1819–2005*, p. 253.
9. H.E. Wilson, *Social Engineering in Singapore: Educational Policies and Social Change
    1819–1972* (Singapore: Singapore University Press, 1978), p. 156.
10. Ibid., pp. 140–1.
11. Liok Ee Tan, *Politics of Chinese Education in Malaya, 1945–61* (Kuala Lumpur:
    Oxford University Press, 1997), p. 67.
12. Federation of Malaya, *Report of the Special Committee Appointed by the High Com-
    missioner in Council to Consider Ways and Means of Implementing the Policy Outlined*

in the Education Ordinance, 1952 in the context of diminishing financial resources of the Federation (Council Paper No. 67 of 1954).

13. Tan, *Politics of Chinese Education in Malaya, 1945–61*, pp. 70–6.

14. *SCJP*, 16 October 1954. See also *NYSP*, 8 November 1954, 15 November 1954; *SCJP*, 9 November 1954, *CSJP*, 10 November 1954, *NEP*, 10 November 1954.

15. *NYSP*, 12 October 1954.

16. *NYSP*, 21 October 1954.

17. *NYSP*, 24 October 1954.

18. *NYSP*, 16 November 1954.

19. All Chinese dailies [*NYSP*, *SCJP*, *CSJP*] 18 November 1954; *NEP*, 18 November 1954.

20. *NYSP*, 20 November 1954.

21. *NYSP*, 9 December 1954.

22. *CSJP*, 20 November 1954; *NYSP*, 23 November 1954.

23. All Chinese dailies, 24 November 1954.

24. Turnbull, *A History of Modern Singapore, 1819–2005*, p. 252.

25. Ibid., pp. 263–7.

26. Ibid., p. 250.

27. Turnbull, *A History of Modern Singapore, 1819–2005*, p. 252.

28. *NEP*, 20 November 1953; *Sin Chew Weekly*, 26 November 1953; *NYSP*, 27 November 1953, 19 March 1954; *CSJP*, 18 March 1954, 27 March 1954.

29. *NYSP*, 27 November 1953, 16 December 1953, 19 March 1954.

30. *NYSP*, 16 March 1954.

31. *NEP*, 11 January 1954.

32. *SCJP*, 5 April 1954; *NYSP Saturday Review*, 24 April 1954; *SCJP*, 15 May 1954.

33. *NEP*, 23 April 1954.

34. *NEP*, 6 April 1954; *SCJP* 6 April 1954.

35. *NEP*, 22 April 1954; *NYSP Saturday Review*, 1 May 1954; *NYSP*, 14 May 1954.

36. Hong Liu and Sin-Kiong Wong, *Singapore Chinese Society in Transition: Business, Politics, and Socio-Economic Change, 1945–1965* (New York: Peter Lang, 2004), p. 146.

37. *NEP*, 23 April 1954.

38. *NYSP*, 14 May 1954, 24 May 1954; Ting Hui Lee, *The Open United Front: The Communist Struggle in Singapore 1954–1966* (Singapore: South Seas Society, 1996), p. 49n2.

39. *NYSP*, 14 May 1954; Colony of Singapore, Proceedings of the Second Legislative Council, 4th Session, 1954/55 (Singapore, 1956), B126–B131.

40. *NEP*, 11 January 1954.

41. *SCJP*, 14 May 1954.

42. *NYSP*, 23 January 1953; *SCJP*, 11 February 1953.

43. *NEP*, 13 May 1954, 14 May 1954; *NYSP*, 14 May 1954; *SCJP*, 14 May 1954, 15 May 1954; *CSJP*, 14 May 1954, 15 May 1954; *Singapore Standard*, 14 May 1954.

44. *Warta*, 18 May 1954.

45. *Straits Times*, 14 May 1954.

46. *Sin Chew Weekly*, 20 May 1954.

47. *NYSP*, 19 May 1954; *SCJP*, 19 May 1954; *CSJP*, 19 May 1954.

48. *SCJP*, 21 May 1954; *NYSP*, 21 May 1954; *CSJP*, 21 May 1954.

49. *NYSP*, 16 June 1954; *SCJP*, 16 June 1954; *CSJP*, 16 June 1954.

50. *NEP*, 22 June 1954; *SCJP*, 22–24 June 1954; *NYSP*, 22–24 June 1954; *CSJP*, 22–24 June 1954.

51. *NYSP*, 24 June 1954, 25 June 1954; *SCJP*, 25 June 1954; *CSJP*, 25 June 1954.

52. *NEP*, 5 July 1954.

53. *NYSP*, 6 July 1954.

54. *NYSP*, 7 September 1954, 13 September 1954, 14 September 1954; *SCJP*, 8 September 1954.

55. *NYSP*, 19 September 1954; *SCJP*, 19 September 1954.

56. Colony of Singapore Annual Report 1954, pp. 25–9. See also Singapore Labour Department Annual Reports 1947–1953.

57. Colony of Singapore Annual Report 1954, p. 27.

58. Charles Gamba, *The Origins of Trade Unionism in Malaya: A Study in Colonial Labour Unrest* (Singapore: Eastern Universities Press Ltd, 1962), pp. 352–3.

59. *SCJP*, 4 February 1953; *NEP*, 29 January 1953; *NYSP*, 12 March 1953.

60. Kim Wah Yeo, *Political Development in Singapore, 1945–55* (Singapore: Singapore University Press, 1973), pp. 233–6. When a reporter from the *Straits Times* tried to form a union, he was promptly sacked. For a deeper discussion of labour politics until 1955, see Yeo, 1973, pp. 202–50.

61. *NEP*, 30 December 1953, 17 February 1954, 13 May 1954, *NYSP*, 4 January 1954.

62. *NEP*, 2 August 1954.

63. *NYSP*, 4 August 1954, 5 August 1954.

64. *SCJP*, 25 August 1954, 26 August 1954.

65. All Chinese dailies, 24 February 1955.

66. Lee Kuan Yew, Legislative Assembly Debates [henceforth LAD], 16 May 1955, Col 2043–206.

67. *NYSP*, 29 April 1955.

68. *NEP*, 29 April 1955.

69. Lee Kuan Yew, LAD, 16 May 1955, Col 2083–210.

70. Ibid.

71. *NEP*, 11 May 1955.

72. All Chinese dailies, 10 May 1955.

73. David Marshall, LAD, 16 May 1955, Col 2353–6.

74. Turnbull, *A History of Modern Singapore, 1819–2005*, p. 263.
75. Ibid., p. 262.
76. Ibid., p. 264.
77. Lee Kuan Yew, LAD, 16 May 1955, C209–10.
78. Lee Kuan Yew, LAD, 16 May 1955, C214.
79. William Goode, LAD, 16 May 1955, C176.
80. For example, Andrew Teo, Kenneth Koh.
81. Freedom Press No. 61, May 1955.
82. Lee, *The Open United Front: The Communist Struggle in Singapore 1954–1966*, pp. 79–84.
83. *NYSP*, 31 May 1955.
84. See for example *NYSP*, 27 May 1955, 19 June 1955; *SCJP*, 19 June 1955, *SCJP*, 15 February 1957.
85. Turnbull, *A History of Modern Singapore, 1819–2005*, p. 280.
86. *NYSP*, 16 August 1962.
87. Thum, "Chinese Newspapers in Singapore, 1945–1963", pp. 70–2.
88. Turnbull, *A History of Modern Singapore, 1819–2005*, p. 15.

Bibliography

Gamba, Charles. *The Origins of Trade Unionism in Malaya: A Study In Colonial Labour Unrest*. 1st ed. Singapore: Eastern Universities Press Ltd, 1962.

Lee Ting Hui. *The Open United Front: The Communist Struggle in Singapore 1954–1966*. Singapore: South Seas Society, 1996.

Liu Hong and Wong Sin-Kiong. *Singapore Chinese Society in Transition: Business, Politics, and Socio-Economic Change, 1945–1965*. New York: Peter Lang, 2004.

Sai Siew Min and Huang Jianli. "The 'Chinese-Educated' Political Vanguards: Ong Pang Boon, Lee Khoon Choy and Jek Yueng Thong." In *Lee's Lieutenants*, ed. Peng Er Lam and Kevin Y.L. Tan. Singapore: Allen & Unwin, 1999, pp. 132–68.

Tan Liok Ee. *Politics of Chinese Education in Malaya, 1945–61*. Kuala Lumpur: Oxford University Press, 1997.

Thum Ping Tjin. "Chinese Newspapers in Singapore, 1945–1963 — Mediators of Elite and Popular Tastes in Culture and Politics". *Journal of the Malaysian Branch of the Royal Asiatic Society* 83, 1 (2010): 53–76.

Turnbull, C.M. *A History of Modern Singapore, 1819–2005*. Singapore: NUS Press, 2009.

Wilson, H.E. *Social Engineering in Singapore: Educational Policies and Social Change 1819–1972*. Singapore: Singapore University Press, 1978.

Yeo Kim Wah. *Political Development in Singapore, 1945–55*. Singapore: Singapore University Press, 1973.

5

Historical Sketch of the Settlement of Singapore

John Bastin

Sir Stamford Raffles listed among his losses in the disastrous fire on the ship *Fame* on 2 February 1824 a "detailed account" of the establishment of Singapore which, he said, contained "the principles on which it is founded; the policy of our Government in founding it; the history of commerce in the Eastern Islands; its present state and prospects; [its] ... rapid rise ... ; its history until I gave over the charge; with all the original documents connected with the discussion with the Dutch, and every voucher and testimony which could have been required to make good the British claim, and uphold measures I had adopted".[1]

This description is given in a letter to the Directors of the East India Company dated 8 February 1824, but in a general letter to his friends in England describing the fire on the ship, he writes only of his "intended account of the establishment of Singapore", indicating that it had not been written at the time he boarded the *Fame*, and that his losses related only to the documentary materials he had assembled for the work. This is confirmed by a statement contained in a letter to his brother-in-law, Peter Auber (1788–1848), Assistant Secretary of the East India Company, three months earlier, on 4 November 1823: "I propose on the voyage ... [to England], if my health admits, to sketch out something like an account of the establishment of Singapore, with a description of the place, map, &c. Something of the kind seems necessary for general information".[2]

How Raffles envisaged this account is outlined in a letter he wrote to his friend, Thomas Murdoch (1758–1845/6), ten days later, on 14 November 1823: "I notice what you say regarding the publication of some account of the establishment of Singapore, with a map annexed, and thank you for the hint. I have little to say on the subject, more than has been repeated over and over again in my official despatches, though perhaps in different words; but as these are likely to moulder away in Leadenhall-street, without perhaps being twice read, it may be useful should I attempt a more public exposition of my sentiments and views. Indeed, after what has taken place, and particularly with reference to the extraordinary assertion of Lord Bathurst as to the nature of my appointment [that he was merely a commercial agent of the East India Company without political authority], something of a public nature will be required from me; and although I am far from wishing to obtrude myself or my proceedings on the public, I feel confident, that the more my conduct is investigated and known, the more credit will at any rate be given to my motives; so that, in this point of view, I have rather an inducement to publish than otherwise. Should, therefore, my health admit, I shall probably devote a few hours in the day, during the voyage home, to condense into a convenient space what I think may be interesting on the subject, to be revised after my arrival in England, according to circumstances ... According to my present notion of the subject, it occurs to me that, by way of introduction, I might enlarge on the course and value of the trade of the Eastern islands and China, its past history and present state, with a description of the more interesting points of character among the inhabitants, and some account of the geography and natural history of the different countries. I might then give a short, but pointed account of the question with the Dutch; the reasons which induced the establishment at Singapore; how that establishment was effected; the principle on which it was maintained, and the rapidity of its rise; a short description of the place, its inhabitants, productions, and localities, might follow, with an account of its institutions, and an appendix, containing the regulations for the Chinese and Malay College, &c."[3]

It is to be regretted that Raffles never wrote this account of Singapore. He enjoyed few opportunities for writing during the horrendous homeward voyage to England on the *Mariner* (John Herbert), and what leisure he had was spent in drawing up a summary of his administrations in the East for submission to the Directors of the East India Company. This was entitled *Statement of the Services of Sir Stamford Raffles*, and was printed by Cox and Baylis of Great Queen Street, Lincoln's-Inn-Fields, shortly after his arrival in London. It was a somewhat perfunctory effort because of the loss of his papers in the fire on the *Fame*, but on pages 56–7 of the work he repeated his determination to write a detailed account of Singapore: "Of the present circumstances of Singapore, of its rapid rise and prosperity, and of the prospects which it holds out of greatly extending and improving our commerce in the East, I shall refrain from particular notice in this place. These particulars it is proposed to give to the public in a separate memoir, in which its progress from the commencement will be stated in detail."

Raffles again refers to having "pledged" himself "to give the public a memoir on Singapore" in a letter to Charlotte, Duchess of Somerset (1772–1827), dated 2 November 1824,[4] but in the period between then and his death on 5 July 1826, he appears to have done little. This was partly due to ill-health, and partly to the press of business, including the founding of the Zoological Society of London, but the main reason for his failure to produce the account was because of the lack of documentary materials. He attempted to repair some of his losses in the *Fame* by soliciting records from his friends in Singapore, and from his sister, Mary Ann Flint (1789–1837), wife of the Master Attendant at Singapore, Captain William Lawrence Flint, R.N. (1781–1828), but to little avail. His intention, therefore, of writing a "Memoir" on Singapore came to nothing.

Yet, there is in print, though it has never been recognised, a brief "Historical Sketch of the Settlement of Singapore", which was written in large part by Raffles, and published anonymously in July 1823 in *The Asiatic Journal and Monthly Register for British India and its Dependencies* XVI, 91: 24–30. That it was largely written by him is established by the following points. First, the argument about British rights to Singapore is the same as he expressed in his various despatches on the subject, and second, the wording of some of the passages in the "Historical Sketch" is the same, or similar, to that in his long despatch to the Supreme Government of 13 February 1819 in which he reported the founding of the British settlement.[5] Indeed, the fourth paragraph of this despatch contains a description of the Karimun Islands which is virtually identical to that given in the tenth paragraph of the "Historical Sketch": "Geographically the Carimons seem to be well situated for giving to a strong Naval Power the Command of the Straits during War; but they are yet uninhabited, and are covered with an almost impenetrable forest — The Northern part of the larger Island is mountainous, but to the

Southward, a portion comprehending at least three fourths of its extent, … is low and apparently swampy — The only harbour the Carimons possess is formed to the North East, by the position of the lesser Island, and altho' there is a sufficient depth of water on one side of this harbour to enable Ships to approach the Shore in the event of their finding it necessary to seek protection from a battery, yet when this advantage is afforded, the mountains rise abruptly from the Sea, and the Settlement must necessarily be established at a considerable distance, where level land may be found — the nature of this land is such as to justify a doubt of its salubrity, and on the whole, the position did not appear to me to be sufficiently inviting to be made our Chief object of attainment …"[6] Similar brief passages in the "Historical Sketch" relate to other parts of the despatch.

This was a "Secret" despatch addressed to the Chief Secretary to the Supreme Government in Calcutta and restricted to the Governor-General and members of his Council. Yet less than three months after it was written, sections of it had been leaked to the *Calcutta Journal*, and were printed in the issue of 1 May 1819, cols. 325*–328*, together with a description, and map of the harbour of Singapore by Captain Daniel Ross of the Bombay Marine, who had been present at the founding of the British settlement. Raffles is the most likely person to have supplied this material to the *Calcutta Journal*, though he may have done so through the agency of his Secretary, Dr. William Jack (1795–1822), whose known admiration for his master may explain the laudatory reference in the account to "the active and penetrating mind of Sir Stamford Raffles, (than whom no man has given to the world a more splendid proof of his intimate acquaintance with every thing connected with out eastern possessions)". This sentence could, of course, have come from the grateful pen of the editor of the *Calcutta Journal*, James Silk Buckingham (1786–1855), though it has to be said that similar flourishes can also be found in articles supplied directly by Raffles to the London press describing his activities in Sumatra. Indeed, even in the "Historical Sketch", we find the advantages of establishing a British station south of the Melaka Straits attributed to "the active mind of Sir Thomas Stamford Raffles".

Four years after its publication in the *Calcutta Journal*, the account was revised and formed the basis of the "Historical Sketch", published in *The Asiatic Journal and Monthly Register* XVI, 91. Additions were made, including extracts (pp. 27–8) from a private letter of Raffles to the third Marquess of Lansdowne (1780–1863) dated 15 April 1820 which had been appended to the *Report relative to the Trade with the East Indies and China* issued in May 1821 by a Select Committee of the House of Lords of which Lansdowne was Chairman. Other new material in the "Historical Sketch" is extracted from *The Prince of Wales Island Gazette* of 10 October 1822, copies of which would have reached Singapore shortly after Raffles' arrival in the island on his third and final visit, and provide a satisfactory chronology for the "Historical Sketch" having been despatched from Singapore to London in time for its publication in *The Asiatic Journal* in July 1823. This, of course, is on the assumption that it was sent by Raffles, but one can think of no one else who would have wanted to publish a revamped version of the earlier account in the *Calcutta Journal*, with suitable updated additions, in order to publicise the commercial importance and legal status of Singapore at the resumption of the discussions in London relating to Anglo-Dutch dissensions in the East.

Yet there are elements in the "Historical Sketch" which suggest that its author was writing at a distance from Singapore, and with out-of-date information, such as on page 29 where it is stated that "Sir Thomas Raffles was expected ... to establish his government at the settlement [Singapore], instead of Bencoolen, if the sanction of the Court of Directors could be obtained for that measure". This statement clearly relates to Raffles' position earlier in 1822, and not to the period later in the year when he was at Singapore, so one must suppose that if he was involved, the outline of the "Historical Sketch" was drawn up at Bengkulu and revised in Singapore before being despatched to London. The only qualification to this supposition is that the "Historical Sketch" contains references to "Sir Thomas", and not to "Sir Stamford", which was the form Raffles preferred at the time.

Whatever revisions and alternations may have been made to the "Historical Sketch", and whatever the precise manner of its composition, it does not alter the fact that the work draws substantially on material written by Raffles. It cannot be said that it is a major work on the history of Singapore, and it is a poor shadow of what he intended to write on the subject, but it is the only contemporary printed account of the events leading to the establishment of the British settlement.

The accounts in the *Calcutta Journal* and the "Historical Sketch" both contain a verbatim report of a survey of Singapore harbour made in February 1819 by Captain Daniel Ross of the Bombay Marine. A copy of his manuscript chart, which accompanied the survey, found its way at the time into the hands of the editor of the *Calcutta Journal*, who had it engraved for publication in the issue of 1 May 1819. It is the first map or chart of Singapore published after the British settlement on the island, and is reproduced here to accompany the facsimile report of the "Historical Sketch of the Settlement of Singapore", published in *The Asiatic Journal and Monthly Register for British India and its Dependencies* XVI, 91 (July 1823): 24–30.

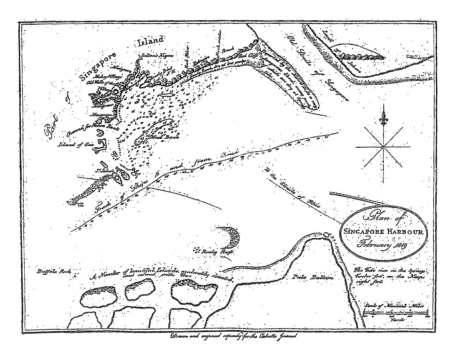

Chart of Singapore Harbour by Captain Daniel Ross, February 1819
Engraved for the *Calcutta Journal*, 1 May 1819

HISTORICAL SKETCH OF THE SETTLEMENT OF SINGAPORE.

THE island of Singapore is situated at the extremity of the peninsula of Malacca, in what is called the Straits of Singapore, through which lies the route of vessels to and from the China seas. The town stands on a point of land near the western part of a bay, and is easily distinguished by a pleasant hill behind it, partly cleared of trees, which abound on the island.

The motives which influenced the Government of India to establish a free port in this quarter, and the circumstances which led to the choice and occupation of this spot for the settlement, are briefly these:

When the peace of 1814 transferred to the Netherlands' Government their Eastern possessions, they acquired a very serious preponderance of power in this quarter. Besides Java and the Moluccas, the Dutch were masters of the best trading stations on Borneo, several settlements on Sumatra, and likewise Malacca, which enabled them to exercise a powerful influence over the petty Malay princes. It was believed, upon pretty sure grounds, that this selfish people contemplated the placing their Eastern possessions under such a system of restraint, as to secure to themselves a monopoly of the commerce in those possessions, and in fact entirely to engross the Malay trade.

The advantages that would attend the occupation of some station in the Straits of Malacca, to obviate this exclusive system of the Dutch, as well as to facilitate the objects of our trade in general, first occurred to the active mind of Sir Thomas Stamford Raffles: who no sooner suggested the scheme, than it was immediately concurred in by the Supreme Government of Bengal; and in the latter end of the year 1818, Sir Thomas was selected as the fittest person to carry the project into execution.

Sir Thomas accordingly sailed from Calcutta, vested with discretionary powers as to the selection of an ap-

propriate station for a British Settlement, which might in some degree command the free navigation of the Straits of Malacca; being fettered with no other restrictions than the just ones of not violating the rights of the Netherlands' Government, nor using force or improper influence with the natives.

Some jealousy, it appears, was felt at Penang respecting this scheme, from motives which can easily be imagined; and when the expedition arrived at that place, the hopes entertained of receiving every assistance requisite to the full accomplishment of its object, were disappointed: A decided want of cordial co-operation was perceived, which did not, however, prevent the expedition from proceeding to its destination.

It is disagreeable to observe that the hostility, if we may so term it, between the two settlements of Penang and Singapore, grows every day more decided. A letter we have seen in the Penang Gazette, 10th October 1822, is full of invective against the improper artifices of those who labour to misrepresent " the increasing importance and prosperity " of its rival, and of endeavours to show that the latter has not increased so much as it ought, under the favourable circumstances in which it is placed; and that Penang, on the contrary, has greatly added to the amount of its exports and imports.[*]

---

[*] " The value of imports and exports, in Penang amounted in 1818-19 to upwards of half a million of dollars more than the preceding year. In 1819-20, in which year Singapore had more trade than it has had since, or fully as much, the value of imports and exports at this island (Penang) was upwards of 500,000 dollars more than in 1818-19; and in 1821-22, the value of merchandize exceeded that of 1817-18, the year preceding the Settlement of Singapore, upwards of $15,000 dollars. I may add, that the present year will bear a comparison with the most favourable one since the formation of this colony. These are satisfactory results, Mr. Editor, and I hope conclusive, that the Singapore writers not only mistake, but misrepresent."—Extract of Letter referred to:—On the other hand, a letter in the Calcutta John Bull of October 5, 1822, states, that Penang " had suffered much by the produce of Sumatra going to Singapore."

At the period when the expedition sailed, the Dutch claimed sovereignty over Rhio, and the whole of the ancient empire of Johore, as a former dependency of Malacca; and they spoke openly of preventing the Rajah from making any cession of the Carimons to the English. So far had they effected their purpose, as to have formed an establishment at Rhio under a treaty with the chief, the terms of which were not publicly known, but the nature of which must have been extremely limited. No Dutch flag had been actually hoisted either at Lingen, Johore, or Pahang, the other three great divisions of the empire; so that, in truth, the Dutch influence might have been considered as strictly confined to Rhio, which port was governed by a Bugguese Chief, the Rajah Mooda, or Vizier; while the legitimate Sultan of Johore was still a free agent, and under no engagements to the Dutch.

Though Rhio was thus so far secured to the Dutch as to give any interference with their claims there an appearance of injustice, or violation of right, yet Johore remained free for examination; but, as it was advisable, before deciding upon any particular spot, to examine the whole of those which were eligible, the expedition proceeded first to the Carimons.

These islands, in a geographical point of view, are admirably situated for giving to a strong naval power the command of the straits; but they are uninhabited, and are covered with primeval forests. The northern part of the larger island is mountainous; but to the southward, for an extent of three-fourths of the whole island, it is low, and apparently swampy. The only harbour is found to the north-east, by the position of the little Carimon; and although it has sufficient depth of water on one side to enable ships to lie under the protection of batteries, where this advantage is offered the mountains rise abruptly from the sea, and the defences must

necessarily be distant from the principal settlement, which would require to be fixed where level land is to be found. Doubts were entertained as to the salubrity of the place, and, under all circumstances, the Carimons did not present sufficient claims for selection.

The expedition next proceeded to Singapore, where it was understood that the chief authority of Johore had now fixed his residence. This town was founded by the Malays so early as the twelfth century; it was their first station in the Archipelago, and long the rival of Maning-Kabue, in Sumatra. In the neighbourhood of the town there was found to be sufficient cleared land for the immediate accommodation of the troops; the surface of the country was elevated without being mountainous; the harbour unrivalled in those seas as to capacity and security, and in every respect this station appeared to be admirably adapted for the proposed establishment.

Upon inquiry, it was found that there had never been any Dutch Settlement either here or at Old Johore, and that that nation had not even attempted hitherto to exercise an authority or even influence over these ports. Johore Lama had long been deserted, and the chief authority now resided at Singapore, where the Dutch flag had never appeared, and where it would not be received or admitted on any terms.

The Toomoongong, who now exercised authority here, held the lands of Singapore, Johore, and of all the islands about the Straits, with the exception of Rhio and Lingen, as his own inheritance, his family having always enjoyed the revenues of them since he held his commission as an independent chief of this division of the empire, from the late Sultan of Johore, Mohammed Shah, whose independence the English had always acknowledged; and since the death of that chief, there had not even existed a contention for supremacy throughout these dominions.

It having been previously ascertained, by a visit of Major Farquhar to Rhio, that no claims to the exercise of authority over Singapore were set up in that quarter, and the actual governor of the island, whose *legitimacy* (a material point in these ticklish times) was fully established by the fact of his being the twenty-sixth monarch of his line, having solicited the friendship and protection of the British, an arrangement was concluded for establishing a British settlement there, on grounds unobjectionable to any of the parties concerned,* and the British flag was hoisted with due honours and ceremony.

" It cannot be wondered at, when the Netherlands' Government discovered the advantages likely to accrue from this settlement, that its removal became a very important and desirable object to them. It was at first contended that the whole of the eastern stations enumerated before were dependencies of Malacca, and as such belonged to the Dutch; and that, besides, the Rajah of Rhio had absolutely ceded Singapore by treaty to the Dutch nation.

Now a plain and satisfactory answer may be made to the first objection; Rhio, or rather the empire of Johore, was not a dependency of Malacca; when the latter place came into the possession of the British in 1795. On that occasion the military and naval commanders of the expedition demanded of the Dutch authorities at Malacca, whether Rhio, &c. were dependencies. The Dutch governor replied, that all engagements between the chief of Rhio and the governor-general of Batavia had ceased and determined, and they were consequently considered and acknowledged by the British as independent states, and a document to this effect was actually given to the Sultan.

* It would appear, that a sort of rent was paid for the island in shape of a monthly stipend to the prince.

The second objection may be removed by a reference to what has already been advanced, namely, that the Rajah of Rhio, with whom the Dutch are said to have concluded the treaty, by which a cession of all these other ports are made to them, has really, according to his own confession, and the general understanding of all the Eastern chiefs, no authority beyond his own immediate territory. Singapore was found by the British Expedition in the quiet and undisputed possession of its legitimate sovereign, reigning as much by the suffrage and consent of the subjects over whom he exercised his rule, as by his own right to the throne, occupied as it had been by his ancestors for several generations.

These are the chief and only important objections that have been publicly announced in regard to our occupation of Singapore. So bent were the Dutch Government upon dislodging the settlers, that it was expected for some time that our Government at home would yield to the remonstrances of the former, and issue orders for the abandonment of the island, an apprehension which excited no little interest in India, and checked the progress of the Settlement. One of the Dutch governors, it appears *threatened* to drive the English away by force. The futility of the Dutch pretensions, however, and the policy and expediency of maintaining such a post as Singapore, became so apparent in England, that our ministers refused to give way. The consequence shortly was, the comparative ruin of Malacca, During the last year it was represented to be quite deserted; not a vessel resorting there except for refreshment, or a few peculs of spices; and the best part of the inhabitants removing to Singapore, notwithstanding the prohibitory capitation tax levied upon those who emigrate.

The hostility of the Dutch to this Settlement arose not merely from the natural jealousy which a rival power may be expected to feel on such an occasion, and from the effectual check which the establishment of a free port would offer to the revival of that pernicious system of oppression and monopoly they meditated; but from a consciousness, inspired by past experience, of the anxiety of the native inhabitants of all their possessions, to withdraw themselves from their authority,* and to seek the mild and fostering rule of the English. During the revolts in the Moluccas in the year 1817, which nearly ended in the expulsion of the Dutch from those islands, the brave but unfortunate islanders not only fought under an English flag, but constantly declared their intention of placing themselves under the protection of the British.

The rapid progress made by this settlement is truly astonishing, and fully demonstrates the sagacity by which the measure was conceived. In the first two months no less than one hundred and seventy-three vessels are stated to have arrived there. Its central situation with respect to India and China, from the latter of which it is distant only five days' sail; its position in regard to Java, the great islands of Borneo and Sumatra, and the Eastern Archipelago; its physical advantages, being placed on a rich soil, surrounded by fertile tracts of land, that bid fair to become hereafter a vast commercial and agricultural establishment perhaps only inferior to Calcutta, are circumstances which, when duly considered, lessen in some degree our wonder at the influx of trade, especially when combined with the freedom from imposts.

In little more than a twelvemonth after the settlement was formed (which was placed under the direction of Major, now Colonel Farquhar, formerly Resident at Malacca), Sir Thos.

* By a communication received at Singapore, 1st October last, from the Dutch Commissioner at Borneo, the trade with Sinkawang is interdicted, on account, it would appear, of the revolt of the whole Chinese population, amounting to 90,000, against the Dutch Government.

Raffles gave the following statement of its condition, in a letter to the Marquess of Lansdowne, dated April 15, 1820:

" The rapid rise of this important station, Singapore, during the year that it has been in our possession, is perhaps without its parallel. When I hoisted the British flag, the population scarcely amounted to two hundred souls. In three months the number was not less than three thousand; and it now exceeds ten thousand, principally Chinese. No less than a hundred and seventy-three sail of vessels of different descriptions, principally native, arrived and sailed in the course of the first two months, and it has already become a commercial port of importance. I consider myself extremely fortunate in the situation, and in not having had to complain of any one of the almost invariable difficulties attending the establishment of new settlements. The establishment has more than equalled my anticipations; and its effects have been more marked and sudden than I could have contemplated, though not more so than I wished.

" If our object in the Eastern Seas and in China is commerce, and commerce alone, I am not aware of any plan so easy of adoption, or so unobjectionable, as that of making our station *free ports.* In a political point of view, it will have the effect of preventing and deterring other European nations from settling on the neighbouring coasts; for our continental possessions will enable us to do that, without considering it as a loss, which no other nation could do, except at a dead loss, in consequence of the greater distance of their power: this is particularly applicable to the French, Russians, and Americans. We can not only afford to maintain our Eastern stations without levying duties at them, but by doing so we improve the general trade, and consequent prosperity of our continental possessions. No other nation could afford to maintain such stations without levying duties.

"In a few years, if the system on which I have commenced is followed up, the whole of the Eastern Archipelago will be clothed from Great Britain; and I see no reason why Ava, Siam, Cochin China, and even a large portion of China, may not follow the example."

A very interesting and minute detail of the state of the settlement is given in a letter, dated Nov. 1, 1821, published in a Calcutta paper, from whence the following particulars are extracted:

A large population of various races were comfortably settled upon the island, whose soil furnishes an inexhaustible quantity of every requisite for building, of excellent quality. A well-built town is fast rising along the banks of the inlet which penetrates into the interior. This inlet is about three hundred feet wide towards its mouth; has regular tides, and is capable of admitting vessels of two hundred and fifty tons.

Between the inlet and a parallel rivulet, at the distance of a-quarter of a mile is a square plain, faced with a high sandy beach, free from surf, and terminated on the inner side by a steep hill, of a sufficient elevation to possess a beautiful and commanding view of the surrounding country and the Straits. On the further side of the inlet is, on one hand, a regularly built Chinese town; and on the other, beyond the rivulet, an extensive plain, in front of which the sandy beach stretches into an inner bay, and whence another inlet, resembling a river, encompasses it behind. The nearer part of this plain is marked out for a European town, and intersected by roads at right angles to each other. That more remote is partly occupied by natives; and it is there the Sultan resides.

The interior of the island, which, from a late general survey by the Resident, is found to be several times

larger than was supposed, or is laid down in the charts, consists of undulations of hill and dale, and is adapted to the growth of various and valuable commodities. Plantations of gambier, pepper, and spices are already making their appearance in many parts; cultivation is also extending to the neighbouring islands, which, from a nest and harbour for pirates, may soon be expected to become the abode of industrious and civilized people. An overland communication is meditated between Singapore and the interior of some of those Malay states on the east side of the peninsula, whose ports are shut up during the violence of the north-east monsoon.

The writer declares, that greatly as his expectations were raised by all he had heard respecting this much talked of settlement, they met with no disappointment; and he expresses his astonishment at finding so large a population of Malays, Bugueses, Chinese, &c., industriously employed upon a spot, that for ages past had been covered by impenetrable forests.

The advantages possessed by Singapore are not confined to those we have already enumerated; its facilities and resources are in many other respects admirable. Goods may at all times be shipped and landed; wood may be procured in abundance; the water is excellent; the soil rich and fruitful; the temperature surprisingly cool; and such is the salubrity of the climate, that the inhabitants have been almost totally exempted from sickness of any kind. Whilst that scourge of the human race in the eastern world, the *cholera morbus*, was ravaging most of the surrounding stations, and had approached its immediate neighbourhood, by visiting Malacca on one side, and Lingen on the other, Singapore was scarcely molested by it; a circumstance which, it seems, the natives attributed to the *good luck* of the English. The only drawback is what might be expected from a rapidly increasing settlement, the dearness of all provisions except fish.

The latest account we have seen is from a gentleman who halted at Singapore on his way to China, who was so charmed with the place, that he intimated his probable design of returning thither from China, instead of proceeding to England; and he had already secured some land at the settlement whereon to plant coffee-trees, &c.

The competition for land is represented to be very great, and the prosperity of the place in every respect most encouraging. Bengal produce was greatly in demand, and likely for a long time to continue so, particularly piece-goods and coarse chintz; and the returns were certain and favourable. Pepper, gold-dust, tin, betelnut, rattans, and even tea, which can be procured there from Europe vessels always cheaper than from China. "In short," adds the writer, "a more fortunate spot was never selected; and when the resources of Siam, Cochin-China and China are considered, it is difficult to calculate the extent to which, through a free intercourse with these vast kingdoms, the commerce of Singapore may rise." Sir Thomas Raffles was expected there to establish his government at the settlement, instead of Bencoolen, if the sanction of the Court of Directors could be obtained for that measure.

We shall conclude this sketch with the following description of the port of Singapore, by Capt. Ross, of the Bombay marine, which accompanies a chart of the harbour and vicinity, from a survey taken February 1819.

"Singapore harbour, situated four miles to the N.N.E. of St. John's Island, in what is commonly called the Singapore Straits, will afford a safe anchorage to ships in all seasons, and being clear of hidden danger, the approach to it is rendered easy by day or night. Its position is also favourable for commanding the navigation of the Straits, the track which the ships pursue being distant about five miles; and

it may be expected from its proximity, to the Malayan Islands and China Seas, that in a short time numerous vessels will resort to it for commercial purposes.

"At the anchorage, ships are sheltered from E.N.E. round to north and west, as far as S. by W. by the south point of Johore, Singapore, and many smaller islands, extending to St. John's; and thence round to the north point of Batang, bearing E.S.E., by the numerous islands forming the south side of Singapore Strait; the bottom, to within a few yards of the shore, is soft mud, and holds well.

"The town of Singapore, on the island of the same name, stands on a point of land near the western part of a bay, between which there is a creek; in which the native vessels anchor close to the town, and it may be found useful to European vessels of easy draught to repair in. On the eastern side of the bay, opposite to the tower, there is a deep inlet lined by mangroves, which would also be a good anchorage for native boats; and about north from the low sandy point of the bay there is a village inhabited by fishermen, a short way to the eastward of which is a passage through the mangroves, leading to a fresh water river.

"Ships that are coming from the eastward, have nothing to apprehend in rounding the small peaked island which is in the east side of St. John's, as the reef does not extend above a cable's length off it; and just without that the depth of water is from twelve to fourteen fathoms.[*] Having rounded the peaked island, at half a mile, a north or north by east course will lead to the anchorage, and twelve or fourteen fathoms be the depth; but when at one mile and a half from the island, it will decrease to five or four

[*] Capt. Ross has not noticed in his description the extensive shoal, reported by the natives to be a very dangerous one, extending, in his chart, from the N.W. corner of the island, in a S.W. direction, many parts of which are stated to be dry at spring tides.

and three-quarter fathoms at low water, on a flat which is two miles and a half long, and is parallel to the coast: there is no danger whatever on this bank, being soft mud. Continuing the north or north by east course, you will deepen into a channel of twelve or thirteen fathoms, and again shoal rather quickly to six fathoms on the shore bank, after which the depth decreases gradually to the shore. Large ships will find the best anchorage to be with Peaked Island, about south by west; and the eastern extreme of Singapore Island about north-east by east, in five fathoms at low water, where they will have the tower, bearing N.W. by W., distant one mile and a half. Ships of easy draught can go nearer into three fathoms at low water, with the Peaked Island bearing S.W., and Johore hill on, with the eastern extreme of Singapore Island, where they will be distant about three-quarters of a mile from the tower, and about half a mile from the eastern low sandy point of the bay.

"The coast to the eastward of the town-bay is one continued sandy beach; and half a mile to the eastern point of the bay, or two miles and a half from the town, there is a point where the depth of water is six or seven fathoms, at three or four hundred yards from the shore; and at six hundred yards a small bank, with about three fathoms at low water; the point offers a favourable position for batteries, to defend ships that may in time of war anchor near to it.

"The tide during the neaps is irregular, at two and three miles off shore, but close in it is otherwise. The rise and fall will be about ten or twelve feet, and it will be high water, at full and change, at 8 h. 30 m. The latitude of the town is about 1° 15½'N., and the variation of the needle observed on the low eastern point of the bay is 2° 9'E."

Notes

1. Lady Raffles, *Memoir of the Life and Public Services of Sir Thomas Stamford Raffles, F.R.S. &c.* ... (London: John Murray, 1830), facsimile reprint with an Introduction by John Bastin (Singapore: Oxford University Press, 1991), pp. 572–3.
2. Lady Raffles, *Memoir of the Life and Public Services of Sir Thomas Stamford Raffles*, p. 556.
3. Ibid., pp. 558–9.
4. Letters from Sir T.S. Raffles to Charlotte, Duchess of Somerset, 1817–24 (MSS. Eur. D.742/24, British Library); Lady Raffles, *Memoir of the Life and Public Services of Sir Thomas Stamford Raffles*, p. 584.
5. *Bengal Secret Consultations* 308, no. 26 (Asia, Pacific & Africa Collections, British Library).
6. T.S. Raffles, "Sir Stamford Raffles's Account of the Founding of Singapore", in John Bastin, *Letters and Books of Sir Stamford Raffles and Lady Raffles: The Tang Holdings Collection of Autograph Letters and Books of Sir Stamford Raffles and Lady Raffles* (Singapore: Editions Didier Millet, 2009), pp. 258–9.

Bibliography

Primary Sources

Bengal Secret Consultations, Vol. 308. Asia, Pacific & Africa Collections, British Library.
Letters from Sir T.S. Raffles to Charlotte, Duchess of Somerset, 1817–24. MSS. Eur. D.742/24, British Library.

Printed works

Calcutta Journal. Calcutta, 1818–19.
House of Lords. *Report [Relative to the Trade with the East Indies and China] from The Select Committee of the House of Lords, appointed to inquire into the means of extending and securing the Foreign Trade of the Country, and to report to the House; together with the Minutes of Evidence taken in Sessions 1820 and 1821, before the Said Committee: — 11 April 1821.* Ordered by The House of Commons, to be Printed, 7 May 1821.
Raffles, T.S. "Sir Stamford Raffles's Account of the Founding of Singapore". In John Bastin, *Letters and Books of Sir Stamford Raffles and Lady Raffles: The Tang Holdings Collection of Autograph Letters and Books of Sir Stamford Raffles and Lady Raffles*. Singapore, 2009, pp. 245–81.
_____. *Statement of the Services of Sir Stamford Raffles*. London, 1824. Facsimile reprint with an Introduction by John Bastin. Kuala Lumpur: Oxford University Press, 1978.

————. "Historical Sketch of the Settlement of Singapore". *The Asiatic Journal and Monthly Register for British India and its Dependencies* XVI, 91 (1823): 24–30.

Raffles, Lady. *Memoir of the Life and Public Services of Sir Thomas Stamford Raffles, F.R.S. &c.* ... London, 1830. Facsimile reprint with an Introduction by John Bastin. Singapore: Oxford University Press, 1991.

Wurtzburg, C.E. *Raffles of the Eastern Isles*. London, 1954.

6

Singapore's Role in Constituting the "Malay" Narrative

*Anthony Milner**

IN PUBLIC AND TO A LARGE EXTENT academic discussion, Singapore history has been focused on two great men: Sir Thomas Stamford Raffles and Lee Kuan Yew. The Malay history of Singapore, perhaps understandably, has received less attention. Partly because of my re-reading of Robert Pringle's classic study of Sarawak, I have begun to see just how central Singapore might be in the "Malay" narrative. Pringle speculated that the term "Malay" became "widely used in Sarawak today only because in 1841, James Brooke (the future 'Rajah' of the territory) brought it with him from Singapore."[1] The comment suggests that Singapore, far from being a side-show in Malay history, was critical in the constituting of the idea of a pan-Archipelago "Malay" racial identity. Furthermore, focusing on Singapore's role, I will suggest, provides the opportunity for a closer examination of not just why but also how the European discourse on race contributed to this process, particularly in its early stages.

---

* I should like to thank Peter Borschberg, Jane Drakard and Claire Milner for their assistance in the writing of this chapter.

The Malay History of Singapore

The outline of the Malay history of Singapore is now quite well-established. The island was by no means a major Malay centre in January 1819, when Raffles signed a preliminary treaty to establish a trading post on the island. Mary Turnbull (in the first edition of her fine *A History of Singapore, 1819–1975*) suggested Singapore might have had a thousand inhabitants. The vast majority were members of several tribes of *"orang laut*, or sea nomads" and there were also "twenty to thirty Malays" in the entourage of the local chieftain, the Temenggong, and a "similar number of Chinese".[2] The earlier, pre-Raffles history of Singapore (as Turnbull saw it) was "obscure": the physical remains encountered by Raffles included an earth wall running inland from the sea, a royal grave, "some sandstone foundation blocks and old fruit trees", and a long inscription on a large stone; also, the written records "relating to Singapore in ancient times are fragmentary".[3] Nevertheless, Turnbull reported that the chronicle of the great 15th-century sultanate of Melaka — the so-called "Malay Annals" — claims that the founder of Melaka had come from Palembang (in Sumatra) and then ruled in Singapore, and that in his time, "foreigners resorted in great numbers (to Singapore) so that the fame of the city and its greatness spread throughout the world."[4]

In recent decades, the Malay history of Singapore has been given increasing attention (and this is reflected in the most recent edition of Turnbull's *History*).[5] Chinese, Malay, Portuguese and Dutch records have been further examined, as well as archaeological remains. What has been called a "classical Malay port-city" — dating at least back to the 14th century and including what appears to be a temple on a square sandstone platform — has been identified, and contains evidence of a lively trade with China and other parts of the Archipelago.[6] From the 16th century, the Singapore region was central in the political and commercial contests between Johor, Aceh, the Portuguese and the Dutch: in fact, it has been observed that the "Straits of Singapore and Melaka have for centuries stood at the forefront of geo-strategic concerns."[7] The tendency to neglect the earlier, pre-Raffles, Malay history of Singapore, it has been argued, has "exacerbated Singapore's post-1965 identity crisis" — it has prevented Singaporeans having "a deeper understanding of their place in the region ..."[8] One important question about this period of Singapore's past, however, concerns at what stage the locals living there would have seen themselves as part of a specifically Malay narrative. As John Miksic has argued, the evidence suggests that "we cannot equate Singapore's indigenous population of the 14th century with the identity glossed as 'Malay'."[9]

Although Singapore became part of a British colony in the 19th century, and the Chinese had become the largest community by 1827,[10] the continuing importance of the island as a religious, cultural and political centre for people who would at least today be identified as "Malay" has certainly been acknowledged. Colonial rule brought opportunities as well as restrictions — in particular, as I'll discuss in greater detail, a degree of freedom from the traditional ruling elites of the sultanates (or *kerajaan*) in the surrounding region. The migrant to Singapore entered a strongly urban settlement — and a hub for ideas as well as commerce. Singapore became the gathering point in the Archipelago for the pilgrimage to Mecca — and the place where people would be likely to encounter new religious doctrines. New non-royal elites came to the fore in Singapore — and important divisions emerged in the "Malay" and "Muslim" community. One internal challenge to the *ancient regime* in the first years of the settlement is associated with the writer Abdullah Abdul Kadir, a radical thinker who was in close touch with the British founders of the new Singapore. Modern schools were soon established in the settlement, and then newspapers that promoted public discussion. In the early decades of the 20th century, newspaper editor Mohd. Eunos Abdullah became leader of the Singapore Malay Union, a pioneer political organisation. With respect to religious reformism — also benefiting from the measure of ideological freedom in Singapore — the pioneering paper *Al Imam* (1906–1908) helped to develop an explicitly Islamic template for the restructuring of local society, and was succeeded by numerous other Islamic periodicals over the following decades.[11]

The two main centres where people who were increasingly labelled "Malay" gathered were Kampong Glam — where the Temenggong and his following had been based — and Geylang, which attracted mainly new immigrants. By the 1930s, the political activists in Singapore had begun to be viewed as a threat to British rule — by contrast, in the Japanese occupation period, they tended to be given encouragement. After the Pacific War, as Khoo Kay Kim has explained, "Malay political activities became more widespread on the Peninsula"; but Singapore "remained the centre of Malay literary and journalistic activities" and also of the "Malay movie industry". When Malaya gained independence in 1957, "most of the writers, journalists and movie stars, especially those who were not Singapore-born, relocated as Kuala Lumpur emerged as the new centre of the Malay world..."[12] After Singapore had first joined (in 1963) and then separated from Malaysia (in 1965), the Singapore "Malay/Muslim community" became a minority in the new Singapore nation, and began to occupy "a position which is not unlike, but by no means identical to, that of the Muslims in Mindanao (Philippines) and Patani (Thailand)."[13] The first President of independent Singapore, Yusuf bin Ishak, was in some ways a model for this minority: in Turnbull's words, he "stood for multi-racialism and secular modernisation and worked to lift the condition of the Malays through their own efforts and through education."[14] The social and economic condition of the Malay community has certainly been a major theme of scholarly investigation.[15]

The claim that Singapore was a 14th-century precursor to Melaka, together with its status as a hub for religious and social reform in colonial times and its role as an early focus for modern political activity — all give Singapore a special role in a retrospective "Malay" history, quite apart from the Raffles/Lee Kuan Yew narrative of the building of a city-nation of global significance. The Pringle comment about Brooke bringing the term "Malay" from Singapore to Sarawak, however, suggests an even more fundamental role.

The Concept of "Malay"

The term "Malay", of course, is by no means an invention of the early 19th century. Writings from an earlier period refer to "Malay customs and ceremonial", "Malay music", "Malay dress", "Malay dance" and "Malay people" (*orang Melayu*). But these references are primarily concerned with the sultanate of Melaka and its successor the sultanate of Johor, and those polities closely associated with these kingdoms. Virginia Matheson Hooker observed long ago that in the *Malay Annals* — the royal chronicle of Melaka (and Johor) — the term "Melayu" is "reserved exclusively for those descended from Sumatran-Palembang forebears, and thus were close to the siGuntang-Melayu dynasty."[16] That is, "Malay" is used in the text for those people who were said to have come with the ruling family from Sumatra to Singapore, and then Melaka. When we turn to royal writings from outside the Melaka-Johor sphere — for instance, from Patani or Kedah — the local people are not described as "Malay".[17] The Acehnese text, the *Hikayat Aceh* — which is rare in being available in an early (17th-century) manuscript — makes a clear link between "Johor" and "Malay"; and it does not refer to Aceh itself, or Deli (in northeast Sumatra), as "Malay".[18]

Just why the word "Malay" was used at all is unclear. One possibility, however, is that the "Malay people" (the *orang Melayu*) who came with their royal leader to Melaka from Sumatra, had been named after a river called *Melayu*. There are *Melayu* rivers in both the Palembang and Jambi regions — both areas with which the people coming to the Peninsula were said to have had close association. The *orang Melayu* would thus have been people "of the *Melayu* river", just as the *orang Pahang* are people "of the *Pahang* river".

From the 16th century, Europeans would refer to people living in many parts of the Archipelago as "Malay", but the specific use of the word in Malay writings from this period tends to underline the danger of assuming that the people described would have defined themselves in the same terms. In fact, those officials who were scholarly enough to be precise in their use of language tend to confirm the need for such caution. Thus, William Marsden — who spent many years at a British post on the west coast of Sumatra in the late 1700s and became the English authority on that island — noted that in all the letters from "Malay" states that he received in his official capacity, the writers "very rarely" referred to themselves as "Malay".[19] A description that was often used, according to Marsden and numerous other observers,[20] was "people beneath the wind" (*orang dibawah angin*), or people located below the typhoon belt; but this term was applied as well to others in the Southeast Asian region, including Thailand and Java. The descriptions "*Jawah*" or "*Jawi*" also had a wider application. People who would later call themselves "Malay" were certainly referred to as *Jawi*, but so were many others across the Archipelago and even from mainland Southeast Asia.[21] Often, a person was identified with reference to a specific location, usually a river. We see *orang Johor* or *orang Sarapat* (a river in Borneo) — but as Tim Babcock stressed some decades ago, identification with a particular place should not be confused with "racial identity". Writing particularly of Sarawak, he explained that indigenous conceptions of identity were "characterised by impermanence", with "frequent change of group membership and assimilation of one group into another."[22]

It is in Malay writings of the early 19th century — particularly those of Abdullah Abdul Kadir — that we begin to see the use of "Malay" to describe people beyond the Melaka-Johor sphere. His writings focus on races rather than kingdoms. He used the term "*bangsa*" for "race" — writing of the English *bangsa*, Chinese *bangsa* and Arab *bangsa* — as well as the Malay *bangsa*. The inclusiveness of his concept of "Malay"

— the use of the term to describe many people beyond Melaka-Johor
— is evident in particular in the way he defined himself. Although he was
described by a contemporary as a "Tamilian of Southern Hindustan",
and although he tended sometimes to write of "the Malays" as an outsider, in his later work, he used the phrase "we Malays".[23] In a number
of publications, I have sought to trace the way the idea of the "Malay
race" gained influence in the 19th and 20th centuries.[24] In Singapore
Malay-language newspapers of the early 1900s, for instance, we encounter
careful ideological work relating to the *"Bangsa Melayu"* — refining, or
rather building the concept, giving it definition and emotive substance.
A "Malay" history began to be composed, to supplement or replace the
chronicles of individual sultanates. Books written in the new "novel"
genre were dedicated to the *Bangsa Melayu*, lauding the idea of "loving
one's race"; service to the *Bangsa Melayu* was described in the same language that had once been employed to depict devoted service to a sultan.
"Malay" associations were formed — teachers', craft, literary, and political associations. The manner in which the *bangsa* was constructed, so I
have argued, has a special interest for the student of the history of ideas.
It involved a significant revision or "localisation" of the concept of "race"
usually encountered in Europe.

This chapter, however, is not concerned to consider in detail the
ideological development of the *Bangsa Melayu* — but rather to examine the
origins of the process. Singapore — or rather, the colony of the Straits
Settlements (which included also Melaka and Penang) — and the British
colonial leadership made contributions at a number of levels to the
building of a Malay racial identity.

Singapore and the Building of the Idea of Race

First, the development of radical concepts — and from the perspective of
the royal elites, "race" could be seen as dangerously radical — is difficult
without a degree of freedom, and here Singapore provided an opportunity. Like Melaka and Penang, Singapore offered ideological space to
adopt or construct new social visions which might antagonise members
of the local *ancien régime*. In Singapore (as Turnbull has explained), the
influence of the Johor aristocracy was much reduced, leaving a leadership
vacuum among the indigenous population.[25] Abdullah was one of those
who took advantage of this to expound doctrines that were subversive
from the perspective of the royal courts. He wrote of the "tyranny and

injustice of the government of the rajas, especially towards their own subjects";[26] and also identified the British colony as a model of egalitarianism — a place where ordinary people could "sit with rajas": and "if we are rich, we can build houses and wear clothes just like rajas."[27] With respect to religion, Christian missionaries — who had good reason to be close observers — drew attention to the growing power of a specifically religious elite, able to exercise enhanced authority in the absence of strong royal leadership. The missionaries suggested that Islamic doctrine was more strictly observed in the British colony than the independent sultanates, or *kerajaan*. People from the sultanates tended to be more open to Christian teachings, and the moment these people "came on shore they (were) always cautioned not to go near us". The "Hajies of Singapore", in the words of one missionary, "refuse(d) themselves, and prevent(ed) others as far as they can from receiving or reading (Christian literature)". "Mohomedan bigotry" was more prevalent in Singapore than in the independent states of the region.[28]

By the opening of the 20th century, Singapore had become well-established as an Islamic centre where (in William Roff's words) students came to sit at "the feet of itinerant scholars from the Hadhramaut, and from Patani, Aceh, Palembang and Java — most of whom had themselves studied in Mecca."[29] Members of the religious elite were directly critical of the rajas in the region, accusing them in particular of not enforcing Islamic law, the *shari'ah*. Some rulers, according to the journal *Al Imam*, squandered money on customary (or *adat*) celebrations and even on "glasses and goblets and dancing girls."[30] A theme in this journal is the assertion of religious leadership — of the claims of religious scholars, the *ulama*. Not only is it said to be critical for rulers to take advice from the *ulama*, but (as one article explained matters) "if examined closely it is (the *ulama*) who are the rajas in Islam."[31]

The notion of a racial identity — a racial community — that transcends individual sultanates, and might provide an alternative focus of loyalty to the raja or sultan, certainly had the potential to provoke royal opposition. To speak of "Malay" in the Melaka/Johor context was one matter — here "Malay" could be articulated in terms of a single sultanate — but membership of a pan-Archipelago community was something different, and dangerous not only as a competing demand on allegiance. As Alexis de Tocqueville observed in the early 19th century, there is an element of complementarity between race and democracy. Under aristocratic institutions, men would "often sacrifice themselves for other men";

in the case of democracy, the "duties of each individual to the race are far more clear."[32] Prioritising race is implicitly egalitarian in the sense that all levels of society partake in the racial heritage — the racial blood is not the monopoly of royalty and aristocracy.

There is, in fact, plenty of evidence of Sultanate antagonism in the early stages of Malay ethnic/national activism. In the 1930s, on the Peninsula, the prominent leader Ibrahim Yaacob found that the royal courts "still hold firmly to the old feeling and strongly oppose the new desire to unify the Malay people."[33] In Kedah, members of the ruling elite had opposed the formation of a Malay association on the grounds that Kedah "possesses a raja";[34] in Perlis, Ibrahim was frustrated to find the people "did not know how to love their bangsa"; they were "loyal only to their raja."[35] In Brunei, as D.E. Brown's study of the sultanate explains, ethnic distinctions were not prominent "within the indigenous population for all indigenous groups enjoyed the common status of subject of the Sultan". The rulers, Brown observes, would not be likely to have encouraged "broad-scale ethnic identities", but rather preferred a "classificatory "fragmentation" of ethnic groups by local identification". They took steps to "hinder coalitions of people under them."[36]

In the sultanates of East Sumatra, the *kerajaan* leadership ("the tengkus and datuks" in such sultanates as Deli, Langkat and Asahan) was described in the post-Pacific War period as having "never cared for the suku Melayu" ethnic identification.[37] It is true that the sultanates fostered "associations" in the late 1930s — and these were intended to serve the interests of the segment of the population that was increasingly identifying as "Malay" — but these organisations did not use the term "Malay" in their names. Examples include the "Association of Native Sons of Deli" and the "Loyal Langkat Association".[38] The royal elite, in addition, tended to go on referring to commoners as "*rakyat*" (subjects), rather than "Malays".[39]

In many polities on the Peninsula and elsewhere, sultans eventually made a vital accommodation with the "Malay" movement — presenting themselves not as rivals but as promoters and unifiers of the Malay race (*bangsa*). They began to be described even as "symbols" or "emblems" of "Malayness".[40] But this extraordinary achievement of ideological adaptation should not be allowed to disguise the real contest between monarchy and race that was present in the 19th and early 20th centuries. It is the fact of this contest too that gave Singapore and the other Straits Settlements a special role in providing an enabling context for the building of the Malay *bangsa*.

The "Founder of Singapore" and His Colleagues

Apart from being enclaves in the Archipelago, the British settlements were also important sites where a European contribution to Archipelago racial thinking was made. Charles Hirschman has pointed to the impact made by British census classification in the Straits Settlements to the growing importance of the category "race" in Malayan and Malaysian thought and behaviour.[41] The Malaysian anthropologist Shamsul A.B. has discussed the way in which, at the everyday level, colonial administrative policies — the introduction of the Malay Reservation Act (1913); the development of separate "Malay", "Chinese" and "Indian" education; the establishment of a Department of Chinese Affairs — "drove home the point" that racial categories mattered.[42] These are critical observations, but a history of ideas also needs to focus on the decades around the founding of Singapore — an ideologically formative period when the idea of "race" was being formulated in Europe, and influenced the thinking and imperial planning of some of the key British officials in the Archipelago.

At this time, as Christopher Bayly has put it recently, the category "race" was increasingly used as part of a European attempt to identify the "whole map of mankind".[43] Napoleon, the greatest figure of the age, had "at first emphasized race and ethnicity, rather than dynasty and tradition in his reorganization of Europe";[44] scholars on the Continent and in Britain worked busily at the task of identifying and describing the different peoples or races of the world, including in the Asian region. In England, Sir Joseph Banks — a leader in many aspects of scientific observation and analysis — was a supporter of William Marsden, who was a pioneer in Sumatran and Malay studies. After his appointment as an official in Penang in 1805, Thomas Stamford Raffles frequently corresponded with the much-respected Marsden, initially to help the senior man with his scholarly work. Raffles also quickly established close relations with John Leyden, the author of an important essay on the "Indo-Chinese nations" — and, in earlier days, a literary collaborator of Sir Walter Scott. Another figure in the British contribution to "Malay studies" in the earlier 19th century was John Crawfurd, who had also been posted to Penang (1808), worked with Raffles in Java (where Raffles was Lieutenant Governor during the British occupation, 1811–1816), published a three-volume History of the Indian Archipelago in 1820, and became Resident of the newly-established Singapore in 1823.

After arriving in Penang, Raffles' attentions were soon focused on defining the different races or "nations" around him — and in a way that would influence the conceptualising of the "Malay race". He observed in particular that: "I cannot but consider the Malayu nation as one people, speaking one language, though spread over so wide a space, and preserving their character and customs"[45] — and it seems to me that this was more than an exercise in description. He was seeking to formulate a category: he was contributing to a developing system of classification. He suggested that it was in the "Malay states in the Peninsula" that "the Malays" were "least adulterated in their character, usages, and manners",[46] and described in detail the "character of a Malay" ("indolent", "polite", "alive to insult").[47] Later, his colleague John Crawfurd went on to try to determine the different classes of Malay and the "parent country of the Malay race".[48] Raffles, it should be said, also alluded to "the Malays" as a biologically-defined group when he wrote of their physical stature and form.[49] Such biological emphasis was very much in line with thinking in Europe itself. When "race" was discussed in this period — for instance, by Friedrich Schiller, Johann Gottfried von Herder and Walter Scott — blood ties certainly tended to be stressed.[50]

When Raffles considered Britain's future role in the Archipelago, like Napoleon, he thought largely in terms of "race and ethnicity, rather than dynasty". He referred frequently to "Malay chiefs" and "Malay states", including under the latter heading sultanates such as Aceh and Palembang (as well as a number of states in Borneo) that were unlikely to have described themselves in such a way at that time. Looking to the past, he wrote of two great empires in the region — one "Malayan", the other "Javan".[51] He suggested in 1811 that "the present Malay chiefs" might "easily be prevailed upon by suggestions to invest the Governor General of India with the ancient title of Bitara" — a title used centuries earlier by the ruler of Majapahit in Java, who was acknowledged as suzerain by the Malay sultans or "Rajahs". By taking this title, the British would gain "a right of superintendence over, and interference with, all the Malay states."[52] John Leyden had made similar proposals, writing of the need to create "a general Malay league" and "a general parliament of the Malay states" — all "under the protection" of a British "Governor of Java".[53]

Majapahit was not the only focal point these officials had in mind in their efforts to build a race-based, British-backed "Malay" empire. In 1808, Raffles had opposed the intention of the East India Company to leave Melaka in Dutch hands, pointing out that Melaka had once been "the capital of the Malay straits", and suggesting that from this base, "the whole of the Malay Rajahs in the Straits and to the Eastward might be rendered not only subservient but if necessary tributary."[54] In 1818, he proposed a territorial rather than racial basis for a revived Archipelago empire when he visited Pagaruyung in Sumatra — the capital of the old Minangkabau empire. He noted that the "sovereignty of Menangkabau" had once been "acknowledged over the whole of Sumatra", and made the proposal that by "upholding (Minangkabau) authority, a central government may easily be established: and the numerous petty states, now disunited and barbarous, may again be connected under one general system of government". In this way, "Sumatra, under British influence" would again "rise into great political importance."[55] With the establishing of Singapore in 1819, Raffles returned to the race paradigm. He did not merely see the establishing of a British settlement on Singapore as a measure towards protecting Britain's trade through the Straits of Melaka — though this had been the objective agreed to by his superiors in Calcutta.[56]

Raffles saw Singapore as "classic ground", where it was still possible to see the "lines of the old city, and of its defences."[57] He drew on his historical researches — particularly his knowledge of the chronicle of the ruling dynasty of Melaka and Johor, a text which Leyden (in the fashionable race language of the period) called the "national poem" of the Malays.[58] This text — which was translated into English by Leyden, and published after Leyden's death by Raffles under the race-emphasising title *Malay Annals* — gives prominence to Singapore as a pre-Melaka capital for the famed dynasty that later ruled from Melaka and other locations in the western Archipelago. Singapore — presumably in the 14th century — is described by the text as "a great city ... (whose) fame and greatness spread throughout the world", and in recent decades archaeological excavations have helped to support the view that Singapore was at that time "a thriving port."[59] As Christina Skott has pointed out, in his Singapore negotiations with the Johor elite, Raffles referred to his proposed treaty as a "means of resurrecting the line of the ancient kings" and was soon referring to Singapore as the original seat of the "Malayan empire", noting that "the Malays" called it the "Navel of the Malay countries."[60]

To "revive" such a concept of Malay nation or race, so Raffles appears to have thought, might entail both a return to a pre-Islamisation past and the adoption of new institutions and doctrines. Singapore had the advantage that "in the minds of the natives it will always be associated with their fondest recollections, as the seat of their ancient government, before the influence of a foreign faith had shaken those institutions for which they still preserve so high an attachment and reverence."[61] Raffles had long been something of an opponent of Islam and "the Arabs".[62] In urging that the religious influence of "the Arabs" among "the Malays" be countered, he argued that the former "inculcate the most intolerant bigotry, and render (the Malays) incapable of receiving any species of useful knowledge."[63] Noting that "the Malay nations" had "made considerable progress in civilisation before the introduction of the religion of Islam among them",[64] he saw in a positive light the fact that "the Malays" continued to be attached to their "own peculiar usages and customs."[65] Looking to the future, he believed "the Malays" were more "open to instruction than the votaries of Islam in general",[66] and even advocated the propagation of Christianity among them.[67] In 1811, Raffles had proposed another measure to rejuvenate "the Malays": he encouraged the British Governor to "invite the Malay chiefs to a revisal of their general system of laws and usages". This, said Raffles, might be done on a "grand scale", with "every Malay chief" in the first instance furnishing a copy of the laws "current in his own state". It would provide the opportunity to "procure the abandonment of some of those maxims and usages which have the strongest tendency to prevent (Malay) progress in information and the habits of civilised life". To carry out such a "reform of Malay laws", Raffles urged, would be "one of the means by which the benefit of the Malay nations will be secured from their connexion with the English."[68]

Proposals and views such as these — focused on a race not on one or more specific kingdoms, and spelt out by key officials in the government of the rising power in the Archipelago — reveal much about the political ambitions and ideological structure which informed the founding of a British settlement on Singapore in 1819. More important for the present purposes is the influence on local peoples — or at least local elites — of these views, and the way of thinking that underpinned them. Noting the influence of racial categorisation on British administrative measures pointed to by Hirschman and Shamsul — I have written elsewhere of other, even more explicit ways in which racial thinking was promoted by Europeans. A race-focused, Malay-language geography textbook of the mid-19th century, for instance, was likely to have been used by Johor ruling-class students in a European-run, Singapore school. Also, the writings of Abdullah Abdul Kadir, so clearly concerned with the fortunes of a race, not individual sultanates, were printed and distributed in the colonial education system from the late 1800s.[69] A recent publication of a collection of Malay-language letters written to Raffles — and only "discovered" (by John Bastin) in 1970 — throws further light on the propagation of the *Bangsa Melayu* idea. The letters provide an insight into how Raffles and other proponents of the new discourse of race began to influence members of the sultanate ruling class from the earliest years of the 19th century.

Royal Letters and the Dissemination of a New Discourse of Race

Translated and introduced by Ahmat Adam, these letters — most of which were written in 1810 or 1811 — illuminate numerous aspects of the history of the region as well as the role of the British. For our purposes here, they add to the knowledge of how sultans of the period represented themselves — and seem also to suggest ways in which that representation was changing, including as a result of an encounter with European racial categorisation. As already noted, in the late 1700s — specifically the 1780s — Marsden observed that the authors of the letters he read as an official "very rarely" referred to themselves as "Malay". In the letters to Raffles, however, written only a few years later, there is somewhat more evidence of the use of "Malay", including from rulers beyond the Melaka-Johor sphere. The letters themselves suggest that one reason for this might be the influence of British racial terminology.

Looking through the letters, we see that the rulers in Pontianak and Banjarmasin in Borneo do not use "Malay" in their letters; nor did the ruler in Aceh in Sumatra. The ruler in Jambi writes of Raffles' "fame" among "all rajas at this time", but does not use the phrase "Malay rajas".[70] The sultan in Palembang writes of "rajas of dark complexion beneath the winds" (*raja-raja jenis kulit hitam di bawah angin*),[71] or "rajas of dark complexion on this eastern side",[72] rather than "Malay rajas". Not surprisingly, the sultan in Lingga — who claimed also to rule in Johor and Pahang, and who would presumably have long been comfortable with the description "Malay" — referred to Raffles' intention to "conduct major deliberations with all the Malay rajas in these *negeri* in these eastern regions."[73] In the case of Siak in Sumatra — which, as Ahmat points out, had been "an integral part of the Johor empire"[74] — the "Old Raja" (Sultan Sayid al-Syariff Abdul Jalil Saifuddin) refers to the "customs (*adat*) of all Malay rajas" as being significant in Siak, and also to having received gifts from Raffles in the formal manner "of Malay rajas".[75]

The surprising cases, as I understand things, are Kedah and Sambas — and it is here especially that we might detect the European influence at work. The ruler from Kedah — where (as suggested above) we would not expect "Malay" to have been used for self-description — does refer to the British Governor-General in Bengal as "ruling over all Malay rajas" and as "wishing to deliberate with the Malay rajas in every *negeri* (settlement)"; he also presents Raffles with a dagger and other items "worn by Malays (*orang orang Melayu*).[76] The Kedah sultan does not, however, refer explicitly to himself or his people as "Malay". The sultan in Sambas tells Raffles that he (Raffles) is "famous in all the Malay countries (*negeri*)" and notes that Raffles wishes to "promote relations between every raja of the Malay countries". In this instance, as Ahmat Adam points out, there are signs of confusion — as in both of the sultan's statements the Jawi letters of the original text spell out "m-l-a-y-w-a" rather than "melayu".[77]

Despite a need for caution with respect to the Sambas letter, the increased use of "Malay" outside the Melaka-Johor context is of interest. Furthermore, asking why it might have been occurring may provide an insight into how Raffles, the so-called "Founder of Singapore", and other European officials in the Dutch as well as British territories, were able to contribute to the promotion of a broad racial consciousness among the people of the Archipelago polities. In this period, so soon after the category "race" was being promoted and developed in Europe, Raffles' role as the representative of a rapidly growing power in Southeast Asia needs to be emphasised. The British were known to be moving against the Dutch: in 1811, the sultan in Siak said he had heard "an expedition of innumerable men-of-war" was being assembled by the British to "strike against the Dutch and the French".[78] Raffles in his own letters to rulers at this time described the Governor-General as the "raja above all rajas dependent on the English flag of the great king of England from above and below the wind",[79] and the rulers themselves echoed such description of the Governor-General in their own letters to Raffles.[80]

As Ahmat Adam explains, most of the letters from rulers in 1810 and 1811 were written in the context of this British expansionism. They were, in fact, "replies to the letters that Raffles sent from Malacca, appealing for the support and assistance of the indigenous rulers of the archipelago in the British invasion of Java, particularly requesting sailing vessels and supplies of food and livestock for the British invasion force."[81] When Raffles wrote on behalf of the "raja above all rajas" in Bengal, and even called himself a "great raja" (*Radja besaar*), the language as well as the content of his letters may well have been influential. In letters he wrote to the ruler in Palembang, for instance, Raffles described himself as a "true friend of all the Malay rajas in the eastern settlements (*negeri*) and districts, including Palembang"[82] and announced that the Governor-General wished to hold "important deliberations with all the Malay rajas, including that of the country of Palembang."[83] In such statements, he was in effect inviting his respondents to join him in the use of this language of race — and some did. As we have seen, the Palembang ruler (like a number of rulers in Sumatra and Borneo) did not respond positively to Raffles' invitation to classify his polity as "Malay" — he preferred to group the sultanates of the region under the phrase "rajas of dark complexion on this eastern side". But the sultans in Kedah and Sambas (or their scribes) may well have been influenced by Raffles' categories when they decided upon a collective term. Here we seem to encounter a process of ideological influence — the communication (and endorsing) of a concept that was increasingly influential in Europe, and had shaped the way Napoleon himself conceptualised his empire-building.

The sultans at this point were not writing of a "Malay race" that extended across a range of monarchies, and could be brought together as a political unit, possibly under British stewardship. But at least two of them — in responding to the "Founder of Singapore" — might be viewed as making tentative, early steps in a process that would eventually lead to the consolidation of a "Malay race". The idea of a *Bangsa Melayu* — which had the potential to challenge the rulers themselves as a focus of loyalty and identity — was promoted by Raffles in Kedah and Sambas, as it was later to be propagated in other ways in Sarawak.

Conclusion

The suggestion that James Brooke brought the term "Malay" from Singapore to Sarawak in 1841 is a reminder of the novelty of a pan-Archipelago Malay ethnicity, and of the European role in introducing this new configuration. Brooke's comment is an invitation to explore in a different way the "Malay history" of Singapore. In this chapter, I have drawn attention to the role of Singapore as an enclave in the Archipelago world — a site where novel social or religious visions (including a race-based vision) were able to be developed and expressed beyond the political reach of the surrounding sultanates. From a *kerajaan* perspective, the notion of a racial community and identity that transcended individual sultanates was radical — subversive in the sense that it urged a focus of loyalty and a form of egalitarianism that could potentially threaten monarchy.

The impact of 18th- and 19th-century European thinking on the building of the *Bangsa Melayu* — and also the manner in which local ideologues reformulated, or localised, the concept — must be recognised as a vital theme in "Malay history".[84] The present chapter, dedicated to the leading international specialist on Singapore history, focuses in particular on the early stages of the propagation of racial thinking among "the Malays", particularly on the part played by Raffles and other British officials who were critical in the Singapore story. The establishing of British power on Singapore needs to be understood, at least in part, in terms of the race-based ideological structure which was gaining potency in Europe in that period. It was an initiative influenced by the hope to revive or, more accurately, construct under British tutelage a widespread "Malayan empire". Such British thinking about "race" — the prestigious ideology of a new, conquering power — was disseminated around the Archipelago in ways which I have discussed here. Local ideologues in Singapore and elsewhere then proved to be critical in localising the specific concept of the "Malay race". Present-day Singapore, of course, has not been restored to its role as the "Navel of the Malay countries": Singapore's aspirations and achievements lie elsewhere.

Notes

1. Robert Pringle, *Rajahs and Rebels: The Ibans of Sarawak under Brooke Rule, 1841–1941* (Ithaca: Cornell University Press, 1970), pp. xviii–xix.
2. C.M. Turnbull, *A History of Singapore, 1819–1975* (Kuala Lumpur: Oxford University Press, 1977), p. 5.
3. Ibid., p. 1.
4. Ibid., p. 3.
5. C.M. Turnbull, *A History of Modern Singapore, 1819–2005* (Singapore: NUS Press, 2009).
6. Kwa Chong Guan, Derek Heng and Tan Tai Yong, *Singapore: A 700-Year History* (Singapore: National Archives of Singapore, 2009); John N. Miksic, "14th-Century Singapore: A Port of Trade", in *Early Singapore, 1300s–1819: Evidence in Maps, Text and Artefacts*, ed. John N. Miksic, Cheryl-Ann Low Mei Gek (Singapore: Singapore History Museum, 2004), pp. 41–54.
7. Peter Borschberg, *The Singapore and Melaka Straits: Violence, Security and Diplomacy in the 17th Century* (Singapore: NUS Press, 2010), p. 1; Kwa Chong Guan, "Sailing Past Singapore", in *Early Singapore*, ed. Miksic and Low, pp. 95–105.
8. Kwa Chong Guan, "From Temasek to Singapore: Locating a Global-State in the Cycles of Melaka Historiography", in *Early Singapore*, ed. Miksic and Low, p. 137.

9. John N. Miksic, "Temasik to Singapura: Singapore in the 14th to 15th Centuries", in *Singapore from Temasek to the 21st Century: Reinventing the Global City*, ed. Karl Hack and Jean-Louis Margolin, with Karine Delaye (Singapore: NUS Press, 2010), p. 105.

10. Turnbull, *Singapore*, 1977, p. 36.

11. Willam R. Roff, *The Origins of Malay Nationalism* (Kuala Lumpur: University of Malaya Press, 1967); see also Anthony Milner, *The Invention of Politics in Colonial Malaya* (Cambridge: Cambridge University Press, 2002).

12. Khoo Kay Kim, "Overview", in *Malays/Muslims in Singapore: Selected Readings in History 1819–1965*, ed. Khoo Kay Kim, Elinah Abdullah and Wan Meng Hao (Singapore: Pelanduk, 2006), pp. xxv–xxvii.

13. Khoo, "Overview", p. xxviii.

14. Turnbull, *Singapore*, 1977, pp. 272–3.

15. Tania Li, *Malays in Singapore* (Singapore: Oxford University Press, 1990); Lily Zubaidah Rahim, *The Singapore Dilemma: The Political and Educational Marginality of the Malay Community* (Kuala Lumpur: Oxford University Press, 1998).

16. Virginia Matheson, "Concepts of Malay Ethos in Indigenous Malay Writings", *Journal of Southeast Asian Studies* X, 2 (1979): 360.

17. Matheson, "Concepts", p. 362; A. Teeuw and D.K. Wyatt, eds., *Hikayat Patani: The Story of Patani* (The Hague: Martinus Nijhoff, 1970).

18. Teuku Iskandar, *Hikajat Atjeh* ('s-Gravenhage: Nijhoff, 1958), p. 153.

19. William Marsden, *A Grammar of the Malayan Language* (Tokio: Mitake Torie, 1930 [orig. publ. 1812]), p. ix.

20. Anthony Milner, *The Malays* (Oxford: Wiley-Blackwell, 2011), p. 96.

21. Ibid., pp. 96–8.

22. Tim Babcock, "Indigenous Ethnicity in Sarawak", *Sarawak Museums Journal* XXII, 43 (1974): 196.

23. Anthony Milner, *The Invention of Politics in Colonial Malaya* (Cambridge: Cambridge University Press, 2002), p. 12.

24. Milner, *Malays*; Milner, *Invention*.

25. Turnbull, *Singapore*, 1977, p. 52.

26. Quoted in Milner, *Invention*, p. 15.

27. Kassim Ahmad, *Kisah Pelayaran Abdullah* (Kuala Lumpur: Dewan Bahasa dan Pustaka, 1964), p. 104.

28. Quoted in Milner, *Invention*, p. 154.

29. Roff, *Origins*, p. 43.

30. Milner, *Invention*, pp. 139–41.

31. Ibid., p. 176.

32. Louis Dumont, *Homo Hierarchicus* (London: Paladin, 1972), pp. 52–3.

33. Ibrahim Yaacob, *Melihat Tanah Ayer* (Kota Bharu, 1941), pp. 11–2.

34. Ibid., p. 72.

35. Ibid., p. 81.

36. D.E. Brown, *Brunei: The Structure and History of a Bornean Malay Sultanate* (Brunei: Brunei Museum, 1970), pp. 4, 9.

37. Ariffin Omar, *Bangsa Melayu: Malay Concepts of Democracy and Community 1945–1950* (Kuala Lumpur: Oxford University Press, 1983), p. 78.

38. Ibid., pp. 23–4.

39. Ibid., pp. 71, 77.

40. Anthony Milner, "How 'Traditional' is Malaysian Monarchy?", in *Malaysia: Islam, Society and Politics*, ed. Virginia Hooker and Norani Othman (Singapore: Institute of Southeast Asian Studies, 2003), pp. 169–93.

41. Charles Hirschman, "The Meaning and Measurement of Ethnicity in Malaysia: An Analysis of Census Classifications", *JAS* 42, 3 (1987): 555–82.

42. Shamsul A.B., "Debating about Identity in Malaysia: A Discourse Analysis", *Southeast Asian Studies* 34, 3 (1996): 14; Shamsul A.B., "Identity Contestation in Malaysia: A Comparative Commentary on 'Malayness' and 'Chineseness'", *Akademika* 55 (1999): 17–37.

43. C.A. Bayly, *The Birth of the Modern World 1780–1914* (Oxford: Blackwell, 2004), p. 110.

44. Bayly, *Birth*, p. 108.

45. S. Raffles, *Memoir of the Life and Public Services of Sir Thomas Stamford Raffles* (Singapore: Oxford University Press, 1991), p. 15.

46. Ibid., p. 16.

47. Ibid., 235–6.

48. John Crawfurd, *History of the Indian Archipelago* (London: Frank Cass, 1967), vol. 2, p. 372.

49. T.S. Raffles, *The History of Java* (Kuala Lumpur: Oxford University Press, 1965), p. 59; Raffles, *Memoir*, p. 172.

50. Ivan Hannaford, *Race: The History of an Idea in the West* (Washington: The Woodrow Wilson Center Press, 1996), pp. 225, 231; Robert J.C. Young, *The Idea of English Ethnicity* (Malden: Blackwell, 2008), pp. 37–8.

51. Raffles, *Memoir*, p. 358.

52. Ibid., p. 71.

53. Ibid., p. 25.

54. Christina Skott, "Imagined Centrality: Sir Stamford Raffles and the Birth of Modern Singapore", in *Singapore from Temasek to the 21st Century*, ed. Hack and Margolin, with Delaye, p. 162.

55. Raffles, *Memoir*, p. 363.

56. Turnbull, *Singapore*, 2009, p. 27.

57. Raffles, *Memoir*, p. 376.

58. Skott, "Imagined Centrality", p. 161.

59. Kwa Chong Guan, "Singapura as a Central Place in Malay History and Identity", in *Singapore from Temasek to the 21st Century*, ed. Hack and Margolin, with Delaye, pp. 141–2.

60. Skott, "Imagined Centrality", p. 168.

61. Ibid., p. 169.
62. Syed Muhd. Khairudin Aljuneid, *Raffles and Religion: A Study of Sir Thomas Stamford Raffles' Discourse on Religion amongst the Malays* (Kuala Lumpur: The Other Press, 2004).
63. Ibid., pp. 73, 82.
64. Raffles, *Memoir*, p. 80.
65. Ibid., p. 81.
66. Ibid., p. 81.
67. Ibid., p. 83.
68. Ibid., p. 81.
69. Milner, *Invention*, Chapters 1–4.
70. Ahmat Adam, *Letters of Sincerity: The Raffles Collection of Malay Letters (1780–1824)* (Kuala Lumpur: Malaysian Branch of the Royal Asiatic Society, 2009), p. 225.
71. Ibid., pp. 257, 253.
72. Ibid., p. 270.
73. Ibid., p.126.
74. Ibid., p. 137.
75. Ibid., pp. 169–70.
76. Ibid., pp. 54, 51, 48.
77. Ibid., p. 300.
78. Ibid., p. 198.
79. Ibid., p. 198.
80. Ibid., pp. 51, 125, 192.
81. Ibid., pp. 2–3.
82. Ibid., p. 357.
83. Ibid., p. 359.
84. Milner, *Malays*; Anthony Milner, *Race or Civilization: The Localizing of 'The Malays'* (Bangi: Institute of Malaysian and International Studies, 2010).

References

Ahmat Adam. *Letters of Sincerity: The Raffles Collection of Malay Letters (1780–1824)*. Kuala Lumpur: Malaysian Branch of the Royal Asiatic Society, 2009.

Ariffin Omar. *Bangsa Melayu: Malay Concepts of Democracy and Community 1945–1950*. Kuala Lumpur: Oxford University Press, 1983.

Babcock, Tim. "Indigenous Ethnicity in Sarawak". *Sarawak Museums Journal* XXII, 43 (1974): 191–202.

Bayly, C.A. *The Birth of the Modern World 1780–1914*. Oxford: Blackwell, 2004.

Borschberg, Peter. *The Singapore and Melaka Straits: Violence, Security and Diplomacy in the 17th Century*. Singapore: NUS Press, 2010.

Brown, D.E. *Brunei: The Structure and History of a Bornean Malay Sultanate*. Brunei: Brunei Museum, 1970.

Crawfurd, John. *History of the Indian Archipelago*. London: Frank Cass, 1967.

Dumont, Louis. *Homo Hierarchicus*. London, Paladin, 1972.

Hack, Karl and Jean-Louis Margolin, with Karine Delaye, eds. *Singapore from Temasek to the 21st Century: Reinventing the Global City*. Singapore: NUS Press, 2010.

Hannaford, Ivan. *Race: The History of an Idea in the West*. Washington: The Woodrow Wilson Center Press, 1996.

Hirschman, Charles. "The Meaning and Measurement of Ethnicity in Malaysia: An Analysis of Census Classifications". *JAS* 42, 3 (1987): 555–82.

Ibrahim Yaacob. *Melihat Tanah Ayer*. Kota Bharu, 1941.

Iskandar, Teuku. *Hikajat Atjeh*. 's-Gravenhage: Nijhoff, 1958.

Kassim Ahmad. *Kisah Pelayaran Abdullah*. Kuala Lumpur: Dewan Bahasa dan Pustaka, 1964.

Khoo Kay Kim. "Overview". In *Malays/Muslims in Singapore: Selected Readings in History 1819–1965*, ed. Khoo Kay Kim, Elinah Abdullah and Wan Meng Hao. Singapore: Pelanduk, 2006, xvii–xxviii.

Kwa Chong Guan, Derek Heng and Tan Tai Yong. *Singapore: A 700-Year History*. Singapore: National Archives of Singapore, 2009.

Kwa Chong Guan. "Sailing Past Singapore". In *Early Singapore, 1300s–1819: Evidence in Maps, Text and Artefacts*, ed. John N. Miksic, Cheryl-Ann Low Mei Gek. Singapore: Singapore History Museum, 2004, pp. 95–105.

_____. "From Temasek to Singapore: Locating a Global-State in the Cycles of Melaka Historiography". In *Early Singapore, 1300s–1819: Evidence in Maps, Text and Artefacts*, ed. John N. Miksic, Cheryl-Ann Low Mei Gek. Singapore: Singapore History Museum, 2004, pp. 124–46.

_____. "Singapura as a Central Place in Malay History and Identity". In *Singapore from Temasek to the 21st Century: Reinventing the Global City*, ed. Karl Hack and Jean-Louis Margolin, with Karine Delaye. Singapore: NUS Press, 2010, pp. 133–54.

Li, Tania. *Malays in Singapore*. Singapore: Oxford University Press, 1990.

Marsden, William. *A Grammar of the Malayan Language*. Tokio: Mitake Torie, 1930 [orig. publ. 1812].

Matheson, Virginia. "Concepts of Malay Ethos in Indigenous Malay Writings". *Journal of Southeast Asian Studies* X, 2 (1979): 351–71.

Miksic, John N. "14th-Century Singapore: A Port of Trade". In *Early Singapore, 1300s–1819: Evidence in Maps, Text and Artefacts*, ed. John N. Miksic, Cheryl-Ann Low Mei Gek. Singapore: Singapore History Museum, 2004, pp. 41–54.

_____. "Temasik to Singapura: Singapore in the 14th to 15th Centuries". In *Singapore from Temasek to the 21st Century: Reinventing the Global City*, ed. Karl Hack and Jean-Louis Margolin, with Karine Delaye. Singapore: NUS Press, 2010, pp. 103–32.

Miksic, John N. and Cheryl-Ann Low Mei Gek, eds. *Early Singapore, 1300s–1819: Evidence in Maps, Text and Artefacts.* Singapore: Singapore History Museum, 2004.

Milner, Anthony. *The Invention of Politics in Colonial Malaya.* Cambridge: Cambridge University Press, 2002.

_____. "How 'Traditional' is Malaysian Monarchy?". In *Malaysia: Islam, Society and Politics*, ed. Virginia Hooker and Norani Othman. Singapore: Institute of Southeast Asian Studies, 2003, pp. 169–93.

_____. *Race or Civilization: The Localizing of 'The Malays'.* Bangi: Institute of Malaysian and International Studies, 2010.

_____. *The Malays.* Oxford: Wiley-Blackwell, 2011.

Muhd Khairudin Aljuneid, Syed. *Raffles and Religion: A Study of Sir Thomas Stamford Raffles' Discourse on Religion amongst the Malays.* Kuala Lumpur: The Other Press, 2004.

Pringle, Robert. *Rajahs and Rebels: The Ibans of Sarawak under Brooke Rule, 1841–1941.* Ithaca, NY: Cornell University Press, 1970.

Raffles, S. *Memoir of the Life and Public Services of Sir Thomas Stamford Raffles.* Singapore: Oxford University Press, 1991.

Raffles, T.S. *The History of Java.* Kuala Lumpur: Oxford University Press, 1965.

Rahim, Lily Zubaidah. *The Singapore Dilemma: The Political and Educational Marginality of the Malay Community.* Kuala Lumpur: Oxford University Press, 1998.

Roff, William R. *The Origins of Malay Nationalism.* Kuala Lumpur: University of Malaya Press, 1967.

Shamsul A.B. "Debating about Identity in Malaysia: A Discourse Analysis". *Southeast Asian Studies* 34, 3 (1996): 8–31.

_____. "Identity Contestation in Malaysia: A Comparative Commentary on 'Malayness' and 'Chineseness'". *Akademika* 55 (1999): 17–37.

Skott, Christina. "Imagined Centrality: Sir Stamford Raffles and the Birth of Modern Singapore". In *Singapore from Temasek to the 21st Century: Reinventing the Global City*, ed. Karl Hack and Jean-Louis Margolin, with Karine Delaye. Singapore: NUS Press, 2010, pp. 155–84.

Teeuw, A. and D.K. Wyatt, eds. *Hikayat Patani: The Story of Patani.* The Hague: Martinus Nijhoff, 1970.

Turnbull, C.M. *A History of Singapore 1819–1975.* Kuala Lumpur: Oxford University Press, 1977.

_____. *A History of Modern Singapore, 1819–2005.* Singapore: NUS Press, 2009.

Young, Robert J.C. *The Idea of English Ethnicity.* Malden: Blackwell, 2008.

7

Reappraising the Aftermath of War:

The Problems of the British Military Administration and Singapore's Place in the Changing Strategic Environment of Empire, 1945–1946[1]

Kelvin W.K. Ng

A Problematic Epilogue to the Far Eastern War

WRITING ON THE BRITISH MILITARY ADMINISTRATION (BMA) in *A History of Modern Singapore, 1819–2005*, Mary Turnbull observes:

> In its seven months it destroyed the goodwill that existed at the time of liberation and brought British prestige in Singapore to an even lower point than in February 1942.[2]

Turnbull's claim is a bold one. The disastrous Malayan campaign of 1941–1942 which culminated in the surrender of Singapore and a 130,000-strong imperial field army represented a catastrophe of British arms not seen since Yorktown, and left a stain on British military prestige that even the spectacular run of victories in Burma during 1944–1945 could not erase.[3] Since the tide of war turned in the Far East, British politicians and military commanders had been spoiling for a dramatic *Overlord*-style re-invasion of Malaya, which alone, they believed, could redeem the failures of 1942. The sudden death of the Japanese Empire in the ruins of Hiroshima and Nagasaki denied them the battlefield achievement that they assumed would restore the image of British rule in the eyes of their Malayan subject peoples. If one is to accept Turnbull's assertion, the seven months of post-war military government that came in place of a hard fought campaign of liberation dealt an even harder blow to the British Empire than the collapse of its armies in 1942, and severely compromised the re-imposition of colonial authority.

The BMA assumed the government of Singapore and Malaya upon the return of British Empire forces in September 1945 and lasted till the handover to civilian rule on 1 April 1946. Its mission was the political stabilisation and economic resuscitation of these once prosperous territories, so vital to Britain's post-war fortunes. But it was an administration fraught with problems whose legacies undoubtedly paved the way for the Communist Emergency and the bitter post-war experience of radical and racial politics. Yet its significance is obscured by a problematic historiography that overlooks some of the important issues of this episode.

This epilogue to the Far Eastern campaigns occupies an understandably marginal place in the historiography of the Second World War, the British Empire's last years, and the postcolonial histories of its successor states. The brief moment of military rule was overshadowed by more dramatic developments: Field Marshal Slim's sweep through Burma; the atom bombs; the Communist Emergency; the independence of Malaya and Singapore. Allied triumphalism regarded it as a successful postscript to the war against Japan.[4] Alternatively, it appeared as a small chapter in the story of progressive Malayan nationhood.[5] But by the later 1960s, when the turbulent secession of Singapore from the Federation, intensifying communal violence, Indonesian aggression and an escalating war in Vietnam made the entire post-war British enterprise in the region seem prodigal and vain, the tone of writing changed. Rudner's 1968 article "The Organisation of the BMA" presented a scathing attack on the BMA, in particular the rampant black marketeering and corruption, a posture which was similarly adopted by subsequent historians.[6] For instance, the Andayas' *A History of Malaysia* depicts an impotent military government reliant on communist assistance to restore law and order,[7] while Turnbull emphasises the "false hopes [and] disappointments" of the period, noting its widespread poverty and unemployment.[8]

The problems in the historiography are evident. The assessment of the BMA has been overwhelmingly concerned with political and civil affairs, a natural focus given the BMA's mission but one that neglects important issues. The BMA was essentially a military organisation operating along military lines. Operational factors therefore governed the BMA's conduct of its civil affairs duties, and were crucial to post-war problems and their long-term repercussions, while the changing strategic environment threw up dilemmas which further complicated the BMA's mission.

Approaching this topic from a more overtly military angle is a task long overdue. Since the *Official History*, little has been written about this. Murfett's military history of Singapore, *Between Two Oceans*, only briefly alludes to the re-occupation,[9] while Harper and Bayly's *Forgotten Wars*, though devoting much attention to the BMA, is more concerned with the political and social dynamics of a radicalised Southeast Asia and does not fully explore the military realities which framed these developments. Nor do the histories of the Emergency properly examine the link between the security legacies of the military government and the origins of the communist insurgency. For instance, Short's account emphasises the internal crisis of the Malayan Communist Party (MCP) and the dislocation of British intelligence,[10] while Mackay focuses on the Emergency's racial character and the discontent over the Malayan Union scheme.[11] When the re-occupation is invoked, they largely fixate on developments relating to the MCP instead of considering the importance of British military dynamics in the post-war period. A military analysis of the re-occupation is essential if one is to better appreciate the significance of the period of military government.

A problem with the existing writing is that of perspective. The *Official History* treats the subject from an oppressively general staff viewpoint that depicts troop movement with a tabletop simplicity. Yet the sometimes worm's-eye account that Harper and Bayly produce, while powerfully evoking the atmosphere of political intrigue that hung over post-war Singapore, misses out on some of the harder military questions that must underlie an appreciation of the BMA. A variety of military sources is available to bridge these two extremes. Although the high command perspective is often a skewed one, it nonetheless dictated the parameters in which subordinate bodies operated, and it is worth examining the regular reports and memoranda produced by the BMA and its associated higher military headquarters (HQ). Further down this hierarchy, the war diaries of individual formations and units, with their detailed accounts of operational experience, prove particularly revealing. The private papers of military personnel also give insights into how events unfolded on the ground. A more complex story of the re-occupation thus emerges when one links the strategic context with the local.

The immediate post-war period was as important to Singapore's history as the Japanese rampage of 1941–1942. While the collapse of British rule in the face of Japanese aggression arguably sounded the death knell for British imperialism, the British military had the opportunity in 1945–1946 to manage the end of empire better. Turnbull's analysis of the political and civil dimensions of the military government leaves little doubt as to its myriad problems and their consequences for post-war Singapore. Yet these socio-political developments can only be properly understood against the operational experience of returning British forces and the wider strategic context that this episode was situated in. It is by bringing military affairs back into focus that the complexities and significance of the period of military government become more fully apparent.

"The Seedy Atmosphere of a Bourbon Restoration"

Paraphrasing Victor Purcell, an officer of the pre-war Chinese Protectorate who returned to Singapore as a colonel in the BMA, Mackay opines that there was "something of the seedy atmosphere of a Bourbon restoration in the picture presented by the reimposed British regime".[12] The old regime, which had collapsed in visible disgrace three years previously, had now amazingly been returned on the basis of (to the locals) unheard-of victories in distant battlefields. Popular disenchantment with and opposition to the British grew when it became apparent that they were out of touch with new political realities, as evinced by the attempt to foist the Malayan Union scheme upon an unreceptive population or Lord Mountbatten's naïve believe that left-wing opinion could be easily won over through constitutional changes.[13] Purcell emphasises this in a report on the political situation. "Are the political parties so active in this country and with such a great following to be ignored? … Like the Bourbons do we never learn?"[14]

As Turnbull argues, the economic woes of post-war Singapore went hand-in-hand with the febrile political atmosphere. The inability of the BMA to address food shortages, unemployment, and overcrowding fuelled the growth of the communist movement, while the indecision of the BMA in the face of communist politics and labour actions further disrupted economic recovery.[15] Amidst all these problems, the BMA acquired a reputation for corruption and graft, which led Rudner to memorably pronounce that the "banana colonels" of the BMA, like the "banana dollars" of the Japanese before them, had proven worthless in reality.[16]

Senior BMA officers admitted as much. Writing to Brigadier Donnison, official historian of the British wartime military governments, the head of the BMA Major-General Hone admitted that it was "all too true that the period of Military Administration in Malaya has left bad memories behind it".[17] Aside from their failure to resuscitate the economy and keep a lid on radical politics, the new military masters of Singapore impinged heavily upon civilian life. Poor traffic discipline, high-handed officers, and commandeering of private vehicles were frequent complaints made by civilians.[18] Indeed, the people of Singapore seemed to have merely exchanged one set of wartime occupiers for another, and were again victims of looting on a grand scale. General Hone recalled that:

> Time after time when troops were moved in Malaya, I and my advisers saw lorries being loaded up with furniture, pianos, frigidaires, cooking stoves, china, glass and cutlery. The officers were as bad if not worse than the men ... the sight at the docks was indescribable ...[19]

These problems were hardly surprising when one considers the composition of the BMA. There were, as Turnbull notes, "honest men of high calibre", and more importantly, officers who had pre-war experience of government in Singapore and Malaya. Hone, although himself coming from an African and Middle Eastern background, counted several seasoned "Malaya hands" among his subordinates. His deputies, Brigadiers McKerron and Willan, were pre-war Malaya Civil Service (MCS) officials; the aforementioned Victor Purcell was drafted into the BMA as a colonel, as was M.C. Hay, a previous advisor to the Sultan of Johore; A.W. Wallich, formerly of the shipping house Boustead, was put in charge of the supply situation.[20] And while Turnbull, Harper and Bayly note that the decision to repatriate government employees who had been interned during the war deprived the BMA of much expert knowledge, some renegades successfully resisted this policy and provided valuable assistance to the BMA.[21] Then of course there was the criminal and opportunistic element to be found in all armies in any period of history.[22] But more significant was the fact that the majority of the BMA had neither experience of public service nor of Singapore and Malaya, but comprised young regimental officers who had spent their war in Northwest Europe, General List officers reassigned from supernumerary staff posts as hostilities wound down, and others looking for future careers in the colonies after demobilisation[23] — in short, all the human flotsam associated with a conscript military at the end of a long global war.

With the sudden end to the war in August 1945, the carefully laid plans to thoroughly prepare BMA officers for their impeding duties went awry. Instead of language courses at the London School of Oriental and African Studies, instruction at the civil affairs staff centre at Wimbledon, and intensive training in field craft,[24] later batches of BMA personnel saw their civil affairs training reduced from eight weeks to six, and then to three,[25] while others were rushed straight to a forward depot in Palla-varam in southern India for a crash course.[26] Training naturally suffered despite the best efforts of Brigadier Willan and a group of ex-MCS offi-cers to improve instruction while BMA personnel were being concentrated in India.[27] The combat units earmarked for Malaya — the military muscle through which the BMA would re-impose British rule — were not in significantly better shape. Although the divisions of XXXIV Corps — the principal corps formation committed to Malaya and Singapore — were at a satisfactory state of training, they suffered from widespread defi-ciencies in signals equipment, engineer stores, and motorised transport.[28] *Python*, the plan to repatriate British servicemen who had served a mini-mum of three years and four months in the Far East, further denuded many units of veteran officers and NCOs, with Indian engineer and British signals and logistics units worst hit.[29]

Organisational factors therefore reveal that the BMA was not suitably prepared to cope with the complexities of local politics, the provision of public services, and economic resuscitation. Nor were the combat forma-tions assigned to Malaya and Singapore adequately equipped to perform the range of tasks expected of them, as shall be later evident. However, these failings by themselves cannot explain the severity of the corruption, political uncertainty, economic misery, and the air of irreversible malaise that set colonial rule on its terminal trajectory. One turns elsewhere to seek explanations, and some other important factors become apparent when one analyses the operational experience of returning British Empire forces.

Seven Troubled Months of Military Administration

Despite the many problems which the BMA proved unable to resolve, it was not without its successes. In several instances, military resources and wartime experience were brought to bear on civil affairs, to generally good effect. Civil affairs officers filling public works appointments were attached to engineer units to ensure that urgent requirements were given due attention, and heavy engineering units had Singapore's docks operating at pre-war capacity by the end of military rule.[30] In fact, the resuscitation of the docks began paying dividends by February 1946 when food supplies from Australia and China began arriving in appreciable quantities.[31] Pest consumption of rice stocks in Singapore was also drastically reduced through experimentation with new anti-weevil treatment.[32] In the field of medicine, troop mobility helped to avert a malaria epidemic with the organisation of mobile medical columns and dispensaries that brought healthcare to rural communities.[33] With the local police compromised by their collaboration with the Japanese, and the paramilitary civil affairs police recruited in India during 1944–1945 sorely under-strength,[34] law and order proved a serious challenge to the BMA. In Singapore at least, the time-tested solution of stiffening poor quality police with crack combat troops yielded much success. Elements of the elite 5 Parachute Brigade — amongst whom were veterans of Arnhem — were attached to the city's degraded police force and by December 1945 had restored its confidence and effectiveness.[35]

But such successes seemed almost trivial when set against the three towering and seemingly insoluble problems which plagued the period of military government: the economy, corruption, and political unrest. Operational factors underpinned many of the failures in these areas, and in this regard, one must also examine the developments on the peninsula, as they were intertwined with the problems experienced in Singapore.

Although the BMA achieved some notable progress in its attempt to resuscitate the economy, it was a task that was far from concluded by the handover to civilian rule. Indeed, food production remained dismal well into the period of civil rule. In May 1947, the rice ration had actually fallen to an amount equal to the lowest level during the Japanese occupation, and the general economic situation and standards of living only experienced significant improvement in 1948.[36] Food shortages, inflation, and the lack of essential services owed much to military supply difficulties. Based on his African experience, General Hone knew that the Royal Army Service Corps was not prepared to stock or handle such civilian items as clothing, yarn, and agricultural implements, and so introduced a system whereby the BMA ran independent supply lines outside the main ports and depots.[37] However, both the BMA and the combat formations suffered from shortfalls in motorised transport. As shown earlier, the divisions of XXXIV Corps arrived in Malaya under-establishment in terms of transport, while over the course of this period, the BMA never received the number of vehicles it needed. In January 1946, the number of BMA vehicles fell short of the month's target figure by almost 300, and by the end of March, the deficiency amounted to 1,020 four-wheeled vehicles and 312 motorcycles.[38] Stocks of captured Japanese vehicles became a precious commodity over which civil affairs officers and their colleagues in the combat units fought desperately. In Johore, Colonel Hay, the senior civil affairs officer in the state, was of the opinion that his greatest enemy was not the various ethnic militias and armed communist groups, but 161 Brigade, which hoarded most of the confiscated motor transport for their own use.[39] Insufficient transport for civil affairs use caused serious delays in distributing rice, salt, and sugar rations in Johore, and at its worst point during October 1945, only four trucks were available per day to move foodstuffs.[40] If, as Turnbull points out, commodity shortages were a key reason for inflation and rampant black market-eering,[41] it was poor military logistics that ultimately lay behind this.

These logistical problems were intimately linked with the problem of corruption. As mentioned above, the inability to ensure deliveries of essential commodities led to the grand level of inflation which made the black markets and corruption possible. At the same time, given the supply and manpower difficulties that the BMA faced, many economic pro-grammes had to be farmed out to extra-governmental bodies. Much of the imported relief supplies were handled by the Supplies Distributing Unit, a body officially sponsored by the BMA but comprising private traders and merchants, thereby opening the way for the deliberate mis-allocation of supplies. The appointment of civilian food controllers to relieve the overworked civil affairs officers and their strained military supply system also allowed for the confusion of public service and private advantage.[42] Was it any wonder then, that the Sydney police warned British authorities about known Australian gangsters attempting to join the BMA because of black market opportunities?[43] The endemic corrup-tion of 1945–1946 that damaged the image of the British Empire far more than the temporary defeat of its forces in 1942 was therefore not the result of a notional moral collapse of society during the war years or the convenient arrival of an inferior post-war breed of British official,[44] but was fundamentally created by the severe logistical and organisational problems that the returning British military suffered from.

General law and order in Singapore may have been at a satisfactory state by the end of 1945, but political troubles continued to grow in a worrying manner. Labour actions and demonstrations took place with

increasing frequency and on a crippling scale, and finally brought about
a showdown between the BMA and the unions.[45] The temporary victory
won by the BMA during that episode proved to have little impact on the
longer-term political scene; the volatile politics of 1950s Singapore hardly
need repeating here. Growing political unrest was undoubtedly fuelled by
economic misery and corruption, while the "Bourbon restoration" had
underestimated the popular support for left-wing politics. But it also owed
its terrible potency to the military government's inability to re-establish
the colonial state's monopoly of force.

The British had after all returned to a Malayan landscape seething
with multiple armed groups. In the last months of the war, the Japanese
had successfully set the Malays against the Chinese, and ethnic self-
protection organisations — vigilantes — thus abounded throughout the
countryside. With the removal of Japanese suppression, *Kuomintang* (KMT)
organisations and Chinese triads resurfaced. Simple banditry also flou-
rished in the vacuum of law and order created by the retreat of Japanese
forces into urban areas following the general surrender. But the most
capable amongst these groups were the wartime communist resistance
forces — nominally Allied and largely Chinese, but with an undisguised
anti-imperialist mission — and in the weeks between Japanese surrender
and British return, they took responsibility for law and order in various
parts of the country. In certain places, they managed to restore basic
infrastructure, thereby setting themselves up as an alternate, functioning
government before the reappearance of the British.[46] Furthermore, in
the absence of the British, the communists gained much political capital
by being the only armed force that was willing and able to protect the
Chinese community in this time of heightened racial animosity. It was
therefore imperative that returning British Empire troops succeed in
pacifying the restive countryside. Failure to do so would make it impossible to negotiate from a position of strength with local political factions
— either in the rural areas and or in the urban economic nerve-centres
like Singapore. As long as these armed groups, and above all the communists, continued to present a challenge to the colonial state, popular
political opposition to British rule could only gain in momentum.

The first weeks of the re-occupation were therefore crucial ones.
Instead of a scenario in which military rule was gradually phased across
Malaya as enemy forces were rolled back, the Japanese surrender had
turned over the whole of the Malay peninsula to the British all at once.
What was needed in the immediate aftermath of the landings at Singa-
pore and Morib, on 5th and 9th September 1945 respectively, was the

rapid projection of a British military presence throughout Malaya. Upon the speed of troop movement hinged the political position of the BMA and its mission of reconstructing the country.

Acknowledging that it would take time for the combat units of XXXIV Corps to spread out across Malaya, the British devised the solution of sending small parties of civil affairs officers in advance of the ponderous troop columns to establish the rudiments of government in the various states. This expedient achieved not inconsiderable progress, and a week after the landings at Morib, civil affairs detachments (CADs) were in every state save Trengganu and Pahang, where British liaison officers with the guerrilla forces there took on civil affairs duties instead.[47] The CADs proved relatively well-adapted to their role as the vanguard of the military government. Many CAD officers had prior experience of Malaya and were well-acquainted with local conditions, which helped them in their key tasks of establishing essential services and liasing with local communities and their leaders. For example, the CAD in Kelantan had as its commander Lieutenant-Colonel David Somerville, who had been an MCS official before the war.[48] On the whole, they fared well in their civil affairs role. In Selangor, for instance, Colonel James Calder and his executive officer John Gullick displayed great energy in re-opening banks, running electricity substations, and holding meetings with local communities to dampen racial tensions.[49] However, while the CADs could get a skeleton form of government operational, they only represented a thin veneer of British authority and lacked the military muscle needed to tame the restive countryside. Without effective local police forces, the most common response to reports of ethnic tensions was for a lone civil affairs officer to drive out to the disturbance and single-handedly attempt to calm tempers.[50] Colonel Hay's diary records his relief when significant numbers of soldiers from 1/16th Punjabs finally deployed to his area of responsibility in late September,[51] while during September and much of October, there were only three British officers in Kelantan against a — admittedly well-behaved — Japanese infantry battalion and the better part of a communist regiment![52]

The CADs were therefore an incomplete solution to the central problem of the reoccupation. The key to the reoccupation was the projection of military force across Malaya, which alone could bring to heel the variety of armed groups that prowled the country, create a security environment conducive for the reconstruction effort, and foster a more manageable political climate in urban centres. This, however, was not to be. The *Official History* describes the troop movement conducted after the landings as proceeding smoothly and suggests that the task of re-occupying Malaya was complete by 25 September 1945; subsequent lite-rature is similarly vague, and from these writings, one cannot appreciate just how long it took to push British and Indian line battalions and other combat units across the country. The sudden end to the war had already lost the invasion force several divisions which were despatched to other parts of Southeast Asia. The two corps plus independent formations ori-ginally earmarked for Malaya were thus effectively reduced to a single corps, though some of the independent brigades were retained.[53] As men-tioned above, these divisions were under-establishment in motorised transport, and to this one must add Malaya's difficult geography with its central mountain range complicating lateral communications across the peninsula, and the neglected state of roads and rails, especially in the east where infrastructure had been underdeveloped even before the war.

The initial days saw swift consolidation in the south and the west. Control over Singapore was quickly established upon the landing of troops on 5 March 1945. 5th Indian Division moved into Johore two days after their return to Singapore, and a week later, elements reached northern Johore where they gained touch with units of 23rd Indian Division deploying southwards.[54] In the west of the peninsula, the main economic centres were rapidly reoccupied after 23rd and 25th Indian Divisions were landed at the Morib beaches on 9 September. Port Swettenham was taken by 7/16th Punjabs on the day of the landings, Port Dickson by 3/5th Gurkhas the next, and 51 Brigade entered Kuala Lumpur on 12 September. In the week of 9–16 September, elements from these two divisions, 23rd exploiting southwards and 25th northwards, took control of Selangor, Seremban, and Malacca.[55]

Movement into the northern states, where large numbers of commu-nist guerrillas were based, only took place in the week of 17–24 Septem-ber. A single company of 9th Royal Sussex entered Alor Star on 17 Sep-tember, troops from 53 Brigade only arrived in force in the major Perak town of Taiping on 21st September, while a company of 14th Baluchs took over the garrison of Baling near the Thai border — an area swarming with armed groups — on 27 September. But it was in the eastern states that troop movement was at its most appalling. 5/6th Rajputs only arrived at the important eastern port of Kuantan on 28 September, while poor road and rail communications with Kelantan meant that 7/16th Punjabs was routed through a railhead in southern Thailand to reach the state capital, and thus British Empire combat troops only arrived in Kota Bahru at the northeastern tip of Malaya — where the Japanese had first landed in 1941 — on 18 October.[56] It was therefore at least a month — in some places even two — after the Japanese surrender before significant numbers of British and Indian soldiers made their presence felt in many parts of the country.

The arrival of British Empire forces did not bring an immediate end to the restiveness in the countryside. While a lid was soon put on urban crime, the activities of armed groups continued in many rural areas. Matters were worsened by the fact that until the wartime guerrillas were stood down in December 1945, communist forces nominally under the direction of British liaison officers were used to patrol and keep the peace in areas where the British were shorthanded — further ruining British military prestige, boosting the standing of the communists in the eyes of the Chinese, and providing the opportunity for more mischief.[57] The existence of ethnic militias continued to provoke racial conflict. Clashes entailing significant loss of lives took place on a regular basis; in Negri Sembilan in December 1945, while reprisal followed massacre in Pahang during February and March 1946.[58]

The security situation was especially grave in the north. The official disbandment and disarmament of guerrilla forces in December had little impact on military realities. In early September, Chinese guerrillas around Alor Star took advantage of the slowness of British troops in reaching the north to buy arms from renegade Japanese and prepare for a post-war struggle. Throughout the period of military government, communist groups actively opposed British authority in the countryside, and it was noted that the growth of subversive elements in areas like Larut, Matong, and Selama in Perak, kept pace with the increasing numbers of security forces.[59] Clashes with the communists could take place on a frighteningly large scale. On 26 February 1946, an assistant district officer was murdered near Grik in the far north of Perak; the platoon sent to investigate ran into roadblocks manned by Chinese guerrillas armed with Bren guns and grenade dischargers; it took a week for 33 Indian Brigade, with the support of armour from 16th Light Cavalry, to clear this stubborn hostile force from the Grik-Lenggong-Betong road.[60]

These troubles were not confined to communist activities. The British found themselves dealing with a much more complex, shifting patchwork of minor local powers. Most surrendered Japanese — the last of whom were repatriated in 1947 — behaved perfectly well and were usefully employed as labour units. But in November 1945, a party of renegade Japanese terrorised villages in Pahang, while a mixed gang of heavily armed Chinese and Japanese — the latter joining their wartime enemies

rather than surrendering to the British — roamed the Selama region of
Perak. The KMT proved another powerful locus of anti-British activity.
It was only in 1947, for instance, that security forces managed to round
up a rogue KMT group that was running what was in effect an alternate
state in the depths of rural Perak, raising taxes, enforcing their own laws,
and executing criminals (in an interesting twist, these men were inducted
into the Special Constabulary to fight against their communist arch-
enemies when the Emergency began).[61] By the end of military rule, the
British had yet to gain the initiative in the countryside, and the situation
in rural Malaya was an insurgency in all but name. Under such circumstances, negotiating from a true position of strength with political factions
in Singapore was impossible.

Dilemmas: Strategic Confusion in British Southeast Asia

While shedding some light on Singapore's post-war travails, such operational factors as the difficulty of communications and supply, the slowness
of troop movement, and the persistence of armed groups, do not by themselves fully explain the failures of the military government. There was a
wider strategic dimension to the way in which these problems unfolded.
The British mission in Southeast Asia — of which Singapore was the
fulcrum — was evolving rapidly during these seven months of military
rule. In mid-1945, the British Empire was preparing for a drawn-out reconquest of the Malayan peninsula; in August, her main aim had become
the disarmament of the surrendered Japanese formations not just in
Singapore and Malaya, but throughout Southeast Asia; by late 1945, it
was clear that British Empire forces were fighting not only a budding
insurgency in Malaya, but full-blown wars against nationalist groups elsewhere. The changing strategic mission made for difficult choices, and the
confusion they caused lay at the heart of the BMA's troubles.

The failure to re-establish a monopoly of force during the opening
weeks of the reoccupation was after all caused by an inability to recognise
the changing strategic situation. The lethargy in moving sufficient British
forces into areas like Kelantan with large numbers of communists was
not due to a failure of intelligence. Reports from liaison officers meant
that British high command knew where guerrilla forces were located.[62]
However, British commanders had misread the changing nature of their
post-war mission, and still thought in terms of the recently ended conventional war. Rounding up Japanese units was thus of greater importance
to them than dealing with the dormant threat of communist groups.

States like Pahang and Kelantan were low on British priorities because their remoteness meant that few Japanese units were to be found there. Ironically this very fact made the presence of armed groups possible, and should have warned against any complacency in projecting force into these regions.

The wider British mission in Southeast Asia also complicated the security situation. By late 1945, the liberation of Singapore was no longer the endpoint of the Far Eastern war, but the island had now become the only secure forward base for continued British operations elsewhere in Southeast Asia. In the wake of victory over Japan, the British Empire saw its authority temporarily extended over the entirety of Southeast Asia, and in Indonesia and Indochina, its forces were quickly embroiled in the first wars of the European succession in Asia. The period of military rule saw a constant cycling of units out of the country and their replacement by fresh troops. 23rd Indian Division left for Java in October 1945, for instance, and 5th Indian Division and 5 Parachute Brigade followed suit by year's end.[63] British forces in Singapore and Malaya thus lost much newly-gained and valuable local experience, which was a setback for overall security efforts.

Furthermore, Singapore had become a transit point for Dutch forces returning to Indonesia. The requirement to host and train the Dutch was an added strain on resources. By January 1946, 16 Dutch battalions were in Singapore and Malaya, and each British infantry battalion — but not the Indian ones — had one or even two Dutch units attached to it. British units were ordered to carry out command, weapons, and support arms courses for their Dutch colleagues, with temporary exchanges of personnel conducted at the sub-unit level.[64] This reduced the efficiency of combat teams within British infantry units and distracted them from what should have been their primary task of pacifying the countryside.

The wider strategic situation had implications for British force disposition too. Before long, troops were being concentrated in key population centres, thereby limiting their presence in the countryside. For example, the original plan of assigning Perlis and Kedah to 51 Brigade was modified to concentrate the formation in the Kuala Lumpur area, while the former two states were added to 74 Brigade's area of responsibility which was initially just Province Wellesley, thereby causing its soldiers to be thinly stretched across all three regions.[65] This situation was further exacerbated when Lieutenant-General Messervy, who took over Malaya Command in December 1945, instituted a policy of keeping his forces in

brigade-sized formations whenever possible. Messervy saw this as necessary for the conduct of proper training, recalling lessons from the war
about the demoralisation and reduction in effectiveness caused by distributing troops across the country in small garrisons.[66] While this was consistent with keeping troops in fighting trim for conventional campaigns
elsewhere in Asia, it detracted from the mission within Malaya itself,
which was to deal with widespread, low-intensity internal security threats.
For this, the dispersal of British units across the country was necessary.
This then was the fundamental dilemma: optimise dispositions for the
pacification of the countryside, or shape available forces for the wider
regional mission. The former was essential for the post-war reconstruction
of Singapore and Malaya, and arguably more important given that these
were formal British territories. But there was also a pressing need to support Britain's French and Dutch allies and prevent a radical redesign
of the strategic environment in Southeast Asia. The greater emphasis
on shaping forces for the latter objective thus undermined the ability to
deliver genuine security in Singapore and Malaya, and thereby compromised the political and economic mission of the BMA.

The changing strategic environment also had a deep impact on the
logistics of the military government. Singapore's role as a hub for ongoing
operations in Southeast Asia precluded a quick return to normalcy for
the civilian population. The influx of British Empire — and Dutch
— military units and HQs into the city taxed the housing situation to its
limit, with many civilian houses turned over to military use because of
the inadequate number of existing camps. Some of these houses were not
returned to their owners for nearly two years due to a shortage of building
materials that slowed down construction projects.[67] The inability to resolve this problem inevitably contributed to the political grievances of the
population, and Victor Purcell observed in December 1945:

> More acute and bitter than any other resentment is that there are so
> many civilian buildings and houses occupied by the Services ... there
> is not a single Chinese girls' school open because their premises are
> occupied. They cannot receive grants-in-aid, the teachers are unem-
> ployed, the children roam the streets.[68]

But the BMA's logistical difficulties were also shaped by factors
beyond Southeast Asia. Although global post-war shortages created difficulties of importing foodstuffs and other essential items into Singapore
and Malaya, the British Empire was theoretically in a position to short-
circuit these given the tremendous global logistics capacity it had built

up in the course of the war. Yet the changing strategic environment of Britain's worldwide empire meant that this global logistics network served to frustrate rather than assist the BMA. India, heaving with political change, could no longer serve as a limitless supply dump for British Asia, and so supplies for Singapore and Malaya had to be indented from the War Office in London. The flexibility of Britain's global logistics ironically resulted in chaos, with supplies originally earmarked for Singapore and Malaya diverted to other crisis areas along the way, while excess and unwanted surplus from dumps all over Europe and the Mediterranean found their way to the BMA — including tinned beef from Bari which had spent two years beneath the Italian sun, and female winter boots dumped in Norway during the 1940 campaign![69] All this, compounded by unsatisfactory shipping records, created a vast accounting hell wherein £7 million vanished during the period of military government.[70] Changing strategic concerns therefore deprived the BMA of the resources, military and otherwise, which were needed for it to recreate a stable colonial state from the ruins of war-torn Singapore and Malaya.

The Logic and Logistics of Imperial Decline: Some Observations on the Experience and Outcomes of the BMA

For the last half-century, successive historians of modern Singapore have criticised the shortcomings of the BMA: corruption, shortages, black markets, and political unrest were major problems that the returning British military failed to address effectively. Turnbull's assertion that these failures brought British prestige to its nadir, to a point even lower than during the Empire's momentary humiliation in 1942, is perhaps not an overblown one. The long, gradual decline of Britain's global power that had begun well before the Second World War was undoubtedly brought to a point of no return by the collapse of Europe's Asian empires amidst the Japanese rampage of 1941–1942; however, the military government that reoccupied Singapore in 1945 could have helped to better manage the war's consequences. While the BMA achieved some commendable successes, these were not significant enough to offset its other failures, which were responsible for the troubled developments that persisted long after military rule, even into the period of independence. The long-drawn counter-insurgency against the communists that had its toll in military and civilian lives and massive social dislocations; the trauma of Singapore's independence; the troubled racial politics of Malaysia to date;

these were the legacies not just of long-term colonialism and the sudden shocks of the war, but also the period of reoccupation when the British military failed to rein in the destabilising post-war forces that plagued the country, despite the unique advantages enjoyed by an all-powerful military government backed by significant numbers of fighting troops.

While Turnbull and other historians of modern Singapore have correctly identified the crucial failings of the BMA, what they have neglected is the military dimension which was so central to the reoccupation. Political developments and economic factors owed much to the operational and strategic framework that governed the actions of returning British Empire forces. Without the re-establishment of a monopoly of force and a swift resuscitation of the economy, radical political movements opposed to the resurrected colonial state could only grow in strength.

At the heart of this lay logistics. Pondering over the experience of the war, Field Marshal Wavell had noted:

> The more I see of war, the more I realise how it all depends on administration and transportation ... It takes little skill or imagination to see where you would like your army to be and when; it takes much knowledge and hard work to know where you can place your forces and whether you can maintain them there. A real knowledge of supply and movement factors must be the basis of every leader's plan...[71]

The great Allied achievements of the war were after all predicated on logistics, on the ability to feed troops and materiel into battle at a higher rate than the enemy.[72] The post-war peace had to be won likewise by the superiority of the Allied supply system, with sufficient numbers of combat troops to deliver genuine security and extensive supply lines to maintain both the military and the civil population. But just as the Malayan campaign was doomed by strategic dilemmas, so too was the mission of the BMA frustrated by grand strategy.

If anything, the end of the war taxed the Empire's military resources more than the fighting itself, especially outside Europe where it took on new responsibilities. In the Far East, the formations that were gathered for mopping-up operations in Burma and the reconquest of Malaya were all at once dispersed across the entirety of Southeast Asia, China, and Japan.[73] India, on the brink of independence, could no longer be relied upon for additional assistance with continued operations in Asia now that the war was officially ended. Furthermore, American air assets in India and Burma, which represented the bulk of Allied airlift in Southeast Asia, were transferred en masse to China following the capture of Rangoon in May 1945.[74] With American shipping concentrated in the Pacific, the burden of maintaining supply lines between India and maritime Southeast Asia was largely left to the limited sealift of the Royal Navy's East Indies Fleet.

This would not have been as great a problem had peace not suddenly intervened. While planning for the liberation of Malaya, the British had drawn up a shipping timetable for a period of three months, whereby the available maritime transport would have delivered necessary supplies into the country in successive stages as the campaign unfolded.[75] The advent of peace threw these fine calculations into disarray. In addition, the multitude of post-war crises caused supplies bound for Singapore and Malaya to be diverted elsewhere, while unwanted and unsuitable stockpiles were dumped onto the BMA. Singapore's place in the strategic environment of empire was changing, to the detriment of the BMA's mission. Desperately needed manpower and materiel were diverted elsewhere, while the available troops could not effectively conduct their proper tasks of bringing stability to the country. The British Empire's global war was not quite ended, though its battles now went by other names, and Singapore's renewed role as the military hub of British Southeast Asia meant that there could be no true return to a peacetime political and social status quo.

The reoccupation of Singapore was as much a turning point in modern history as its surrender in 1942. The earlier event had damaged the colonial edifice beyond repair, but in the months following the war's end, the British military had the opportunity to make the process of decolonisation a less troubled affair. Better logistics could have hastened economic recovery, improved security, and dampened the support for radical politics; fielding more military assets in 1945 could have spared the British Empire the turmoil of a 12-year Emergency. Yet operational constraints and conflicting strategic demands meant that this was not to be. The ultimate defeat of British rule, the endurance of the MCP as a challenge to the colonial state and its successors, persisting communal strife and acrimonious racial politics, all had roots in the security legacies of the reoccupation. The period of military government and the military factors so central to its experiences had long-term consequences and cannot remain marginal to the history of Singapore.

Beyond its importance in the history of Singapore, Southeast Asia, and the last stage of British imperialism, the reoccupation has an enduring relevance when viewed from a longer military perspective. Wars seldom end with the formal cessation of hostilities, and the hardest part of any military enterprise often comes in managing the subsequent peace. The same problems, causes, and trajectories evident in the experience of the BMA can be observed constantly throughout the modern history of warfare. Political complacency, overly optimistic reduction of military force, and new strategic priorities, have constantly complicated efforts to overcome the timeless post-war problems of ethnic-based insurgencies, black markets, organised crime, and socioeconomic unrest. The pattern of Singapore and Malaya was evident in the interwar experience of the mandated Near Eastern territories, repeated after the Second World War in Greece, Burma, Indonesia, and Indochina, and can be discerned again more recently in the Balkans, Afghanistan, and Iraq. These problems were not new in 1945, and they are with us still.

The story of the BMA therefore is of continual relevance to the study of warfare in general. Through it, one is made to appreciate the unique geopolitical, military, and social forces around which a new world coalesced at the end of the Second World War, and also forced to ponder upon the universality of that experience. The reoccupation presented the British Empire with a set of unique strategic and operational circumstances, but at the same time, it provides one with a reminder about the unchanging character of war.

Notes

1. The ideas found within this chapter were first presented to the University of Oxford's Imperial and Commonwealth History Seminar, convened by Professor J. Brown, Dr. J.G. Darwin, and Dr. J.-G. Deutsch, at which the late Professor C.M. Turnbull was present. This chapter has benefited from the comments offered by the Seminar's members, and the writer is especially indebted to Dr. J.G. Darwin.

2. C.M. Turnbull, *A History of Modern Singapore, 1819–2005* (Singapore: NUS Press, 2009), p. 229.

3. C. Bayly and T. Harper, *Forgotten Armies: Britain's Asian Empire & the War with Japan* (London: Allen Lane, 2005), p. 154.

4. S.W. Kirby, *The War Against Japan, Volume 5: The Surrender of Japan* (London: HMSO, 1957).

5. G.P. Dartford, *A Short History of Malaya* (London; New York: Longman, 1956), pp. 188–9; N.J. Ryan, *The Making of Modern Malaya* (Kuala Lumpur: Oxford University Press, 1963), p. 197.

6. M. Rudner, "The Organisation of the British Military Administration in Malaya, 1945–6", *Journal of Southeast Asian History* 19 (1968).

7. B.W. and L.Y. Andaya, *A History of Malaysia* (London: Macmillan, 1982), p. 266.

8. Turnbull, *Modern Singapore*, p. 252.

9. M. Murfett, *Between Two Oceans: A Military History of Singapore from First Settlement to Final British Withdrawal* (Oxford: Oxford University Press, 1999), p. 282.

10. A. Short, *The Communist Insurrection in Malaya, 1948–1960* (New York: Muller, 1975), pp. 260, 498.

11. D. Mackay, *The Malayan Emergency, 1948–60: The Domino that Stood* (London: Brassey's, 1997), p. 15.

12. Ibid., p. 13.

13. For an examination of wartime planning efforts regarding a post-war Malayan Union, please see C.M. Turnbull, "British Planning for Post-War Malaya", *Journal of Southeast Asian Studies* 5 (1974): 239–54.

14. PRO, WO 32/12193 (BMA Reports): Malaya's Political Climate, 1 October 1945, p. 111.

15. Turnbull, *Modern Singapore*, pp. 232–3.

16. Rudner, "Organisation of the BMA", pp. 105–6.

17. Rhodes House Library (RHL), MSS IND OCN s 271 (H. R. Hone, Papers): Hone to Donnison, 15 June 1953, p. 107.

18. A.J. Stockwell, ed., *British Documents on the End of Empire: Malaya* (London: HMSO, 1995), p. 186.

19. RHL, MSS IND OCN s 271: Hone to Donnison, 15 June 1953, p. 109.

20. RHL, 915. 13 s 6 (H.R. Hone, Report on the BMA), pp. 18–20, 37–41.

21. RHL, MSS IND OCN s 45 (M. C. Hay, Papers), pp. 27–30.

22. Bayly and Harper, *Forgotten Wars*, p. 109.

23. National Archives of Singapore (NAS), 002004 (H. Shaw, Interview); NAS, 002379 (J.M. Gullick, Interview); NAS, 001649 (C. Blake, Interview).

24. Imperial War Museum (IWM), 07/20/1 (L. E. Vine, Memoir), p. 81.

25. F.S.V. Donnison, *British Military Administrations in the Far East, 1943–46* (London: HMSO, 1956), p. 322.

26. RHL 915. 13 s 6, pp. 19–25.

27. NAS, 002379; NAS 001649.

28. Public Records Office (PRO), War Office (WO) 203/429 (State of Readiness of XXXIV Indian Corps), pp. 23–4; PRO, WO 203/393 (Concentration and Training for *Zipper*), p. 5.

29. PRO, WO 203/2821 (*Python*), pp. 5, 8–9.

30. RHL, MSS IND OCN s 200 (C. Noble, Papers): Civil Affairs Operations, p. 29; PRO, WO 172/6891 (HQ No 2 Area Singapore), p. 92: Port Executive Committee, November 1945.

31. PRO, Colonial Office (CO) 537/1572, (BMA Monthly Reports): February 1946, p. 27.

32. NAS, 001656 (H.W. Nightingale, Interview).

33. RHL, MSS IND OCN s 276 (C.H.F. Blake, Papers): Report on General Conditions, 10 September–26 October 1945, p. 20.

34. RHL, 915.13 s 6, p. 20.

35. Ibid., pp. 65–6; IWM, 92/37/1 (L.F. Edwards, Memoir).

36. Turnbull, *Modern Singapore*, p. 237.

37. RHL, MSS IND OCN s 271: Hone to Donnison, 29 November 1952, pp. 73–4; RHL, 915.13 s 6, p. 14.

38. RHL, 915.13 s 6, p. 59.

39. RHL, MSS IND OCN s 45, pp. 23, 28.

40. PRO, CO 537/1572: November 1945, p. 144; PRO, CO 273/675/5 (Re-Occupation of Malaya Fortnightly Reports): 14 October 1945, p. 38.

41. Turnbull, *Modern History*, p. 229.

42. Rudner, "Organisation of the BMA", pp. 101–4; RHL, 915.13 s 4 (BMA Gazette): 1 November 1945, p. 11.

43. Bayly and Harper, *Forgotten Wars*, p. 109.

44. Turnbull, *Modern Singapore*, p. 229.

45. Ibid., p. 233.

46. RHL, MSS IND OCN s 45, p. 24.

47. Donnison, *British Military Administrations*, pp. 154–5.

48. NAS, 001613 (L. Comber, Interview).

49. NAS, 002379.

50. Ibid.

51. RHL, MSS IND OCN s 45, p. 24.

52. NAS, 001613.

53. Kirby, *Surrender of Japan*, pp. 235–6.

54. PRO, WO 172/6965 (5th Indian Division War Diary): Review of Period 5–15 September 1945.

55. PRO, WO 172/7021 (23rd Indian Division War Diary): Summary of Events, 9–16 September 1945; PRO, WO 172/7033 (25th Indian Division): Summary of Events, 9–16 September 1945.

56. PRO, WO 172/7033: Summary of Events, 17 September–18 October 1945.

57. RHL, MSS BRIT EMP s 537/9 (End of Empire interviews): John Davis, p. 100.

58. RHL, MSS IND OCN s 116 (W.L. Blythe, Papers): Victor Purcell, Report on Chinese Affairs, 30 March 1945, pp. 47–8.

59. PRO, CO 537/1572: January 1946, p. 41.

60. PRO, WO 172/9722 (HQ Malaya Command G (Ops) Branch, January–September 1946), pp. 188, 191, 240.

61. RHL, MSS IND OCN s 26 (H.J. Barnard, Papers): Activities of KMT in Northern Perak, pp. 1–6.

62. PRO, WO 203/4333 (Malayan Local Forces).

63. Kirby, *Surrender of Japan*, pp. 274–6.

64. PRO, WO 172/6877 (HQ Malaya Command G (Ops) Branch, June–December 1945), pp. 163–72.

65. PRO, WO 172/7033: Summary of Events, 18 September 1945.
66. RHL, MSS IND OCN s 200: Messervy, Military Requirements in Malaya, p. 3.
67. Ibid.: Report on Accommodation, 11 December 1945.
68. *End of Empire*, p. 186.
69. RHL, MSS IND OCN s 271: Hone to Donnison, 6 February 1953, p. 87.
70. Ibid., pp. 73–4.
71. M. van Creveld, *Supplying War: Logistics from Wallenstein to Patton* (Cambridge: Cambridge University Press, 2004), pp. 231–2.
72. Ibid., p. 206.
73. Kirby, *Surrender of Japan*, p. 234.
74. Ibid., p. 32.
75. PRO, CO 273/674/8 (Civil Affairs Directive during Military Occupation).

Bibliography

Archival and Manuscript Sources

Public Records Office, The National Archives, Kew, London

War Office

WO 32/12193	BMA Reports
WO 172/6829	HQ ALFSEA Civil Affairs, September–December 1945
WO 172/6877	HQ Malaya Command G (Ops) Branch, June–December 1945
WO 172/6888	Malayan Corps of Guides
WO 172/6890	No 1 Detachment, 70 Operations Group, Civil Affairs Section
WO 172/6891	HQ No 2 Area, Singapore
WO 172/6965	5th Indian Division War Diary, G (Ops) Branch
WO 172/7033	25th Indian Division War Diary, G (Ops) Branch
WO 172/7045	26th Indian Division War Diary, G (Ops) Branch
WO 172/7082	5th Parachute Brigade War Diary
WO 172/9752	HQ ALFSEA Civil Affairs, January–May 1946
WO 172/9772	HQ Malaya Command G (Ops) Branch, January–September 1946
WO 203/393	Concentration and Training for *Zipper*
WO 203/427	*Zipper* Supply and Transport Units
WO 203/429	State of Readiness of XXXIV Indian Corps
WO 203/1452	Civil Affairs Master Plan
WO 203/2753	14th Army Training Operations
WO 203/2755	Rehearsal Prior to Zipper
WO 203/2770	Intelligence: Enemy Situation and Reaction to *Zipper*
WO 203/2821	*Python*
WO 203/2833	Civil Affairs Section: Reports
WO 203/2834	Transportation Aspect

WO 203/3880   Malaya: Organisation and Administration
WO 203/3903   Malaya Civil Affairs: Organisation of Units
WO 203/4002   BMA Civil Affairs Plan
WO 203/4333   Malayan Local Forces
WO 203/4675   *Jurist* Report
WO 203/4785   *Tiderace* Report
WO 203/5107   *Zipper* Planning and Exercises
WO 203/5116   XXXIV Corps Concept of Operations
WO 203/5124   *Zipper* Small Operations Groups
WO 203/6173   Handover Committee

Colonial Office
CO 537/1572   BMA Monthly Reports
CO 273/674/8   Civil Affairs Directive during Military Occupation
CO 273/675/6   Re-Occupation of Malaya Fortnightly Reports

Rhodes House Library, Oxford

Barnard, H.J.	MSS IND OCN s 26, 268 (2)
Blake, C.H. F.	MSS IND OCN s 276
Blythe, W.L.	MSS IND OCN s 116
BMA Gazette	915.13 s 4
Dalley, John	MSS IND OCN s 254
End of Empire Interviews, Volume 1 (Transcripts)	MSS BRIT EMP s 527/9
Evacuation of Harbour Board	MSS IND OCN s 46
Hay, M.C.	MSS IND OCN s 45
Hone, H.R., Report on the BMA	915.13 s 6
Hone, H.R., Papers	MSS IND OCN s 271
Noble, C.	MSS IND OCN s 199, 200
Webb, George William	MSS IND OCN s 255
Winston, William Peter	MSS IND OCN s 317

Imperial War Museum, London

Memoirs

Blois-Brooke, Lt-Cdr. M.S.	95/5/1
Campbell, F.M.	P182
Cherns, J.J.,	03/23/1
Edwards, L.F.	92/37/1
Emerton, H.W.	96/42/1
Farrow, Lt-Colonel W.L.	95/33/1
Findlay, Major R.J.	91/13/1
Groves, Captain T.W.	06/43/1
Knight, Captain W.S.	97/7/1
Morton, Surgeon Lt-Cdr. E.V.B.	87/16/1
Vine, Colonel L.E.	07/20/1

Recordings of Oral History Interviews

National Archives of Singapore

Blake, Chris	001649	4 July 1995
Comber, Leon	001613	4 August 1995
Gullick, John Michael	002379	21 June 2000
Nightingale, Herbert Walter	001656	17 July 1995
Oakeley, Rowland Henry	001332	8 November 1991
Pates, Richard	001435	19 November 1993
Shaw, Harold	002004	16 March 1998

Printed Primary Sources

Stockwell, A.J. *British Documents on the End of Empire: Malaya*. London: HMSO, 1995.

Secondary Sources

Andaya, Barbara Watson and Leonard Y. Andaya. *A History of Malaysia*. London: Macmillan, 1982.

Bayly, Christopher and Tim Harper. *Forgotten Armies: Britain's Asian Empire & the War with Japan*. London: Allen Lane, 2005.

————. *Forgotten Wars: The End of Britain's Asian Empire*. London: Allen Lane, 2007.

Chew, Ernest C.T. and Edwin Lee. *A History of Singapore*. Singapore: Oxford University Press, 1991.

Chin Kee Onn. *Malaya Upside Down*. Singapore: Jitts, 1946.

Dartford, G.P. *A Short History of Malaya*. London; New York: Longman, 1956.

Donnison, F.S.V. *British Military Administrations in the Far East, 1943–46*. London: HMSO, 1956.

Jackson, Robert. *The Malayan Emergency: The Commonwealth's Wars, 1948–1966*. London: Routledge, 1991.

Kennedy, Joseph. *A History of Malaya, AD 1400–1959*. London; New York: Macmillan, 1962.

Kirby, Stanley Woodburn. *The War Against Japan, Volume 5: The Surrender of Japan*. London: HMSO, 1957–1969.

Mackay, Donald. *The Malayan Emergency, 1948–60: The Domino that Stood*. London: Brassey's, 1997.

Murfett, Malcolm. *Between Two Oceans: A Military History of Singapore from First Settlement to Final British Withdrawal*. Oxford: Oxford University Press, 1999.

Rennell of Rodd, Baron Francis James Rennell Rodd. *British Military Administration of Occupied Territories in Africa during the Years 1941–47*. London: HMSO, 1948.

Robinson, John Broadstreet Perry. *Transformation in Malaya*. London: Secker and Warburg, 1956.

Rudner, M. "The Organisation of the British Military Administration in Malaya, 1945–6". *Journal of Southeast Asian History* 19 (1968): 95–106.

Ryan, N.J. *The Making of Modern Malaya*. Kuala Lumpur: Oxford University Press, 1963.

Short, Anthony. *The Communist Insurrection in Malaya, 1948–1960*. New York: Muller, 1975.

Turnbull, C.M. "British Planning for Post-War Malaya". *Journal of Southeast Asian Studies* 5 (1974): 239–54.

———. *A History of Modern Singapore, 1819–2005*. Singapore: NUS Press, 2009.

Van Creveld, Martin. *Supplying War: Logistics from Wallenstein to Patton*. Cambridge: Cambridge University Press, 2004.

Winstedt, Sir Richard Olof. *Malaya and its History*. London: Hutchinson, 1966.

8

A Colonial Progress:
Franklin Gimson in Ceylon, Hong Kong and Singapore

A.J. Stockwell

MARY TURNBULL WAS THE IDEAL SCHOLAR TO write the life of Franklin Gimson and at the time of her death she was about to embark on it for the *Oxford Dictionary of National Biography*. I was subsequently invited to take on the assignment. This chapter, which is a greatly expanded version of the *Oxford DNB* entry, is written in Mary's memory.

* * *

FRANKLIN GIMSON WAS A PRIVATE MAN DEDICATED to public service in Britain's eastern colonies. He was not a flyer to be fast-tracked to promotion, but a typical recruit to the Ceylon Civil Service where he remained for 27 years making steady, if unspectacular, progress. At the age of 51 and approaching retirement, he was transferred from Ceylon to be colonial secretary of Hong Kong only to be imprisoned in a Japanese internment camp. When, on the restoration of British rule in East and Southeast Asia, he was appointed governor of Singapore, his scope was curtailed by the daunting tasks of post-war rehabilitation, the paucity of resources at his disposal and the control which London now exerted over colonial governors.

At first sight, Gimson's record and legacy may not appear especially noteworthy. His career repays inspection, however, for two principal reasons. First of all, it illustrates the links between British rule in three territories, which for years the Colonial Office had grouped together in the so-called Eastern Cadetship. It identifies their differences and similarities, and it indicates how an administrator's experience in one of them shaped his approach to the others. Second, closer examination of his life reveals Gimson to have been representative of a generation of progressive officials who emerged in the 1930s and were promoted in the 1940s in order to implement a "new colonialism". During the interwar period, Ceylon was the most politically dynamic and constitutionally advanced of the three eastern colonies. Here, Gimson acquired the skill of administering through representative institutions. In addition, his approach to labour relations won him the reputation of a moderniser. He was then sent to Hong Kong specifically to introduce long-overdue constitutional and social reforms, and, although these were frustrated by war, he left his mark on the colony's history in other ways, notably the pivotal role he played in the restoration of British sovereignty. Finally, as Singapore's first post-war governor, he initiated schemes of social welfare and constitutional change, and, although their implementation suffered from administrative inefficiency, Gimson's commitment to local self-government never wavered.

Early Life, 1890–1914[1]

Franklin Charles Gimson was born on 10 September 1890 in the Leicestershire village of Barrow-upon-Soar. He was the son of the Reverend Charles Keightley Gimson and his wife Mary Ann Rebecca (formerly Dyson). The Gimsons had their roots in Leicestershire. In the 1840s, one branch, led by Josiah and his brother Benjamin, had set up an iron foundry and engineering firm which became one of the largest employers in the town of Leicester. Brought up a Baptist, Josiah later became a major figure in the Leicester Secular Society. He was also a town councillor. Ernest, one of Josiah's 11 children, would be a prominent architect-designer in the Arts and Crafts movement instigated by William Morris. So far as we can tell, however, the Reverend Charles Keightley was not closely related to Josiah; unlike Josiah, Charles was an Anglican, not a lapsed non-conformist, and his family appears to have had no business inclinations. At any rate, the Reverend Gimson was not listed among the mourners at Josiah's funeral in September 1883.[2] At the time of Franklin's birth, his father was headmaster of Barrow Grammar School. He later moved to the curacy of Holy Trinity Church, Cheltenham and then to Bradden in Northamptonshire where he served as rector. The Reverend Gimson died in Bradden on 16 November 1939 at the age of 79, his wife having predeceased him. Franklin, who became known to his friends as Jimmy, had one brother, Frederick, and four sisters, Dora, Kathleen, Edna and Betty.[3]

Franklin Gimson was brought up in the Anglican tradition and would remain an unostentatious but devout Christian. He was educated at Cheltenham Grammar School and in 1908 won a scholarship to read mathematics at Balliol College, Oxford. Having graduated in 1913 with a first class in Moderations and a second in Finals, he passed the examination for entry into the Eastern Cadetship Scheme (for service in Ceylon, or Hong Kong, or the Straits Settlements) and joined the Ceylon Civil Service at the start of the First World War. Neither Franklin's family nor his school appears to have had strong imperial connections.[4] Unlike the public school Cheltenham College, Cheltenham Grammar was not renowned as a cradle of colonial administrators. Balliol was probably more influential in determining his choice of career. In the late 19th century, its Master, Benjamin Jowett, had transformed Balliol. He had set great store by selecting students on merit and preparing them for public service at home and abroad. Aspiring "to govern the world" through his pupils, he would readily recommend imperial service to young men who asked: "What line of life should I choose, with no calling to take orders and no taste for the Bar and no connexions to put me forward in life?"[5] Three successive viceroys of India, Lansdowne, Elgin and Curzon, had been Balliol men and, long after Jowett's time, scores of others, who, like Gimson, lacked family backing or patronage but were not attracted to the church or the courts, embarked on careers in public service overseas.

"The Very Able Mr. Gimson": Ceylon, 1914–1941

On arrival in Colombo, Gimson embarked on the standard course mapped out for the competent cadet. Moving between the secretariat in Colombo, district administration and specialist departments, he gained a variety of experience. He rose steadily through the ranks and did not appear to be plagued by the misgivings about imperialism that had recently persuaded Leonard Woolf, that rising star in the colony, to resign from the Ceylon Civil Service. Military service towards the end of the First World War did not significantly interrupt his colonial apprenticeship spent either in the office of the colonial secretary or the remoter districts of Anuradhapura (North Central Province) and Mannar (Northern Province). In 1924, he was appointed landing surveyor in the Customs Department. Four years later, he was promoted to deputy collector of Customs, and in 1929, he became additional assistant director of Education. At the same time, his family responsibilities had been growing. In 1922, he had married Margaret Dorothy Ward (daughter of Canon Ward and known as Dorothy) and two years later, their first daughter, also called Margaret, was born in Colombo, to be followed, in 1929, by Judith, their only other child.

The 1920s saw an increasing localisation of the Ceylon Civil Service and the emergence in the Legislative Council of a vocal, non-official majority exercising what British officials identified as power without responsibility. Having reviewed the problem, the Donoughmore Commission (1927–1928) refrained from applying the principles of Westminster parliamentary democracy to Ceylon where communalism divided society and political parties were non-existent. It recommended instead a constitution whose principal features were universal suffrage (to include the Indian immigrant community), an elected State Council (with both legislative and executive functions) and a Board of Ministers. Members of the State Council were to be grouped into seven executive committees. These committees would be chaired by Ceylonese ministers who, together with the three British officials holding the most important portfolios, would compose the Board of Ministers. In contrast with the bitter controversies then surrounding constitutional change in India and in spite of the distress caused by the acute economic depression of the early 1930s, Ceylon's transition to the Donoughmore system was relatively smooth. Nevertheless, although these measures were in many ways remarkably progressive, they did not satisfy those Ceylonese leaders who aspired to full responsible government on the lines enjoyed by self-governing Dominions. Moreover, they failed to provide an effective relationship between the executive and the legislature, and as time went by, political wrangling and communal antagonism became more inflamed.[6]

Following the first elections under the Donoughmore constitution in 1931, C.W.W. Kannangara became Ceylon's first minister of education and Gimson was appointed his secretary. Kannangara was a lawyer who had served as an elected member of the previous legislative council. He was a redoubtable campaigner on national dress, national language and national education. His advocacy of universal and compulsory free education from kindergarten to university won him the sobriquet "Father of

Free Education" but was resisted by denominational interests and other members of the Board of Ministers.[7] While Kannangara continued as minister of education until 1947, Gimson's term as his secretary was brief.

In February 1932, he became assistant government agent in Trincomalee, the great naval base in Eastern Province, and in December the next year, he was transferred to the district of Kegalle (between Colombo and Kandy). Gimson's time in Kegalle coincided with a malaria epidemic which hit the island after two seasons of severe drought and crop failure, and was said to be the most devastating in the island's recorded history. The government was bitterly criticised for its inadequate preventative and relief measures: "the anopheles mosquito is as effectively preserved and pampered as the sacred cow in India".[8] Voluntary organisations, especially the left-wing Suriya Mal, were very active in the distribution of medicine and food.[9] In Kegalle, which was one of the worst-hit areas, they worked alongside Gimson and his wife in bringing aid to rural areas. The Suriya Mal won local acclaim while Dorothy Gimson received official recognition: she was appointed MBE in the King's New Year Honours of 1936.[10] In August 1935, Gimson was seconded from district work to a special assignment: preparation for the second general election of members of the State Council scheduled for February–March 1936.[11] He then spent a year as chairman of Kandy's Municipal Council before being transferred in July 1937 to the Department of Labour as acting controller. In October 1938, he was promoted controller of labour. It was to be his last post in the colony and probably the most challenging.

Indian Tamils had been recruited as plantation labourers from the late 1830s by government-appointed agents based in south India. Initially, they worked as indentured labourers on European-owned estates and in appalling conditions scarcely distinguishable from slavery. Migrant workers ebbed and flowed with the economic cycle but by the 1930s, Indian Tamils on European estates, which were predominantly located in the central area, numbered approximately 659,000 (including women and children). In addition, about 200,000 Indians (mostly Tamils) were employed in domestic service or commerce and also by government in, for example, docks, harbours and railways. Despite religious, ethnic and cultural ties, Indian Tamils were distinct from Ceylon Tamils (just over 610,000 in 1931) who lived in the north and east of the island as well as in Colombo. The Sinhalese majority (about 3,560,000 of a total population of 5,306,000 in 1931) increasingly resented the presence of Indian Tamils.[12]

In an attempt to assert some sort of control over the migrant labour force, the government set up the Department of Indian Immigrant Labour and legislated for plantation workers to receive a minimum wage. In 1931, this became the Department of Labour with responsibility for the welfare of both migrant and indigenous unskilled workers, though the former continued to be its prime concern. In this context, welfare meant the implementation of legislation governing recruitment, wage levels and conditions of employment, all of which had been skewed in favour of the large plantation companies.

As controller of labour, Gimson faced disputes and unrest on the estates but his scope for independent action was severely restricted by the discredited constitution, trade union militancy, employers' intransigence and inadequate resources. The controller was answerable to the minister of labour, industries and commerce, but by the late 1930s, ministers had become suspicious of the heads of government departments within their portfolios while Ceylonese members of the State Council in general distrusted British officials.[13] In the wider politics of the island, a new generation of activists now campaigned against the gradualism of their elders and pressed for national independence. Furthermore, Marxist Sama Samajists and trade unionists from the towns sponsored strikes on tea and rubber plantations afflicted by unemployment and the soaring cost of living.[14] Communal tensions were also worsening. Sinhalese perceived Indians as "alien intruders" who were taking their jobs and the Sinhalese-dominated State Council passed a number of anti-Indian measures. One of these ended the employment of non-Ceylonese labourers by government departments. Incensed by this challenge to the position of its people in Ceylon, the government of India retaliated in 1939 by placing an embargo on the emigration of unskilled workers to the colony. Uncertain of their status, Indian Tamils opted to stay on the estates rather than return to India when thrown out of work. In so doing, they swelled the ranks of the island's destitute and their grievances were fanned by a visit from Jawaharlal Nehru who urged them to organise for united action. Plantation owners called for tough action. They blamed trade union agitators for the disturbances and were in no mood to compromise. In 1937, they persuaded the chief secretary and inspector of police to deport Mark Antony Bracegirdle, a young communist from Australia who had taken a job on a tea plantation and sided with trade unionists. The affair provoked uproar and the judiciary overturned the deportation order, but the repercussions were felt long afterwards.

Assuming the office of controller of labour in the aftermath of the Bracegirdle affair, Gimson recognised that "changed conditions call for a changed outlook". Repression was not the answer to labour unrest. After all, he pointed out, the labourer had the franchise and therefore "the right to a voice in determining the conditions under which he is to be employed". Gimson aimed to alter attitudes and working practices on the plantations and in his own department. On the one hand, employers failed to appreciate the basic, social causes of unrest. On the other hand, the staff of the Labour Department had little experience of unrest on such a scale and so far had proved "inadequate" to meet the challenge. Hitherto, he observed, both sides had been accustomed to regard the department's role as merely the enforcement of legal requirements reached as a result of negotiations between government and employers. When trouble occurred on estates, superintendents of labour tended to rush to the police who intervened on insufficient evidence, thereby preventing settlement through arbitration and risking "an outburst on a wider bigger scale". The time had come, he urged, for all to accept that the department's duties included "the adjustment of differences between employer and employee" and to utilise its services to the fullest extent. Whereas the controller and his officers had previously confined their attention "to securing the observance of the various Ordinances dealing with labour", Gimson advocated a strategy "to inspire the labourers with the confidence that this Department existed to secure the improvement of the conditions of the workers". He aimed to "get closer in touch with employees and to induce them to represent complaints to this Department rather than to outsiders who may not necessarily be interested directly in the welfare of the working classes". By improving the calibre and status of inspectors, changing the outlook of planters, educating superintendents of estates in new ways and eliminating fraud and oppression by minor staff, he hoped to substitute negotiation for repression in labour relations.[15]

Gimson's conciliatory approach to labour disputes may not have tallied with that of the planters or even with that of the majority of his own staff. It was shared, however, by the new governor, the supremely able Sir Andrew Caldecott, and by the secretary of state for the colonies, the progressive Malcolm MacDonald.[16] Gimson's analysis of the problems of Ceylon's Indian community certainly had a bearing on Caldecott's attempts to reform the island's constitution. It also interested those in the Colonial Office who were addressing disturbances elsewhere in the colonial empire. The world depression had revealed glaring defects in British administration particularly as regards economic development and social welfare. Responding to riots and popular protest, especially in the West Indies, the Colonial Office urged governors to set up labour departments which would inspect working conditions and resolve disputes in their territories. The Colonial Office also set about putting its own house in order; specialist departments were created and experts appointed to advise on development and welfare issues. In 1938, Major G. St. J. Orde Browne became the secretary of state's adviser on labour, and the following year, the Social Services Department was established whose responsibilities included labour.[17] As we have seen, with its long history of managing migrant workers, the government of Ceylon already had in place a labour department, but it was Gimson who endeavoured to enlarge and reshape its functions in keeping with the pressing needs of the colony and the reformist ideas of the Colonial Office.

Memoranda by departmental heads in a colony generally passed no further than the governor, but in 1940, Caldecott forwarded to London a series of reports by his controller of labour. These were noted not only by the Eastern Department but also by the Social Services Department and Major Orde Browne, and comparisons were drawn between conditions in Ceylon and those in the West Indies, Mauritius and elsewhere. Some officials were pessimistic about the chances of Gimson's success. Others felt that factors such as the postponement of Ceylon's general election or the prospect of an agreement with the government of India would be more effective in reducing tension on the plantations. Yet others, however, were struck by Gimson's grasp of the issues and his commitment to a progressive policy. Because labour relations had become such a sensitive aspect of colonial administration, MacDonald had let it be known that, an official's performance in this field would be taken into account when promotion was being considered. The fact that the head of the CO's Eastern Department, G.E.J. Gent, was impressed by the work of "the very able Mr Gimson" is likely to have strengthened his chances of preferment.[18]

In the absence of an official record, we can only guess at the Colonial Office's reasons for selecting Gimson to succeed Norman Smith when he retired as colonial secretary of Hong Kong in 1941. To replace an officer who had spent his entire career in the Hong Kong Civil Service with a man who was only three years his junior and one whose colonial experience was confined to Ceylon needs an explanation, the more so as many Hong Kong hands, including the outgoing colonial secretary, firmly believed that the attitudes and practices of the Ceylon Civil Service were inappropriate to the circumstances of Hong Kong.[19] Yet, we may assume, the Colonial Office appointed Gimson precisely on account of his record in Ceylon: he was familiar with the workings and hazards of representative institutions and he had emerged as a moderniser as regards welfare provision. It was the view of the Colonial Office that both constitutional and social reforms were long overdue in Hong Kong. So too was rehabilitation of the public service which had been racked by scandal and corruption.[20] "Hong Kong has been terribly neglected in the past in respect of social services of all kinds," wrote the outgoing governor, Sir Geoffry Northcote, to the secretary of state in June 1941. "There is a magnificent field of work here of that kind and I had high hopes of getting something done; and then came the war."[21] The ailing Northcote was soon to be replaced by Sir Mark Young. Young, another former member of the Ceylon Civil Service who had gone on to be an energetic and farsighted governor of Barbados and then of Tanganyika, arrived in Hong Kong in September 1941.

"The Indomitable Gimson": Hong Kong, 1941–1945

Gimson arrived in Hong Kong on 6 December 1941. He travelled alone; his wife and daughters spent the war years in England. The next day, the Japanese attacked the colony. Unlike Singapore, which was regarded as impregnable, Hong Kong was defended by a mere 10,000 men, including two newly arrived Canadian battalions which were not combat ready. Nevertheless, Young obeyed Churchill's instruction to hold out for as long as possible. He repeatedly refused Japanese demands to capitulate and under his leadership the Hong Kong garrison earned the prime minister's accolade of "lasting honour".[22] During this time, Gimson held abortive talks with Chinese communists about the possibility of collaboration against Japan.[23] When the commanding officer, Major-General Maltby, reported that further resistance would be useless and only incur needless brutality and loss of life, Young surrendered on 25 December, "black Christmas". Young was first incarcerated in the Peninsula Hotel; he was later moved to Taiwan and then to Manchuria where he remained until August 1945. Unlike Sir Shenton Thomas, who did not return to Singapore after the war, Young would resume his governorship on 1 May 1946.

Gimson was now the senior British official in Hong Kong. The Japanese at first instructed him to remain at his post together with a few other Europeans who had special expertise.[24] During these weeks, Gimson compiled lists of prisoners of war and internees, and assisted in the transition to the new regime. Some Europeans managed to escape or, posing as neutrals, to remain at large in the colony but the vast majority of defeated soldiers and Western civilians went into captivity. The military, many of whom were later compelled to work as labourers, were imprisoned in Sham Shui Po prisoner of war camp. Civilians, including Asians and Eurasians associated with the British regime, were interned in Stanley Camp.[25]

Western civilians of Stanley Camp comprised three principal groups: British and Commonwealth (approximately 2,400), Americans (300) and Dutch (60). Stanley was far from being a homogeneous and harmonious community united in a common cause. Captivity in internment camps across the region heightened tensions of gender, class, nationality (between the British and Americans), race (between Europeans and Eurasians) and profession (between colonial officials and businessmen). Individuals responded to the Japanese regime in different ways. There were survivors who, as time went by, became something of an elite; dodgers with an eye to the main chance; leaders who represented internees' interests to the Japanese; technicians who were retained in essential services; humanitarians who, like Dr. Selwyn-Clarke, managed to serve the Hong Kong community beyond the camp.

At first, the Japanese left internees to cope with the tasks of allocating accommodation, food distribution and health provision. Later, they devolved routine camp administration as well. By the time Gimson joined the camp on 11 March 1942, internees had established an organisation dominated by leading non-officials of the colony, notably Ben Wylie, manager of the *South China Morning Post*, D.L. Newbigging of Jardines, and L.R. Nielson, a New Zealander and businessman based in the Philippines whom the Japanese had transported to Stanley Camp. The first attempt at self-regulation (the British Temporary Camp Committee chaired by Wylie) was succeeded after elections in February 1942 by the British Communal Council. This was chaired by Nielson and included only one colonial official, John Pennefather-Evans, the commissioner of police.[26] The internees had, in effect, "willed their future to the heads of the big companies".[27] Reporting on the Council's first three months, Nielson wrote that it had secured the cooperation of the American and Dutch communities and had established an "amicable and tactful relationship with the Japanese Administration".[28] He also laid claim to "smooth working" with the colonial secretary. In so far as this was the case, it was in large measure due to the efforts of John Stericker, an elected member of the Council who liaised with Gimson.[29]

Gimson was invited to join the Council "in an ill-defined position as a partner of the chairman".[30] Yet, while he praised senior internees for achieving "order out of chaos" in the early days of camp life, Gimson spurned their aspirations as unrealistic, grew impatient with their bickering and judged their chairman to be "an undesirable representative of the British Community". After several months, he responded to a petition from "a large majority of internees" by securing sole chairmanship.[31] He then replaced the Communal Council with a British Community Council which, despite retaining its elected base, was expanded to include additional officials but was limited to an advisory role. Once in charge of the Community Council, he took the title of Camp Commandant, although this changed to "Representative of Internees as the nominee of the Japanese" in 1944 when a Japanese military officer was appointed commandant.[32]

Gimson felt no compunction about acting as colonial secretary towards fellow prisoners and as His Majesty's representative when dealing with the Japanese.[33] While members of the Community Council came to accept his authority in Anglo-Japanese relations, they persistently carped at his day-to-day running of the camp. They were, he confided to his diary, "fully possessed of that arrogance usually associated with elected representatives".[34] Nielson, Wylie and others protested against what they regarded as Gimson's highhanded action in dissolving the Communal Council. They complained it would damage the reputation of "certain members of the mercantile houses of the colony and would have undesirable results in Hong Kong and London".[35] They questioned its legality, a matter on which Gimson sought the advice of the colony's attorney-general, Sir Chaloner Alabaster, who was also interned at Stanley.[36] The nub of this dispute was loyalty. While Gimson regarded loyalty to the monarch and loyalty to the monarch's vicegerents overseas as inextricable, most expatriates distinguished between steadfast allegiance to the Crown and questionable obedience to the discredited regime which Gimson now personified.

Moreover, as the representative nominated by the Japanese, he bore the brunt of internees' grievances over rations, compulsory labour, punishments, torture, brutality and summary executions. Their resentment was fuelled by his derisive dismissal of the proposal to declare Hong Kong an "open city" and his unwillingness to promote the repatriation of British subjects. After a batch of Americans and Canadians departed Stanley in late June 1942 as part of a reciprocal agreement with the Japanese, the hopes of the remaining inmates were periodically raised and dashed.

Gimson later recalled that "rightly or wrongly" he had argued that "internees as British subjects resident in British territory would not be entitled to repatriation".[37] Understandably, but unfairly, he became the butt of their frustrations. Yet behind the scenes, he succeeded in transmitting a message to London, emphasising that the repatriation of women, children and the aged was an "urgent necessity". In the event, further releases were doomed by disagreements between the British government and its Commonwealth partners, particularly Australia.[38]

Aloof, ascetic and "not blessed with a lively sense of humour",[39] Gimson did not readily win the affection of fellow prisoners. He was an outsider who never rid himself of the initial disadvantage of having to feel his way in Hong Kong. By his own admission, he had "little personal acquaintance of its people and its customs".[40] Though he cherished "the friendship of a few",[41] he lacked close colleagues in the civil service and did not warm to the old guard. James Leasor later described him as "an individualist, austere, untroubled by trends, quite outside the accepted civil service mould".[42] In addition, as we have seen, there was little love lost between him and expatriate businessmen, who focused upon commercial objectives to the neglect of the welfare of Hong Kong's wider community and could not "consider any other world than that in which they can make money and retire".[43]

Liberation did not put an end to recrimination. Back in England but still suffering from nervous strain, Gimson believed that Wylie and others would pursue him in the courts over their displacement as camp leaders. Having breathed the "purer air" of Yorkshire and freedom, however, he came to realise that his fears were groundless.[44] Amongst those who continued to harbour grudges was Sir Alexander Grantham. Grantham, who would succeed Young as governor of Hong Kong in 1947, was said to blame Gimson for the death in Stanley of his brother-in-law which, he felt, could have been avoided had Gimson been firmer in his dealings with the Japanese.[45] Years later, an Australian internee, the journalist Dorothy Jenner, bitterly accused Gimson of blocking both her repatriation during the occupation and her appointment to OBE after it. In an autobiography, from which she herself hardly emerges as a paragon, Jenner called him "a very nasty piece of work" and "the ultimate colonial snob".[46] Indeed, none of the Stanley survivors whom Geoffrey Emerson interviewed in the early 1970s for his study of the camp had much that was good to say about him. The release of further material and the work of other scholars since then, however, have persuaded Emerson to revise this adverse assessment of Gimson.[47]

The length of his term as prisoners' representative set Gimson apart not only from other captives in Stanley but also from prisoners' representatives in other Japanese camps. He attained "a status not achieved elsewhere",[48] but it was a status that carried immense risks and incurred much opprobrium. Ignoring the internees' council, the Japanese dealt only with Gimson and offered him special privileges. These he refused, because "acceptance would prejudice such influence as I had among my fellow-prisoners".[49] Instead he decided to assume total responsibility for British internees so as to shield them from reprisals. "My experiences were in total shared by none as I had the responsibility," he declared. "This I could delegate to no one."[50] As a result, he became both the lightning conductor for the discontent of captives and the captors' whipping-boy for any insubordination amongst prisoners. He was bitterly criticised by internees because he "did not adopt a more vigorous line of action".[51] At the same time, he suffered solitary confinement and risked execution at the hands of the Japanese. When at the end of the war he learned of the fate of prisoners' representatives in other camps, he realised "how incredibly lucky" he was to have survived.[52]

The most debilitating aspect of internment, Gimson tried to explain to his wife in his first letter home after liberation, was "not the boredom, not the uncertainty but the nervous inter-play of personality on personality, the selfishness, the malicious trend given to any scandal, the deliberate misinterpretation of any statement and many other signs of extreme nervous tension & lack of mental balance."[53] As sole intermediary between the British and Japanese, he had "almost daily interviews with the Japanese authorities either to receive orders or to make representations".[54] John Stericker, the camp's administrative secretary who attended many of these meetings, testified to the "strain and responsibility [that] was thrown on that one man, with nearly three thousand starving people on one side of him and the obstinate, impossible, and callous Japanese on the other".[55]

Gimson's commitment to prisoners' welfare was tempered by a keen sense of the possible. Early experience of Japanese mood swings taught him that a forceful approach would be counterproductive. As he explained, "I did not ... regard it as my duty to make 'strong protests' against the treatment accorded to us but to secure better conditions of internment".[56] He felt that discretion was usually the better part of valour as, for example, when the Japanese attempted to make propaganda out of a US bombing raid which inadvertently killed 14 internees in January

1945. When the camp commandant tried to force witnesses to sign affidavits that the Americans were to blame, they objected. Gimson, however, advised compliance. "What," he was reported to have said, "is the use of annoying these people? You only make it bad for everyone."[57] He accepted the occasional invitation to play bridge with Colonel Tokunaga (commandant-in-chief of all prison camps in Hong Kong) in the hope that it might put the colonel in an "amiable frame of mind" in times of crisis, such as in the aftermath of the American bombardment and during a furore over Tokunaga's attempted abduction of a female internee.[58] Gimson could hardly refuse such invitations but his trips up "the Hill" for cards with "the Colonel" did attract "some adverse comment if only because [he] would be sure of a decent meal".[59] This constant criticism wore him down and made him "doubtful whether the close relations I had to maintain with [the Japanese] were in the best interests of the British cause".[60]

The British cause was not only the welfare of internees; it was ultimately the reclamation of Hong Kong, and Gimson never wavered in his commitment to this. "The British Government in Hong Kong," he proclaimed, "is still in being and functioning except where prevented by the Japanese."[61] This was not moonshine but a star to steer by. He was constantly on his guard against making any statement or taking any action that might compromise British sovereignty. Thus, on learning of a possible plan to evacuate Stanley, he urged London to leave him behind with a "nucleus of administration to take control of colony as soon as the Japanese withdraw".[62] Communication between Stanley and London was facilitated by the British Army Aid Group (BAAG), an intelligence unit set up in free China by Colonel Lindsay Ride. It was fraught with danger not only for internees but also for those clandestine Foreign Office negotiations regarding repatriation, and in 1943 BAAG was banned from contacting Stanley until the Japanese surrender.[63] As news leaked out of the camp during the first year of internment, however, officials in London gained a sense of Gimson's courage and determination. Commenting on his willingness to remain in Hong Kong in the event of a general evacuation of civilian internees, L.H. Foulds of the Foreign Office commented: "I admire Mr Gimson's spirit. If we have many like him in the Colonial Service it augurs well for the future of the Empire."[64]

In July 1942, Gimson smuggled out to the Colonial Office a paper containing initial ideas for post-war policy. These included Chinese representation on the legislative council and municipal government for Victoria and Kowloon.[65] Although he "was not, at first glance, one of nature's liberals" and "an improbable advocate of reform", he had arrived in Hong Kong abreast of the latest thinking on development and welfare, and, in Philip Snow's words, "saw himself as the faithful executor of Whitehall's designs". The surrender of the colony in 1941 reinforced his conviction that social, economic and political innovation would be essential if Britain was to have a future in Hong Kong. Gimson "grasped earlier than anyone else that as soon as Japan was defeated a race would be on between the Allies for the *de facto* control of the colony".[66] Much would depend on whether Britain had long-term plans for its progressive development. He contrasted Hong Kong with Ceylon, where "I had naturally identified myself with the local inhabitants", and spent much time in Stanley discussing "the means whereby the political, social and economic conditions of the people ... might be reformed and bettered".[67] As he endeavoured to prepare fellow internees for post-war changes in Hong Kong, he made ready a skeleton administration to take over as soon as the war was over.

When news of Japan's surrender reached Stanley Camp, the inmates rejoiced but they were exhausted and faced an uncertain future. Japanese reprisals against prisoners and China's seizure of Hong Kong both seemed likely. However, "the indomitable Gimson"[68] took immediate action. He convened his provisional government of frail and undernourished civil servants, liaised with Lieutenant-Colonel Simon White (commandant of Sham Shui Po prisoner of war camp) and renewed contact with London. Once a Chinese agent from BAAG had confirmed the Allied victory and delivered a message from the British ambassador to China authorising him to administer government, Gimson ignored leaflets dropped from American planes instructing prisoners to stay in camp and, brushing aside Japanese protests, marched his team out of Stanley. Having been sworn in as acting governor by Sir Atholl MacGregor, the mortally sick chief justice, Gimson established his headquarters in the Old French Mission and broadcast to the world that Hong Kong was once again British.[69]

"Gimson's action", it has been written, "may have changed the course of history."[70] Indeed, over 50 years later, on the day when Britain retroceded Hong Kong to China, a British newspaper published a letter from a veteran of the 2nd (Hong Kong) Battalion, The Royal Scots, insisting that Franklin Gimson and Lieutenant-Colonel White of Sham Shui Po PoW camp "wrested control of Hong Kong from the Japanese" and "to them is due the fact that it is Britain which is now handing back a miraculously vibrant Hong Kong to the Chinese".[71] Yet, notwith-standing his careful preparations, determination and quick thinking, Gimson's bold initiative would have come to nothing had the Americans persisted in their support for China's claim to Hong Kong or had the Japanese allowed Chinese guerillas to occupy the Northern Territories and let armed gangs lord it over Kowloon. As it was, however, President Truman proved more sympathetic towards British colonialism than Roosevelt had been, while Chiang Kai-shek was preoccupied with problems elsewhere. Moreover, the Japanese high command calculated that it would be preferable to surrender to the British than to the KMT. So it was that the reoccupation of Hong Kong turned out to be an Anglo-Japanese affair. Gimson's gruelling negotiations with the Japanese throughout the years of internment appeared to have paid off when "overnight prison camp guards became allies of their former captives."[72]

On 30 August, two weeks after Emperor Hirohito's surrender, a naval task force under Rear-Admiral Cecil Harcourt reached Hong Kong. The flotilla encountered no resistance from the Japanese other than a small number of suicide motorboats which attempted to intercept it on its approach and sporadic snipers who opened fire after its arrival. Judging by the display of nationalist flags and exploding crackers, the local Chinese regarded the victory as theirs. Wearing black shorts and a trilby hat, Gimson went aboard HMS *Swiftsure* to greet Admiral Harcourt.[73] Although Chiang Kai-shek insisted that Harcourt receive the Japanese surrender on behalf of the Chinese government as well as the British, he did not oppose Harcourt's installation as governor or the appointment of Gimson as lieutenant governor. On 7 September, the advance party of the Civil Affairs Organisation (CAO) arrived. It was led by Brigadier D.M. MacDougall who took over from Gimson. Members of the ex-internees administration — some 700 of them — were gradually relieved of their duties and, as shipping became available, returned home for much-needed recuperation.[74]

A younger man than Gimson, MacDougall had been a progressive member of the Hong Kong Civil Service before the war and escaped internment to head the Hong Kong Planning Unit in London. He later regretted that "deep down our arrival was interpreted" by Gimson's staff "as a vote of no confidence in themselves".[75] If this was true of some, it certainly did not apply to Gimson whose crucial role in the successful reoccupation of Hong Kong was duly recognised. He was appointed

CMG and received a personal message of thanks from the prime minister. Gimson may have felt that his provisional government could have continued until colonial administration was fully restored,[76] but, as for his own fitness, he told his wife that "as much as I should like to carry on I fear I can't do so for long".[77] In any case, he did not demur from MacDougall's fundamental belief in the need for a fresh start. He welcomed the plans that had been devised in London for the post-war rehabilitation of the colony, and in his farewell broadcast on the eve of his departure for England, he spoke of "the opportunity of a clean sheet" on which to draw schemes of political and social reform. Gimson looked forward to the fostering of self-governing institutions and the fulfilment of "an enlightened long-term policy for the reconstruction of the new Hong Kong".[78] Indeed, following the restoration of civil rule, proposals were drawn up for constitutional advance but these were later shelved by Sir Alexander Grantham (governor, 1947–1957), who was convinced that the "fundamental political problem of the British Colony is its relationship with China and not the advancement to self-government and independence as is the case with most British colonies".[79]

"The Right Man in the Right Place": Singapore, 1946–1952

Physically weak and mentally drained, Gimson returned to Applegarth, the family home in Thornton-le-Dale near Pickering, Yorkshire, where his wife Dorothy had spent the war looking after their two daughters and tending a large vegetable garden.[80] To his younger daughter, Judith, he was something of a stranger. She had not seen him for eight years and when he returned, she was a teenager. His health improved rapidly and by the beginning of November 1945, he was eager to return to Hong Kong but the Colonial Office appears to have ruled this out. Any ill-feeling lingering from Stanley Camp would have hampered Gimson's reintegration into civil administration. Moreover, MacDougall, who had won the confidence of Whitehall as head of its wartime Hong Kong Planning Unit, had already been earmarked as the first post-war colonial secretary.[81] As regards an alternative post, Sir Charles Jeffries, the senior civil servant handling personnel, commented: "I don't know of any opening at present for Mr Gimson outside Hong Kong, unless," he added, "he is to be Governor of Singapore."[82]

Provided he was both fit and free of the threat of litigation from disaffected internees — and both conditions had been met by the end of the year — Gimson's appointment to Singapore made a lot of sense. In recommending him to the prime minister, the secretary of state drew attention to "his splendid record of service in Ceylon", his "conspicuous courage, ability and discretion" during internment, and "his spirited organization of an impoverished British administration in the days before the British fleet arrived". George Hall assured Attlee that, having met with Gimson since his release, he had "formed a most favourable impression of his personality".[83] His appointment was announced on 29 January 1946 and he was installed on 3 April.[84] Dorothy joined him in October but their daughters remained in England finishing their studies. Margaret was a student at the Royal Academy of Dramatic Art while Judith was still at school in Harrogate. From time to time over the next six years, Margaret and Judith would come to stay at Government House and it was here that they would meet their future husbands.[85]

Although Singaporeans knew little of Gimson, the *Straits Times* was impressed by his reputation and especially by the fact that he had been a captive of the Japanese. This would win him "the sympathy and good will of the people of Singapore" and it was "fitting that this high office should go to a man who shared the sufferings that befell the great majority of those he is to govern".[86] For his part, Gimson's gratitude to the brave Chinese of Hong Kong predisposed him towards those of Singapore. At his installation ceremony, he emphasised that the years in Stanley Camp had shaped his thinking about the future of colonial rule and prepared him for the tasks which he now faced in Singapore.[87]

Singapore was no less significant for the empire than it had been before the war and London was determined to restore the island to its commercial and military pre-eminence in Southeast Asia. Nevertheless, its governorship no longer enjoyed the cachet of a blue-ribbon posting. This was principally because communal differences between the island and peninsular Malaya had resulted in Singapore's exclusion from the Malayan Union (of Malay states, Penang and Malacca) which wartime planners had designed as the first stage in the consolidation of colonial administration and British power in the region. Thus, whereas his predecessors had been responsible for the Straits Settlements and (as high commissioners for the Malay States) for the rest of the peninsula as well, Gimson was put in charge of "so limited an area" that Labour's parliamentary under-secretary at the Colonial Office had at first questioned whether it merited "all the pomp and circumstance of a Governor or Lieutenant Governor".[88] His authority was further circumscribed by a metropolitan government that was much more interventionist than before and also by a new regional organisation led Malcolm MacDonald, the Governor-General of Malaya (later Commissioner-General, Southeast Asia).[89]

MacDonald generally set the pace in policymaking and, although he had no executive function in either territory, he coordinated developments in both. As a former secretary of state for the colonies, he commanded immense influence in Whitehall. He could make or break a governor, as Sir Edward Gent would find to his cost. Gent was governor of the Malayan Union and, on its demise in early 1948, he briefly served as high commissioner of the Federation of Malaya. He was transferred to the field from the Colonial Office where his wide-ranging responsibilities as assistant under-secretary had included wartime planning for Ceylon, Malaya, Singapore, Borneo and Hong Kong. Gimson was the most junior member of this triumvirate whose ranking was symbolised by the peerage offered to (but refused by) MacDonald, the knighthood conferred upon Gent before he left England and the knighthood awarded to Gimson only after he had completed four months as governor. More to the point, when in June 1948 the secretary of state was seeking a replacement for Gent, MacDonald reported that, while Gimson was "doing admirably in the smaller governorship of Singapore" where he was "the right man in the right place", he was "not a strong and firm enough administrator" for the more demanding position in Kuala Lumpur.[90]

When the three appointments were announced in January 1946, the *Straits Times* was reassured: "We could not be in better hands".[91] But not everyone was convinced of the need for such an elaborate administrative structure. Sir Cecil Clementi called it "uneconomic and top-heavy". He pointed out that, when he had been governor and high commissioner of Malaya in the 1930s, he had attempted to centralise the administration of Britain's disparate territories in Southeast Asia upon his own office. He argued that it was "absurd to tear away Singapore from the rest of the peninsula, to place it and the 'Malayan Union' under separate Governors, and then to appoint a Governor-General for the purpose of patching up the rent". In short, he saw "no sense in appointing three officials to discharge duties hitherto effectively performed by one".[92]

What Clementi appeared unwilling to recognise, however, was that new circumstances called for new measures. By 1946, the pressure was on to ditch liabilities (notably India, Burma and Palestine) and develop assets such as Malaya and parts of Africa. Development required central planning and the active involvement, or "partnership", of subject peoples. Partnership was essential if the British were to make the most of their colonies; it was also essential if they were to escape the burdens of empire without sacrificing interests and influence. With these ends in mind, but with an eye on the clock, the British drew up plans for economic development, social welfare, the localisation of administration and constitutional advance from empire to commonwealth. In the process, governors' duties increased dramatically while their autonomy declined correspondingly. As agents of the new colonialism, they ceased to be monarchs of all they surveyed and became managers of political change. Some, like MacDonald and to a lesser extent Gent and Gimson, might even be regarded as proconsuls of new nations, or rather, nations moulded in the British image. Yet, as Gimson would discover, the selection of local partners proved problematic: it might run into resistance or founder in a sea of indifference.

Social welfare was not only fundamental to post-war rehabilitation, it was also part of that debt of honour which the British owed Singapore and a prerequisite for its democratic government. Much of the island was scarred by battle. Docks, roads and railways were severely damaged. Water, power and shipping were in short supply. Traumatised by the Japanese occupation, Singaporeans had soon become disillusioned with the "liberation" offered by the British Military Administration during which they had suffered hunger, rising prices, rationing, disease, homelessness, unemployment, corruption and the black market. The task of the colonial administration was to rectify these ills. Social welfare had formerly been a matter for private charity. Now government assumed responsibility for it. Britain's Labour administration was committed to "an imperialism of the welfare state"[93] and Gimson was its enthusiastic agent in Singapore.

Although welfare provision in the colonies would fall a long way short of the welfare state that was being created in Britain, it exceeded anything that had been envisaged before the war. In June 1946, Gimson established the Social Welfare Department (under T.P.F. [Sir Percy] McNeice) which to begin with concentrated on the relief of exceptional hardship. This was followed by a Public Relations Department and a Labour Department, promoting democratic trade unionism and covering industrial relations generally and not just Indian affairs. A ten-year education programme, launched in 1947, promised all children of school age six years of free, compulsory primary teaching in any of the four main languages. Gimson also took a special interest in teacher training and the inauguration of the University of Malaya (1949) which he, like MacDonald, regarded as essential for grooming leaders of the Malayan nation.

In 1948, a medical plan was approved and a start was also made on the much-needed expansion and improvement of housing stock as well as the development of "new towns". This was a costly enterprise and two years later, Singapore's colonial secretary acknowledged that "the resources of Singapore are inadequate for the quick solution of a problem which has been growing steadily and rapidly during the past thirty years".[94]

Some financial support for these projects came from Britain's Colonial Development and Welfare fund from which youth centres, citizens' advice bureaux, community care, and the new University of Malaya all benefited.[95] Otherwise, Singapore was expected to meet the costs through community self-help and taxation. Lady Gimson energetically promoted self-help projects, as she had in Ceylon. Moreover, as the island's economy revived, so did the tradition of Chinese philanthropy. But a persistent deficit in government finances, together with the projected cost of welfare, convinced Gimson of the need to levy income tax.

Previous attempts to introduce such a measure — in 1860, 1910 and 1921 — had failed and Gimson's proposal provoked a furore. In the end, Gimson (like Gent who was proposing similar legislation for the Malayan Union) forced the ordinance through his Advisory Council in the teeth of the unanimous opposition of unofficial members, one of whom, John Laycock, subsequently campaigned for Gimson's dismissal.[96] Gimson's clash with the unofficial members of his Advisory Council over taxation was the only instance of his resorting to gubernatorial reserve powers. The confrontation did little lasting damage to his standing, since the Advisory Council was only a consultative body of officials and nominated unofficials. It commanded little local support and was due to be superseded by a Legislative Council containing some elected representatives. Nevertheless, the dispute over the introduction of income tax confirmed Gimson in his view that the new Legislative Council should be as representative as possible so as to secure popular acceptance of future, controversial measures.

It had been impressed upon him at the start of his governorship that London attached "the utmost importance to the most rapid development that is possible of a sound and broad-based system of Government on progressively democratic lines."[97] In fact, having consulted local opinion, Gimson went further than the Colonial Office in his proposals for the initial stage of constitutional advance. He favoured, first, a greater proportion of unofficial members on council; second, direct and popular elections rather than the indirect election of representatives through organisations such as chambers of commerce; and, third, an electorate of individuals voting in geographical constituencies and not by racial community. Voting was to be by universal suffrage, although this was restricted to British subjects and persons born in Malaya and British Borneo. The Legislative Council was inaugurated on 1 April 1948. It consisted of 23 members of whom 10 were officials and 13 were unofficials. Four of the unofficials were nominated by the governor, three were elected by chambers of commerce, and six (increased to nine in 1950) were popularly elected.

Reform of the Legislative Council had implications for local government. Since Singapore was no longer the hub of the Straits Settlements but a separate, island city-state, some questioned the continuing coexistence of the Municipal Commission alongside the full panoply of island-wide institutions traditionally associated with crown colony rule. Drawing parallels with Hong Kong, however, Gimson was keen to retain and develop institutions of local government: the Municipal Commission became a fully elected body and in September 1951 it was granted city status by Royal Charter.

Gimson knew from his years in Ceylon that representatives without executive responsibilities were likely to "regard themselves as a party in opposition to Government".[98] He attempted to avoid this state of affairs in Singapore by drawing the unofficial members of the Legislative Council into policymaking, and in 1951, they were permitted to select two from their number to serve on the Executive Council. He was, however, reluctant to jeopardise the long-term development of democracy by allowing the premature devolution of executive responsibilities to Chinese unofficials who, in any case, were fully engaged in extensive professional and business activities. He was also sensitive to the opposition of Europeans to any move, such as the transfer of executive responsibility to local politicians, that suggested Britain was about to cut and run. Gimson, therefore, concentrated on the development of representative institutions. In the Federation, meanwhile, Sir Henry Gurney (who had succeeded Gent as high commissioner in October 1948) adopted a different course. Instead of introducing elections to the Federal Council, Gurney sought to satisfy the aspirations of Malayan politicians with a form of ministerial government — the Member System. To Gimson's consternation, as the constitutional paths of island and mainland diverged, the prospect of territorial merger receded.

At first sight, the advance of representative government in Singapore was astonishing. Indeed, the authorities were gratified by both the conduct and the result of the first election. The boycott mounted by the radical Malayan Democratic Union was a failure: 63% of registered voters went to the polls and candidates of the moderate, non-communal Progressive Party (C.C. Tan, John Laycock and N.A. Mallal) won three of the six seats. For the next election in 1951, the number of elected seats was increased to nine, of which the Progressives won six. However, the vast majority of Singaporeans appeared unmoved by the opportunity to vote. Relatively few bothered to register on the electoral roll. The majority of Chinese-speaking Singaporeans were either indifferent or ineligible. It was the small Indian community (7.6% of the population) that proved the most electorally aware, accounting for 45.3% of voters, 40% of candidates and 50% of elected members. Similarly at the second election in April 1951, a mere 21% of the potential electorate registered and only half of these went to the polls. Once again, Indians were dominant while those Chinese who were eligible to vote were reluctant to participate.

The reason for this apathy, the British believed, was not the absence of political consciousness but inadequate social integration. It stemmed from the polarisation of the English-speaking Chinese minority and the Chinese-speaking Chinese majority, and the latter's lack of identification with Singapore, or in other words, "the Chinese problem" of belonging. Many still looked to China, and supporters of the Kuomintang and Communists clashed over the control of Singapore's Chinese schools. Gimson explored ways of creating a sense of nationality and of extending political rights to Chinese-speaking Chinese, but with little success. Meanwhile, members of the Progressive Party were indifferent to social integration, closer association with the Federation and the importance of a popular mandate. The politics of representative government were divorced from popular concerns; they provided a weak foundation on which to build a national partnership with the new colonialism.

Industrial unrest and popular protest had intermittently rocked Singapore since the British return in September 1945. Working through its Singapore Town Committee and the General Labour Union (later the Pan-Malayan Federation of Trade Unions), the Malayan Communist Party (MCP) established a hold upon the discontented labour force. Strikes, particularly of harbour and transport workers, climaxed with a general strike in January 1946 and continued thereafter. Contending with a spate of unrest in March 1947, Gimson demanded greater authority to banish troublemakers, but MacDonald, while accepting that communism was "Enemy No. 1", reined in the governor's authoritarian tendency and diverted attention to regulating the unions.[99] Communist influence also permeated the Malayan Democratic Union which had been founded in December 1945 as a moderate, progressive party committed to democratic self-government. While improving economic conditions contributed to a reduction in labour militancy, it was the government's tough response to the MCP's premature launch of armed struggle in June 1948 that sapped communist activity on the island. The MCP shifted its activities from the towns to the Malayan jungle and Gimson followed Gent by declaring a state of emergency. Police swiftly rounded up known radicals and suspected subversives. Special Branch remained vigilant. A lid was clamped down on unrest in Singapore for the next 18 months.

Early in 1950, however, urban violence resumed. It was during this surge of bombings, arson and intimidation that an attempt was made on the governor's life. Just before midnight on 28 April 1950, a mills bomb was thrown at Gimson as he left the Happy World Stadium after presenting prizes at the Singapore Amateur Boxing Association's championships. It struck him on the leg, rebounded and exploded about six feet away. It appeared to be an old bomb with a defective charge. No one was injured. A man was detained but later released. Road blocks were immediately set up in the vicinity and during the next 48 hours the police screened 40,000 people as against the normal daily quota of 10,000. Only one person — a British serviceman — came forward to give evidence. "A heavy, ominous, dangerous curtain of silence has," commented the *Straits Times*, "descended on the population of Singapore."[100] Coming five months after the assassination of Duncan Stewart, governor of Sarawak, the incident alarmed Colonial Office officials, although one of them, John Higham, who had recently returned from a visit to the region, expressed surprise that attempts on the lives of senior officials in Singapore and the Federation had not been made before. He noted, presciently as it turned out: "when I went about with Sir H. Gurney (admittedly only in the relative backwater of Penang) the police protection was so inconspicuous that I am sure there would have been little difficulty in a determined assassin carrying out his intention."[101]

A few weeks after this incident, the secretary of state for the colonies (James Griffiths) and the secretary of state for war (John Strachey) visited Malaya and Singapore to examine counter-insurgency operations at first hand. At a conference convened by MacDonald, the commissioner-general and governors of Malaya and Singapore briefed Griffiths on constitutional development. MacDonald and Griffiths agreed that, because factors over which the British had little or no control were accelerating decolonisation, the old assumption that the transition to self-government would take 25 years should be revised to 15. While he did not disagree with this analysis, Gimson said, "it was important to know whether we should encourage the transition towards self-government, or try to put a brake on the pace." It was, he continued, "much easier to retard development at an early stage" whereas it would be much harder once elected members had executive responsibilities.[102]

On one thing he was certain: Singapore could not survive on its own. Not only was peninsular Malaya its historic and natural hinterland but, more significantly, any attempt at separate independence would expose the island to interference from China, or Indonesia, or even India.

In the light of the divergent constitutional routes adopted by Singapore and Malaya, he urged their fusion sooner rather than later and (foreshadowing the discussions over Greater Malaysia ten years later) he suggested that Singapore might be incorporated as a city-state enjoying complete control over its local affairs within a looser federation. "At all costs," he said, "we must not allow ourselves to be driven into the position where we have to say 'we cannot grant you self-government because you are not yet united as one territory'".[103] Griffiths seemed impressed by this analysis and, on returning to London, he extended Gimson's term to April 1952 even though he had reached retirement age. MacDonald was "glad" about this decision and Gimson was delighted, not least because his wife could pursue her keen interest in Singapore's welfare centres, particularly those for children. He himself wanted to expand the programme of social services and see through the Legislative Council elections due in 1951.[104] But his reputation took a knock when violence erupted from an unexpected quarter.

At about noon on 11 December 1950, rioting broke out in the vicinity of Singapore's Supreme Court and spread to the area of the Sultan Mosque. The violence lasted 48 hours. 18 people were killed (nine by rioters and nine by the police or military), 173 were injured and much property was damaged or destroyed including well over 100 vehicles. The uproar was triggered by a dispute over the custody of a 13-year-old girl, Maria Hertogh, and whether she should be brought up a Catholic or a Muslim. The Hertoghs had consigned their daughter to the care of Che Aminah binte Mohamed when the Japanese had invaded the Netherlands East Indies. They claimed it was for temporary safekeeping. Che Aminah (who renamed the girl Nadra) claimed it was permanent adoption. The Hertogh riots stand apart from other violent incidents in post-war Malaya and Singapore. They were not driven by Sino-Malay communal antagonism; Muslim anger was directed against Europeans and Eurasians, not against the Chinese. Nor were they part of what the British had identified as the communist threat, be it the insurgency then raging on the peninsula or the labour unrest and student protest on the island. The grievances of Singapore's Muslims arose from their marginalisation by the post-war colonial state. Their discontent turned to riot as a result of colonial negligence, particularly in intelligence and policing.[105]

The authorities' fixation with the threat from the left is illustrated by their overbearing handling of Singapore's intelligentsia. In January 1951, shortly after the Hertogh riots, the police pounced upon the English-speaking branch of the Anti-British League and arrested over 30 students and other intellectuals. Although most were released, five remained in custody including John Eber whom Gimson regarded as a great danger to public security. The secretary of state was disturbed by this precipitate action: news of detention without trial would expose the British government to criticism at home and abroad. When Gimson proposed to extend Eber's period of detention, he was overruled on the grounds that repressive measures against intellectuals would be counter-productive.[106]

Meanwhile, a commission of enquiry had been investigating the Hertogh riots. Chaired by Sir Lionel Leach, a former chief justice of Madras, it ignored the socio-economic groundswell of Muslim discontent and focused on the immediate causes of rioting, its course and the conduct of the security forces. The Leach report targeted the colonial secretary (W.L. Blythe) and also the police whose conduct became the subject of a separate inquiry. Completed in mid-May 1951, publication of the report was delayed until August to allow the governor and those persons named in the report to respond. During this period, Gimson made strenuous efforts to deflect blame, defend senior colleagues (notably Blythe) and secure changes to the report. Gimson himself escaped extensive scrutiny because, as the sovereign's representative, he could not be put under oath. Nonetheless, he was clearly implicated in what had been a breakdown in government which could have had adverse repercussions for Britain's position in the Federation and elsewhere in the Islamic world. The riots and Gimson's special pleading, coupled with complaints about his unpopularity appear to have convinced the secretary of state that he should be relieved of his post. MacDonald, something of a fair-weather friend, agreed.[107] However, the secretary of state decided to await local reaction to the report before selecting a new governor and, when it became clear in September that renewed violence was unlikely, he decided to defer making an appointment until after the British general election which had been called for October.[108]

So it was that Gimson completed his extended term and retired honourably, followed, also honourably, by Blythe in 1953. Indeed, because of the security crisis surrounding the assassination of Sir Henry Gurney on 6 October 1951, Gimson postponed the leave owing to him in order to remain at his post until March. This was a characteristically selfless gesture by a man exhausted after a career devoted to public service. Equally characteristic was Field Marshal Lord Montgomery's insensitive comment: "Gimson is a worthy soul. But he was prisoner in Japanese hands in the war. He has now 'had it', and he admits it."[109]

Conclusion

A ceremony marking the culmination of Gimson's colonial progress was held on 14 March 1952 in Singapore's Victoria Memorial Hall when he became the first person to be conferred with the freedom of the city. It was attended by councillors, judges, clergy, the chancellor of the university (MacDonald) and its vice-chancellor, a military band, schoolchildren, scouts, guides and other youth organisations. In a "modest" speech of thanks — and Gimson had never been flamboyant — he recalled how six years earlier he had been "most anxious that he should repay by service to the people of Singapore some of the debt of gratitude and of honour" owed by those, like himself, who had been victims of the Japanese occupation. He continued: "I still feel most keenly that debt of gratitude and I also feel keenly that it has not been repaid to the fullest extent that I should have liked," adding, "I feel aghast that so much remains to be done." As he prepared to leave the hall, a group of councillors, "representative of each Asian race", heaved him onto their shoulders and broke into song: "For he's a jolly good fellow!"[110]

When, some months earlier, the Colonial Office had been looking to appoint Gimson's successor, MacDonald had offered a profile of the ideal governor that was shaped by his assessment of Gimson's strengths and weaknesses.[111] He should possess, wrote the commissioner-general, "all Gimson's political wisdom plus what he lacks, i.e. real administrative ability and efficiency". If this comment was a tribute to the range of Gimson's initiatives, it was also a criticism of a civil service that had failed to keep up with the flow of government business. Therefore, in addition to continuing "Gimson's policy of steady advance towards self-government", the incoming governor should "overhaul the administrative machine of the existing government".[112] Turning to other gubernatorial attributes, MacDonald expressed the hope "that the new Governor will have another quality which Gimson only partially has — that is, real social informality and equalitarianism in his relations with the ordinary citizens of Singapore." This was a virtue which MacDonald himself enjoyed in abundance and which he displayed sometimes to the dismay of members of the European community. Although he accepted that Gimson was "an extremely friendly man towards all and sundry", Mac-Donald noted that he "retained (unwittingly, I think) too much of the superiority complex of the old Colonial type of Governors". The "stiffness and starchiness" of Government House was palpable but, in MacDonald's opinion, the fault lay less with Gimson than with his wife who liked "all the old-fashioned formalities". This may seem a harsh judgement on Lady Gimson who was a gracious hostess and, in addition to her good works in the community, had done much to restore and refurbish Government House after wartime neglect. What MacDonald was looking for in the next governor was a less withdrawn figure, someone "who will really throw his doors wide open to the people of Singapore", "a fairly young man" to appeal to Singapore's youth who were "the people most in danger of being diverted to Communist or fellow-travelling ideologies".

Soon after the Conservatives came into office, Oliver Lyttelton (Churchill's secretary of state for the colonies) approved the appointment of John Nicoll. An "outstandingly good" colonial secretary in Hong Kong with "experience of the Chinese", Nicoll was expected to "restore confidence" in Singapore and "jerk up the Civil Service". In addition, he was said to be "progressive in his ideas" while keeping "his feet firmly on the ground".[113] MacDonald welcomed the choice, although Nicoll did not have all the attributes which he had stipulated some months earlier. First, at the age of 52, Nicoll could not be regarded as a "fairly young man". Second, since she was not medically fit for life in the colonies, his wife would be unable to perform the role of "first lady". Third, Nicoll's social skills did not appear to be his strongest suit; while his confidential report recorded that "he fulfils his social obligations fully", it judged him to be "autocratic by nature which makes him respected rather than loved". MacDonald accepted that it was unrealistic to expect to find in one man "all the political, administrative and social perfections", but it was re-assuring that Nicoll looked like being "a new broom" and the ideal part-ner — occasionally the sparring partner — for General Templer who was appointed Malayan supremo at the same time. Certainly, Nicoll addressed head-on the vexed relationship between central and local government as well as that between the executive and the legislature with which Gimson had grappled for six years. It was on Nicoll's recommendation that the Rendell Commission reviewed Singapore's constitution and set the colony on the road to responsible self-government. On the other hand, as *The Times* obituarist put it, "he did not immerse himself easily in the spirit of the races among whom he resided".[114] Moreover, he cut an increasingly lonely figure at government house and, as John Higham observed, after a year as governor, Nicoll had completely demoralised the civil service. "Never have I known a man so detested — and with justification."[115]

Meanwhile, Franklin and Dorothy Gimson settled into retirement in Applegarth, Thornton-le-Dale. Unlike some former proconsuls, Gimson did not spend his new-found leisure sitting on committees or boards of directors, or writing to the press about colonial issues. He became director of the North Riding Red Cross and on its behalf he travelled extensively round Yorkshire in his Austin mini car. He was involved in the local branch of the United Nations, giving talks on current affairs, and for many years, he served as churchwarden of All Saints in Thornton-le-Dale. His principal recreation was walking in the Dales — he might cover up to 15 miles a day — and he was a devotee of Gilbert and Sullivan operas. In spite of the privations of internment, he lived to his 85th year. Franklin Gimson died of heart failure at Applegarth on 15 February 1975. Dorothy placed a plaque in his memory in All Saints Church. She survived him by nine years.

Notes

1. Apart from the record that Gimson kept of wartime internment (see note 31), there are no private papers in the public domain. I am very grateful to Mrs. Judith Snowdon for further information on her father.
2. *Leicester Chronicle and Leicestershire Mercury*, 15 September 1883.
3. His youngest sister, Betty, married Charles Graham Brentford in 1930 in Colombo and later set up home in Calcutta. His other sisters remained unmarried and Franklin helped them out financially as they grew older.
4. Nor, it seems, did the other Gimsons, although Christopher, one of Josiah's many grandchildren and Franklin's senior by four years, entered the Indian Civil Service in 1911.
5. Quoted in Anthony Kirk-Greene, *Britain's Imperial Administrators, 1858–1966* (Basingstoke: Macmillan, 2000), p. 16. See also the entry for Jowett by Peter Hinchliff and John Prest in the *Oxford Dictionary of National Biography*.

6. See S.R. Ashton, "Ceylon", in *The Oxford History of the British Empire, IV: The Twentieth Century*, ed. Judith M. Brown and Wm. Roger Louis (Oxford: Oxford University Press, 1999), pp. 455–60.

7. See Nira Wickramasinghe, *Sri Lanka in the Modern Age: A History of Contested Identities* (London: C. Hurst, 2006), pp. 97, 147, 306; K.M. De Silva, *A History of Sri Lanka* (Delhi: Oxford University Press, 1981), pp. 467–8, 472–4.

8. W. Ormsby-Gore (former secretary of state for the colonies) to P. Cunliffe-Lister (secretary of state for the colonies), 18 December 1934. CO 54/924/17, the National Archives of the UK.

9. The anti-imperialist Suriya Mal movement originated in dissatisfaction over the proportion of funds, collected from poppy sales on Remembrance Day (11 November), which was retained for local use. In 1926, Ceylon ex-servicemen launched their own campaign to support needy veterans by selling the *suriya* flower.

10. De Silva, pp. 431, 434, 465–6; V. Kumari Jayawardena, "Origins of the Left Movement in Sri Lanka", *Social Scientist* 2, 6/7 (January–February 1974): 23–4; Wickramasinghe, *Sri Lanka*, pp. 206–7; *The Times*, 1 January 1936. For official reports on the malaria epidemic, see CO 54/925/8.

11. Gimson's report on the general election was completed in May 1936 and published in April 1937 by the Ceylon Government Press. A copy is at CO 54/942/2.

12. *Ceylon: Report of the Commission on Constitutional Reform*, Cmd.6677, September 1945 (Soulbury Report), pp. 38–9, 140.

13. However, I have read nothing to suggest that Gimson did not have anything other than a satisfactory working relationship with G.C.S Corea, the Minister of Labour, Industries and Commerce, who shared Gimson's conciliatory approach to labour disputes. See K.M. De Silva, ed., *Sri Lanka: British Documents on the End of Empire, I* (London: HMSO, 1997), pp. 82–7. Corea had left the Bar for politics in 1930. Three times president of the Ceylon National Congress, he held the Labour portfolio from 1936 to 1946 when he embarked on a diplomatic career representing Ceylon in London, Washington, Paris, and the United Nations.

14. De Silva, *Sri Lanka: BDEE*, I, p. xlii. The Lanka Sama Samaja Party was formed to contest the general election of 1936. Its principal leaders were detained in June 1940 on the grounds that the party's publications were prejudicial to public safety and defence of the island, not because of its activities in relation to labour disputes.

15. The quotations in this paragraph are taken from Gimson's reports on labour unrest on estates in 1940, CO 54/974/9.

16. Caldecott had served in the Malayan Civil Service from 1907 to 1934 (chief secretary, Federated Malay States, 1931–1933; colonial secretary, Straits Settlements 1933–1935; acting governor and high commissioner 1934). A progressive governor of Hong Kong 1935–1937, after the reactionary regime

of Reginald Stubbs, he was transferred to Ceylon (1937–1944) where he pressed for constitutional reform until plans were shelved on the outbreak of the Second World War. MacDonald, son of the prime minister, was secretary of state for the dominions 1931–1935, 1935–1938, 1938–1939, and for the colonies 1935 and 1938–1940. Having been high commissioner in Canada 1941–1946, he was appointed Governor-General, Malaya in 1946 and commissioner-general SE Asia 1948–1955.

17. S.R. Ashton and S.E. Stockwell, eds., *Imperial Policy and Colonial Practice, 1925 1945, British Documents on the End of Empire, I* (London: HMSO, 1996), pp. lxxxiv–lxxxvi.

18. Minute by Gent, commenting on Gimson's report on unrest on tea and rubber estates, 17 February 1940, CO 54/974/9.

19. In August 1942, Smith sent wartime planners a memorandum which emphasised that Ceylon's constitutional development would not suit Hong Kong; see Steve Tsang, *Democracy Shelved* (Hong Kong: Oxford University Press, 1988), p. 191.

20. Frank Welsh refers to the appalling state of the emergency services, corruption in the immigration department and a full-scale commission of inquiry into the public service which was aborted by the governor, Sir Geoffry Northcote, *A History of Hong Kong* (London: HarperCollins, 1997), p. 418.

21. Northcote to Lord Moyne, 9 June 1941, personal, CO 967/70. It was not only the war but Northcote's poor health that had limited his effectiveness.

22. Steve Tsang, "Sir Mark Aitchison Young", in *Oxford Dictionary of National Biography*; secretary of state for the colonies to prime minister, 17 December 1945, CO 850/206/4.

23. Philip Snow, *The Fall of Hong Kong: Britain, China and the Japanese Occupation* (New Haven and London: Yale University Press, 2003), pp. 76–7.

24. Others who were required to stay at their posts included Sir Vandeleur Grayburn (chief manager of the Hong Kong Shanghai Bank, who later died in camp) and Dr. Selwyn-Clarke (Director of Medical Services).

25. Published accounts by internees include: John Stericker, *A Tear for the Dragon* (London: Arthur Baker, 1958); Jean Gittins, *Stanley: Behind Barbed Wire* (Hong Kong: Hong Kong University Press, 1982); George Wright-Nooth with Mark Adkin, *Prisoner of the Turnip Heads: Horror, Hunger and Humour in Hong Kong, 1941–45* (London: Leo Cooper, 1994); Dorothy Gordon Jenner, *Darlings, I've Had a Ball, As Told to Trish Sheppard* (Sydney: Ure Smith, 1975). This section draws upon the following research monographs: Geoffrey Charles Emerson, *Hong Kong Internment, 1942–1945: Life in the Japanese Civilian Camp at Stanley* (Hong Kong: RAS Hong Kong Studies Series, Hong Kong University Press, 2008); G.B. Endacott with Alan Birch, *Hong Kong Eclipse* (Hong Kong and Oxford: Oxford University Press, 1978); Bernice Archer, *The Internment of Western Civilians under the Japanese 1941–1945: A Patchwork of Internment* (London: RoutledgeCurzon, 2004).

26. Pennefather-Evans had been appointed to Hong Kong in 1941 after more than 27 years in the Malayan Police. In the short time before the Japanese occupation, he had drafted plans for reorganising the Hong Kong force. He took early retirement after the war but in 1951, on the recommendation of Gimson (then Governor of Singapore), he was given a one-year contract to reform the Singapore Police after its reprehensible response to the Maria Hertogh riots. Pennefather-Evans spoke Malay and Chinese dialects, and was renowned for his personal charm and ability to foster a sense of camaraderie. Syed Muhd Khairudin Aljunied, *Colonialism, Violence and Muslims in Southeast Asia: The Maria Hertogh Controversy and its Aftermath* (London: Routledge, 2009), pp. 108–9, 112.

27. Stericker, *A Tear for the Dragon*, p. 161.

28. L.R. Nielson, "British Communal Council: A Review of its Activities during the Past Three Months", 15 June 1942, CO 129/590/24. This report was smuggled out of Stanley Camp and reached the Colonial Office via the British ambassador in Rio de Janeiro.

29. John Stericker regarded himself as a neutral in the struggle for power between internees. Having moved from Shanghai, Stericker was a newcomer to Hong Kong. As administrative secretary, he kept records which he secreted in discarded shell cases; see *A Tear for the Dragon*, p. 160.

30. Gimson, report on internment, n.d., Sir Franklin Gimson papers for Hong Kong, Rhodes House Library, Oxford, Mss. Ind. Ocn. s. 222. The other items in the collection are: "Hong Kong reclaimed", another undated report by Gimson; Gimson's diary for 1943–1945; a copy of a letter from Gimson to his wife, 5 September 1945; and the transcript of Gimson's farewell broadcast to Hong Kong. This material is hereinafter referred to as: Report on internment, RHL; "Hong Kong reclaimed", RHL; Diary, RHL; Gimson to his wife, 5 September 1945, RHL; Farewell broadcast, RHL. I would like to thank Mrs. Judith Snowdon and Rhodes House Library for permission to quote from these papers.

31. Report on internment, RHL

32. "Relations with the Japanese", report by F.C. Gimson, 15 October1945, CO 980/192.

33. Gimson to G.E.J. Gent, 29 November 1945, CO 850/206/4.

34. Diary, November 1943, RHL.

35. Gimson to Gent, 29 November 1945, CO 850/206/4.

36. Ibid. See also Report on internment, RHL. Sir Chaloner Alabaster advised Gimson that, according to international law, "the civil authorities of a country occupied by enemy military forces had the authority to function as far as circumstances permitted" and that, should any legal proceedings result from his action, Gimson could call upon the full assistance of the law officers of the Crown.

37. Report on internment, RHL.

38. Kent Fedorowich, "Doomed from the Outset? Internment and Civilian Exchange in the Far East: The British Failure over Hong Kong, 1941–45", *Journal of Imperial and Commonwealth History* 25, 1 (January 1997): 113–40, particularly pp. 119–20.

39. Welsh, *A History of Hong Kong*, p. 418.

40. Report on internment, RHL.

41. Gimson to his wife, 5 September 1945, RHL.

42. I am grateful to Mrs. Judith Snowdon for this quotation from James Leasor, "The Man who Kept Hong Kong British", *Sunday Telegraph Magazine* 407 (12 August 1984). Leasor, who had fought in Burma and went on to become Lord Beaverbrook's secretary and author of many novels, interviewed Gimson in retirement.

43. Gimson quoted in Jan Morris, *Hong Kong* (London: Viking, 1988), p. 257.

44. See correspondence between Gimson and the Colonial Office in CO 850/206/4.

45. Malcolm MacDonald (commissioner general, SE Asia) to Arthur Creech Jones (secretary of state of the colonies), 29 June 1948; A.J. Stockwell ed., *Malaya: British Documents on the End of Empire*, II (London: HMSO, 1995), pp. 35–6. It was for this reason that MacDonald advised against the appointment of Grantham as high commissioner of Malaya in close proximity to Gimson who was then governor of Singapore.

46. Jenner, *Darlings, I've Had a Ball*, p. 210.

47. In the "New Introduction" to his 1973 thesis published in 2008, Emerson has written: "If I were to rewrite my thesis, the biggest change would be my treatment of the colonial secretary, Franklin Gimson." *Hong Kong Internment*, p. 7. For a favourable yet balanced assessment of Gimson, see: Endacott with Birch, *Hong Kong Eclipse*; Snow, *The Fall of Hong Kong*; Steve Tsang, *Democracy Shelved: Great Britain, China, and Attempts at Constitutional Reform in Hong Kong, 1945–1952* (Hong Kong: Oxford University Press, 1988), *A Modern History of Hong Kong* (London: I.B. Tauris, 2004) and *Governing Hong Kong: Administrative Officers from the Nineteenth Century to the Handover to China, 1862–1997* (London: I.B. Tauris, 2007).

48. "Hong Kong Reclaimed", RHL.

49. Report on internment, RHL.

50. Gimson to his wife, 5 September 1945, RHL.

51. "Relations with the Japanese", CO 980/192.

52. "Hong Kong Reclaimed", RHL.

53. Gimson to his wife, 5 September 1945, RHL.

54. "Hong Kong Reclaimed", RHL.

55. Stericker, *A Tear for the Dragon*, p. 161.

56. "Relations with the Japanese", CO 980/192.

57. Vaudine England, *The Quest of Noel Croucher: Hong Kong's Quiet Philanthropist* (Hong Kong: Hong Kong University Press, 1998), p. 150, see also Stericker, *A Tear for the Dragon*, p. 199ff.

58. Diary, 23 January 1945, RHL; see also "Relations with the Japanese", CO 980/192. After the war, Tokunaga was found guilty of war crimes and sentenced to death, subsequently commuted to life imprisonment.

59. Nooth with Adkin, *Prisoner of the Turnip Heads*, pp. 84, 194.

60. "Relations with the Japanese", CO 980/192.

61. Gimson quoted in Morris, *Hong Kong*, p. 256.

62. Telegram from the British Consul (St Vincent) to Foreign Office, 2 October 1942, reporting a message received in Shanghai from Gimson, FO 371/31671 [F6872/G].

63. Edwin Ride, *BAAG: Hong Kong Resistance* (Hong Kong: Oxford University Press, 1981), pp. 163–4.

64. Wm. Roger Louis, "Hong Kong: The Critical Phase, 1945–1949", *American Historical Review* 102, 4 (October 1997): 1064n40.

65. Letter to secretary of state written by P.V. McLane (former Canadian trade commissioner, Hong Kong) under instructions of Gimson and memo by Gimson received by Colonial Office via McLane, 23 July 1942, CO 129/590/24.

66. Snow, *The Fall of Hong Kong*, pp. 202–5, 289; see also Tsang, *A Modern History of Hong Kong*, pp. 128, 137.

67. Report on internment, RHL, and transcript of broadcast, RHL. When, preparatory to his resumption of the governorship, Sir Mark Young was being briefed on constitutional reform, he was given details of discussions which Gimson had held in Stanley Camp; see N.J. Miners, "Plans for Constitutional Reform in Hong Kong, 1946–52", *The China Quarterly* 107 (September 1986): 467n12.

68. Morris, *Hong Kong*, p. 258. In the congratulatory telegram which the prime minister sent Gimson on 8 September after the British re-occupation, Attlee said: "I should like you and your Civil Officers to know high value I attach to your indomitable courage and splendid service." CO 129/591/17.

69. Ride, *BAAG*, p. 299; for the liberation of Hong Kong and instructions to Gimson, see CO 129/591/17.

70. Morris, *Hong Kong*, p. 258.

71. Drummond Hunter, letter to the editor, *The Independent* (London), 30 June 1997.

72. Roger Buckley, *Hong Kong: The Road to 1997* (Cambridge: Cambridge University Press, 1997), p. 20.

73. Photograph on the front page of *South China Morning Post*, 11 September 1945; see also F.E.C. Gregory, "Sir Cecil Halliday Jepson Harcourt", *Oxford Dictionary of National Biography*.

74. Report on the British Military Administration, Hong Kong, August 1945 to April 1946, CO 129/595/9.

75. Snow, *The Fall of Hong Kong*, p. 421n27.

76. Endacott with Birch, *Hong Kong Eclipse*, pp. 259–60.

77. Gimson to his wife, 5 September 1945, RHL.
78. Transcript of broadcast, RHL.
79. Alexander Grantham, *Via Ports: From Hong Kong to Hong Kong* (Hong Kong: Hong Kong University Press, 1965), p. 105. See also Tsang, *Democracy Shelved* and *Governing Hong Kong*, pp. 60–6.
80. Dorothy's father, the Reverend H. Ward, was vicar of All Saints, Thornton-le-Dale.
81. In the same way, Patrick McKerron and Alexander Newboult (both of whom were Malayan Civil Servants, members of the Malayan Planning Unit and Deputy Chief Civil Affairs Officers, McKerron for Singapore and Newboult for Malaya) would in April 1946 become respectively colonial secretary of Singapore and chief secretary of the Malayan Union.
82. Sir Charles Jeffries, minute, 3 November 1945, CO 850/206/4.
83. Secretary of state for the colonies to prime minister, 17 December 1945, CO 850/206/4.
84. His installation, due to coincide with Sir Edward Gent's as governor of the Malayan Union on 1 April, was postponed to 3 April on account of travel delays.
85. The weddings of Margaret and Judith both took place in 1950, Margaret to Commander (Jeken) Allan Elwin DSC, naval liaison officer in Kuala Lumpur, and Judith to Captain (later Lieutenant-Colonel) Douglas Challoner Snowdon, of the Queen's Royal Regiment and ADC to her father.
86. *Straits Times*, 31 January 1946.
87. *The Times*, 4 April 1946; Gimson to Sir T.Lloyd (CO), 8 December 1948, Stockwell, *Malaya*, II, p. 79.
88. Arthur Creech Jones, minute 24 August 1945, quoted in James H. Pullé, "The Management of Political Change: British Colonial Policy towards Singapore, 1942–1954", PhD thesis, University of London, 1991, p. 67.
89. Singapore also provided the headquarters for Lord Killearn, the Foreign Office's special commissioner, and was awash with military top brass.
90. MacDonald to Creech Jones, 29 June 1948; Stockwell, *Malaya*, II, p. 36.
91. *Straits Times*, editorial, "The Men of Tomorrow", 31 January 1946.
92. Clementi, letter to *The Times*, 30 March 1946.
93. Christopher Bayly and Tim Harper, *Forgotten Wars: The End of Britain's Asian Empire* (London: Allen Lane, 2007), p. 280.
94. W.L. Blythe, *Colony of Singapore Annual Report, 1950* (Singapore: Government Printing Office, 1951), p. 92.
95. Bayly and Harper, *Forgotten Wars*, p. 280.
96. C.M. Turnbull, *A History of Modern Singapore, 1819–2005* (Singapore: NUS Press, 2009), p. 238; Turnbull, *Dateline Singapore: 150 Years of the Straits Times* (Singapore: Singapore Press Holdings, 1995), pp. 158–63; *Straits Times*, 8 January 1948.

97. George Hall to Gimson, 2 April 1946, quoted by Pullé, "The Management of Political Change", p. 154. I have drawn extensively on Dr. Pullé's thesis for this account of Singapore's constitutional development during Gimson's governorship.

98. Gimson to G.F. Seel (CO), 31 May 1948, quoted in Pullé, p. 188.

99. Bayly and Harper, *Forgotten Wars*, p. 341.

100. *Straits Times*, 29 and 30 April, 1 May 1950.

101. J.D. Higham, minute, 16 May 1950, CO 537/5964.

102. Minutes of 15th commissioner-general's conference at Bukit Serene, 7 June 1950; Stockwell, ed., *Malaya*, II, pp. 223–30.

103. Ibid.

104. For the extension of Gimson's term as governor, see CO 537/5956 and CO 850/256/4.

105. Syed Muhd Khairudin Aljunied, *Colonialism, Violence and Muslims in Southeast Asia: The Maria Hertogh Controversy and its Aftermath* (London: Routledge, 2009).

106. CO 717/202/7. John Eber, an affluent Eurasian, had been educated at Harrow School and Cambridge, and had trained as a lawyer. He was a principal figure in the MDU until its dissolution in 1948. On release from detention, Eber moved to London and joined Fenner Brockway's Movement for Colonial Freedom, later serving as its general secretary.

107. Syed Muhd Khairudin Aljunied, *Colonialism, Violence and Muslims in Southeast Asia*, pp. 65, 82.

108. Sir Thomas Lloyd to Oliver Lyttelton (secretary of state), 2 November 1951, CO 877/34/12.

109. Montgomery to Churchill, 4 January 1952; Stockwell, *Malaya*, II, p. 358. Montgomery was writing with regard to appointments to top posts following Gurney's death.

110. *Straits Times*, 15 March 1952.

111. See extract from a letter from MacDonald to the secretary of state, 28 August 1951, CO 877/34/12.

112. In fact, Gimson had already made a start on this by retaining the services of Urwick, Orr and Partners Ltd, a firm of management consultants; see Pullé, "The Management of Political Change", p. 238ff.

113. For correspondence on Nicoll's appointment, see CO 877/34/12.

114. *The Times*, 17 January 1981. This anonymous obituary (as was and remains the practice of *The Times*) provoked a spirited riposte from Sir Robert Black (Nicoll's successor in Hong Kong and Singapore): "Although his downright comments sometimes led to accusations of intolerance, John Nicoll, behind an austere and sometimes remote manner, was, in fact, a shy, sensitive and kindly man, and he was a loyal friend", *The Times*, 28 January 1981.

115. J.D. Higham, secret & personal, to Sir John Paskin (CO), 14 April 1953. Higham was in Singapore on secondment from the Colonial Office.

9

To Negotiate Trade and Avoid Politics:

The Overseas Chinese Trade Missions to China and Taiwan, 1956–1957

*Jason Lim**

Introduction

IN 1949, THE GEOPOLITICAL SITUATION IN EAST and Southeast Asia changed dramatically with the victory of the Chinese Communist Party (CCP) in a civil war. On 1 October, Mao Zedong proclaimed the founding of the People's Republic of China (PRC). In December, the defeated National Government of the Kuomintang (KMT) fled to Taiwan where, under the "Temporary Provisions Effective during the Period of the Communist Rebellion", the Republic of China (ROC) continued its claim to be the legitimate government of all China. Chiang Kai-shek, who had resigned in January 1949, reassumed the position of President of the ROC on 1 March 1950.

---

* The author thanks the Singapore Chinese Chamber of Commerce and Industry for releasing the minutes of meetings held in 1956 and 1957.

In her seminal work on a political history of Singapore, Mary Turn-bull noted that by 1947, more than half of the Chinese on the island had neither revisited China nor sent remittances to their families and concluded that "the link with the motherland [China] was more tenuous than was generally supposed".[1] She also noted that the victory by the CCP over the KMT in China in 1949 hardened the attitude of the British colonial authorities in Malaya and Singapore towards overseas Chinese nationalism and reopened the political fault-line in the Chinese community between supporters of the CCP and the KMT. Nonetheless, Turnbull reckoned that "most Singapore Chinese, whatever their political feelings, were stirred by the Chinese Communist Party's triumph in their motherland" even as the British moved swiftly to ensure that China would not exercise any political influence on the Singapore Chinese community.[2]

The CCP victory not only signalled a new era for China, but it also divided the overseas Chinese mercantile community in the British colonial territories of Malaya and Singapore. Some merchants chose not to recognise the new regime on the mainland but remained sceptical about plans by the KMT to retake the mainland from its base in Taiwan. Other merchants threw in their lot with the PRC but were concerned about the future direction of trade between Malaya and Singapore with a communist regime in China suspicious of private enterprise and free trade. Added to these concerns was the international situation that was the Cold War — any move to raise the profile of the China-Malaya and/or China-Singapore trade would incur the suspicion of the Western powers. From this perspective, it seems incredible that the merchants dared to plan trade missions to China and Taiwan in the 1950s. Yet, very little research is done on the trade mission to China and research work on the trade mission to Taiwan is virtually non-existent. Despite the importance of these missions for understanding overseas Chinese merchants' concerns with trade with China and Taiwan, they remain largely forgotten today. Despite the resurgence of the PRC as an economic power by the last decade of the 20th century, these early trade missions have been consigned to the dustbins of history.

This chapter looks at how the Chinese merchants in Singapore and Malaya responded to the call for trade with the PRC and the ROC. It looks at why trade missions were organised to China in 1956 and Taiwan in 1957 and the impressions of the mission members. It will examine how the PRC and the ROC used trade as a means of winning the overseas Chinese merchants over to their respective political causes. It argues that contrary to accepted belief, the overseas Chinese merchants did not constitute a "fifth column" working to destabilise Malaya and Singapore.[3] Rather, the missions point to the difficulties of conducting trade with China and Taiwan *for* the overseas Chinese. The chapter will look directly at the points of concern for these traders through their experiences on these missions and their reflections upon returning home to Malaya and Singapore.

Why Trade Missions?

By 1955, both Malaya and Singapore had achieved partial self-government. Elections held early that year had resulted in victories by non-communist parties. In Malaya, the Alliance made up of the United Malays National Organisation (UMNO), Malayan Chinese Association (MCA) and the Malayan Indian Congress grabbed 51 out of 52 seats. Tunku Abdul Rahman was then appointed Chief Minister. In Singapore, the Labour Front won 10 out of 25 contested seats and David Marshall became Chief Minister. Marshall resigned a year later but the Labour Front continued in office with Lim Yew Hock as Chief Minister until the party was defeated in the 1959 General Elections.

Trade missions became more important for both Malaya and Singapore as they signalled to the world that both colonies were coming of age and ready to take on new roles in international trade and politics. As the new governments looked beyond the Malay Peninsula for more trade prospects, these missions were organised to look into the possibilities of greater imports into Malaya and Singapore and to clear any stumbling blocks to bilateral trade. The entrepôt trade, moreover, remained important for Singapore. In October 1955, the Singapore Chinese Chamber of Commerce (SCCC) organised a trade mission to Indonesia in order to look for ways to increase trade between both territories.[4] From 29 July to 9 August 1956, the Ministry of Commerce and Industry in Singapore also organised a trade mission to Cambodia and South Vietnam and invited representatives from the Chinese, Malay and Indian Chambers of Commerce.[5]

Any trade mission to China, however, would be a political problem for the British and the non-communist governments in Malaya and Singapore. When it came to the China trade, the overseas Chinese merchants had to overcome hostility from the British and the non-communist governments to the CCP regime in the PRC. For example, an embargo on the rubber trade with the PRC was enforced in Malaya and Singapore in 1951 because of China's participation in the Korean War on the side of North Korea. The overseas Chinese merchants found themselves shut out of a potentially large market.

Changes, however, were afoot. In a change of policy, the Ministry of Commerce and Industry announced on 4 June 1956 that some restrictions on rubber exports to China would be lifted. Recognising that the embargo had been "a source of great dissatisfaction to the trade", the Minister announced in the Singapore Legislative Assembly two days later that "reasonable quantities" of rubber could henceforth be exported to China. J.M. Jumabhoy gave a statement that individual applications for exports would be dealt with by the Ministry but "larger quantities" for export would be referred to the Colonial Office in London. He did not define what constituted "reasonable" or "larger" quantities.[6] The restoration of trade with the PRC became a possibility and a trade mission was soon organised. As the leading trade association, the SCCC was invited to send representatives to the mission. Merchants from the other chambers of commerce were also invited to join the mission.

The Trade Mission to China, 1956

In 1956, Yap Pheng Geck proposed a trade mission to China just as former Chief Minister Marshall received a telegram of invitation from the PRC.[7] On 29 June, after a discussion on the merits of organising such a mission, the Executive Committee of the SCCC appointed Yap, Ko Teck Kin, Chuang Hui-tsuan and Lam Thian as the organisers and called upon any interested merchant to register their names with the Chamber.[8] In order not to give the impression that the merchants were interested in trade with China, the organisers decided that the mission should visit Japan before heading to China through Hong Kong. The organisation of the mission was viewed with consternation by Tunku Abdul Rahman, who strongly discouraged Marshall from going, and by the American consul in Singapore, who tried to arrange a holiday to Taiwan for Marshall instead.[9] A total of 82 merchants eventually went with the Singapore delegation of 54 members headed by Ko Teck Kin and the Malaya delegation of 28 members headed by Lee Yan Lian.[10] After visiting Japan, they arrived in Hong Kong on 25 August.

The SCCC publicly announced that the aim of the mission was to look into ways to open up the trade between Singapore, Malaya and China and for local merchants to have first-hand knowledge of the vast Chinese market. Ko Teck Kin was chosen to head the trade mission. Incredibly, however, the Chamber decided also to ask Marshall, who had just resigned as Chief Minister, to be the adviser to the mission. Marshall opined that as he was known to be a vehement anti-communist who would not accept "any monkey business", it lent some level of respectability to the mission. He also thought that if it were not for his presence, the main leaders of the mission — being overseas Chinese — would be seen as if "they were trying to be indoctrinated in China".[11] In addition, Marshall believed that being non-Chinese, he was "a non-ethnic partisan, with no ethnic axe to grind".[12] Marshall insisted that he would go as the advisor only if delegates in the trade mission from Singapore were drawn from all the communities.[13] The trade mission, however, declared that it would avoid any political discussion with the Chinese leadership.

The mission was organised at a time when the Malayan Emergency had been enforced for the past eight years. In 1948, the Malayan Communist Party (MCP) declared its intention to carry out an armed struggle in order to end British colonialism. The colonial authorities in Malaya and Singapore responded by promulgating the Emergency, which outlawed the MCP. Since then, the British and Commonwealth forces had been engaged in a military conflict with MCP guerrillas in the Malayan jungles. Furthermore, the British colonial authorities suspected that the MCP was supplied with military and economic aid by the PRC.

Marshall planned to go to China for two purposes. One task was to get a better understanding of the mindset of the Chinese Government.[14] The other, more immediate, task was to get the Chinese Government in Beijing to issue a formal statement that encouraged the overseas Chinese in Malaya and Singapore to accept Malayan and Singaporean citizenship. He saw the trip to Beijing as an opportunity to settle the matter of Singapore citizenship for the Chinese community with the Chinese government. Some members of the Singapore Chinese community, however, were not so enthusiastic. Tan Lark Sye, another prominent Chinese community leader in the SCCC, felt that it was not Marshall's business to discuss this topic with the Chinese leadership and sneered that Marshall spoke as one without authority.[15]

It was clear right from the beginning that the Chinese government was interested only in negotiating with the Chinese members of the delegation. Marshall noted the "many overseas Chinese present" who turned up at the railway station in Beijing and mobbed members of the mission. An amused Marshall also noted that the Chinese delegates of the trade mission were "receiving the "Welcome home Overseas Chinese" treatment".[16] The initial reaction of the delegates, however, was subdued. Yap told Marshall that the delegates were "depressed" after witnessing the level of poverty and the effects of authoritarian state control.[17] Marshall shared the same outlook as he encountered "grey poverty and shabbiness everywhere", was escorted everywhere he went and had to move according to a very tight itinerary.[18]

The activities lined up by the Chinese government for the trade mission included luncheons with government officials and business personalities, visits to key tourist spots to awe members of the mission and a grand view of the National Day Parade on 1 October. Members were hosted to dinners by Premier Zhou Enlai, the General Manager of the Bank of China and even the wartime Chinese nationalist leader in Singapore, Tan Kah Kee, who was now the Chairman of the All-China Federation of Returned Overseas Chinese.[19]

On his trip, Marshall had the opportunity to meet both Chairman Mao Zedong and Premier Zhou Enlai. While his meeting with Chairman Mao was very brief — as a guest watching a Peking opera performance in a theatre — Marshall came away with the impression that while the Chinese people had "no sense of the joy of living", Mao was "the only really happy type I met there".[20] Marshall was more impressed with Premier Zhou, whom he felt had "sensitivity, a sense of courtesy and intelligence, a reasonableness [sic], a deep desire to be of help and strong subterranean courage running very deep".[21] He compared Zhou as "sharp as a rapier, delightful as a reindeer" while Mao was "solemn and steady and ponderous and friendly in a slow fashion".[22]

The KMT Government in China (and after 1949, in Taiwan) had always maintained that the Chinese were citizens of China by blood, no matter where in the world they resided. This principle of *jus sanguinis* was a continuation of the policy from the Qing Dynasty that had been overthrown by the KMT in 1911. In the early 1950s, the Chinese government had urged all overseas Chinese to return home to work for the social and economic reconstruction of the country. Within a few years, the Chinese government realised that few were taking the appeal seriously. In response, the Chinese government changed its position on the overseas Chinese. At the Afro-Asian Conference at Bandung in 1955, Premier Zhou proclaimed that the overseas Chinese could take up citizenship in the territories of residence. Yet, in a meeting with Vice-Premier Chen Yi, Marshall criticised *jus sanguinis* as "an outmoded dogma of imperialism", drawing a robust denial from Chen as a consequence. The PRC eventually indicated that the Singapore Chinese could take on Singapore citizenship and that the Chinese government decided not to ask for formal treaties with

Singapore — since it was a British colony — as a precondition for dual nationality.[23]

At the same time, however, Chinese members of the mission were invited to meet Zhou privately. For two hours, the Chinese premier expounded on them the need to "liberate" Taiwan. This was a political ploy to get overseas Chinese support for the CCP cause. It made Yap unhappy as the mission had sought to steer clear from international politics; it also upset non-Chinese members such as Marshall as they now believed that Zhou favoured the Chinese members of the mission.[24] Marshall thought this action by the Chinese premier was "unwise"; Yap also admitted to Marshall that "communism, even Chinese style, would destroy Singapore".[25]

Marshall was clearly unimpressed with the social cost that came with the Chinese Communist Party's agenda for the industrialisation of the country. He noticed that "men and women wore the same costume and looked alike, and you couldn't distinguish a man from a woman unless the woman removed her cap, and she had long hair".[26] He also noted that while there were jobs available, there was "no sense of joy". There was a "dull passivity" in the way people worked and that "they had no sense of the joy of living".[27] Marshall and the trade mission were taken to visit different factories across China, all to give them the impression that China's industrialisation programme was taking off. In their meetings with Chinese government officials and businesspeople, Marshall noted that some of them were "eager to impress" the mission.[28]

Marshall returned to Singapore firmly convinced that communism was not suitable for Singapore. Even before he left for the PRC, Marshall declared that "communism in Singapore would mean our economic death".[29] Looking at the workers in the Chinese factories, he reeled in horror at their plight and considered that "communism today is the most thorough form of human exploitation known to history". As he looked at how people feverishly worked without any passion for their jobs, he wrote that "in China today humanity achieves Anthood". However, Marshall also recognised the immense potential of China long before any other leader. Factories were run with "confident efficiency" and he was convinced that "the West is slitting its own throat in ostracising China".[30]

Marshall never failed to get the impression that the Chinese Government was not interested in trade *per se*, but it was more eager to discuss citizenship for the Chinese community in Singapore and the "liberation" of Taiwan.[31] Indeed, the Chinese officials brushed aside the trade mission itself, insisting that the rubber trade between China, Malaya and Singapore would only be conducted through the Singapore Rubber Trade Association.[32] This was in line with the Chinese government's thinking that trade could only be conducted between an official body from China and a single company or association in Malaya and Singapore. By 1960, even tea merchants in Singapore were forced by the China Tea Company (CTC) to organise a single company to trade with China.[33]

Allington Kennard, the editor of the English-language daily *The Straits Times* who accompanied the trade mission, and several other members of the mission, felt that "it was largely a waste of time and that they should go home".[34] Although the China National Import and Export Corporation did not place any objections to rubber imports from Malaya and Singapore, negotiations were slow and members of the mission soon became dissatisfied. Many of them returned to Singapore in disappointment.[35] The disappointment could have spurred the Chinese government to take action as the mission delegates were suddenly informed that the PRC was willing to purchase 3,000 tons of rubber, a figure which subsequently increased to 7,000 tons.[36] Members of the mission also signed £5 million (then about S$42.5 million) of contracts with the Corporation on 3 October. Both sides recognised that trade had been hampered in the past by "various artificial barriers". The joint communiqué also revealed that both sides discussed shipping and banking problems and that China recognised Malaya and Singapore as "useful sources" of rubber and coconut oil and were "valuable outlets for China's industrial and agricultural products".[37] While the monetary worth of the contracts was small, the members of the mission considered it a first step in improving bilateral trade. Upon the return of the mission to Singapore, Ko and Lam presented a report of the trip to the Executive Committee of the SCCC. Both of them were happy with the trip and gushed out praises on the achievements of the mission. The Chinese journalists also started lapping up any impression the mission members may have had on their trip, if not on China herself. Only Chuang had reservations about the trip — this was not surprising since he was a former KMT leader in Singapore.

Premier Zhou told Marshall in no uncertain terms that China, as a communist state, would naturally be friendlier towards countries with communist governments.[38] Within the context of the ongoing Cold War, Zhou had effectively placed his country within the "communist camp". This was undoubtedly a source of concern for the anti-communist

Marshall — what was at stake for Malaya and Singapore as they headed towards independence? All Marshall ever secured from Zhou was a verbal promise that China would not supply any material aid — whether medicine, food or arms — to the Malayan Communist Party (MCP).[39] Zhou made it clear to Marshall that the only way the Emergency would end was when the MCP was legalised as a political party in Malaya.[40] This would not be enough for Marshall as the Emergency was going on and the MCP was still fighting British and Commonwealth forces in the Malayan jungles, though independence for Malaya had been promised for the following year. While the mission was touring China, the MCP had sent a congratulatory note to the CCP on the occasion of the anniversary of the founding of the PRC. The note stated very clearly that the MCP strove to end British rule in Malaya by violent means even though the route to full independence by 1957 was already confirmed.[41] The trade mission would not have missed Zhou's anger when news filtered through to the political leadership in Beijing of the mass arrests of left-wing student leaders and trade unionists by the Lim Yew Hock Government in Singapore. Zhou questioned the mission aloud about Malaya's consideration of joining the anti-communist Southeast Asia Treaty Organization (SEATO).[42] Clearly, politics was foremost in the minds of the Chinese leadership.

While Marshall said he was "keen on attributing and reverting the loyalty of Chinese (in Singapore) to Singapore",[43] he felt that, in the end, the reaction from the Chinese community in Singapore towards the mission to Beijing on this issue was "apathetic". He called it a "total non-reaction" but was buoyed by the sight of the Chinese taking up Singapore citizenship "largely due to the statement issued by the Chinese Government".[44] In October 1957, the Singapore Citizenship Bill was passed by the Legislative Assembly and the majority of the 220,000 Chinese born in mainland China automatically became citizens.[45]

From the perspective of China, however, the trade mission served as the opportune moment to propagate the fruits of revolution by linking trade with politics and attempting to get the mission to support its ulti-mate aim of a so-called "liberation" of Taiwan. Zhou told Marshall that "all conservatist [sic] rightist thinking will be eliminated by end 1957".[46] While not a member of the mission, Tan Keong Choon knew that "China always viewed her business transactions with Singapore in a political perspective". With the end of private enterprise by the mid-1950s, trade came under the purview of Chinese government officials who were "not very conversant with business transactions" and those who were capable to conducting trade had no real power.[47]

Despite the relative success of the trade mission to China, the Labour Front government remained unimpressed. Not long after the signing of £5 million worth of contracts, the Labour Front government announced new restrictions on rubber exports. China had to prove that their purchase of rubber was for "civilian use" only. The announcement of this restriction dismayed the trade mission still in China. The Chinese government rejected the signing of any document certifying that rubber would be for civilian use. Tan Lark Sye, who did not join the mission, expressed his unhappiness over the new restrictions.[48] A telegram was sent to Chief Minister Lim Yew Hock, urging him to remove the restrictions as the Chinese government was furious. Concerned that trade could be used as a political weapon against Singapore, the Labour Front government did not back down.

Even as late as 1958, there were no plans to establish a permanent Singapore Trade Mission in China. Minister of Commerce and Industry J.M. Jumabhoy reported that he had been advised by the Trade Advisory Council that there was no need for a permanent mission since the Chinese Government made purchases directly from producing countries and there was nothing Singapore could produce to sell to China. Therefore, there was "no useful economic purpose" in having a permanent mission in China.[49] He was extremely critical of those calling for trade representation in China as "people who are out to exploit emotions". He warned that "emotionalism is their stock-in-trade for they have nothing better to offer" and criticised Marshall for "muddled thinking which is misleading the people of Singapore". Marshall was censured for not publicly admitting that imports into Singapore were more than exports to China and Jumabhoy warned that by selling more goods to Singapore, China could dump them on Singapore instead.[50] Jumabhoy was not alone; some in the Singapore Chinese community also warned that any PRC Trade Mission in Singapore was part of a communist conspiracy to dominate Malaya and Singapore.[51]

Jumabhoy's refusal to expand trade ties with China drew criticism from the opposition in the Legislative Assembly. Lim Cher Kiang of the Democratic Party, an organisation started by prominent merchants from the SCCC, wondered why the Ministry could not invite an official trade delegation from China to clear up any problems in the Singapore-China trade. He argued:

> Since we are a British colony and since Britain herself has normal trade relations with Red China, I do not think there is anything wrong in doing so. It only needs a little courage.[52]

Lim argued further two weeks later when he said:

> I consider the year 1958 as the biggest failure in our commerce, particularly regarding trade with China. Despite the good work done by the Chinese Chamber of Commerce in sending a Trade Mission to China in 1956 to improve our trade relations, all the good results achieved have been shattered, and our trade relationship with China has now reached a dangerous point ... Is it the policy of this Government to follow the drastic action taken by the Federation of Malaya which, in the name of anti-communism, has closed down the Bank of China? If so, this is tantamount to a breaking of trade relationship with China.[53]

The Trade Mission organised by the SCCC to China in 1956 was hailed as a success by key delegates in a bid to salvage some pride. The reality was that although the trade mission signed £5 million worth of contracts, the Chinese government was not interested in discussing trade. Marshall met with some success in getting the PRC to recognise that the overseas Chinese in Singapore could take up Singapore citizenship but Chinese delegates in the mission could not escape the propaganda sessions organised by the PRC leaders. Meanwhile, the Labour Front government in Singapore remained suspicious of the PRC and tried to keep Chinese influence and presence out of the island. It led several Chinese community leaders such as Lim Cher Kiang to lash out at what they perceive to be an anti-PRC agenda by the Labour Front government. The mission failed to increase Singapore's share of the Southeast Asian trade with China and "the business actually gained could have just as easily have been achieved without any mission going to China at all".[54]

The Trade Mission to Taiwan, 1957

In early 1957, the Chinese National Federation of Industries (CNFI), the Chinese National Association of Industry and Commerce (CNAIC) and the Republic of China Chamber of Commerce in Taipei invited representatives from three trade associations in Singapore — the Singapore Chinese Tea Importers and Exporters Association (SCTIEA), the Singapore Chinese Contractors Association (SCCA) and the Sim Lim Siong Giap Kong Huay (Singapore Forestry Association) — to visit Taiwan in

order to witness the "progress" of industrialisation in Taiwan and to discuss prospects for furthering trade between Singapore, Malaya and the
ROC.[55] The Mission was an obvious response to a visit by Singapore
Chinese merchants to mainland China the year before. The associations
brought the invitation to the notice of the SCCC who appointed four
representatives after it was reassured that the mission would benefit
Malaya and Singapore economically and that there would be no political
discussions in Taiwan.[56] The SCCC seemed determined to ensure that
after enduring unwanted political discussions in Beijing, its representatives
should not be discussing politics with the KMT government in Taipei.

The associations responded by inviting other merchants from Malaya
and Singapore. A trade mission crudely named as the "Singapore-Malaya
Commercial and Industrial Mission to Formosa" was quickly arranged.
It included five merchants who had visited the PRC the year before,
including Chuang Hui-tsuan.[57] The mission to Taiwan was led by Lim
Keng Lian, Chairman of the SCTIEA and a former member of the
KMT. Lim and the first batch of 48 delegates arrived in Taipei on 25
July. The remaining 15 delegates arrived the next day. Lim explained
that the purpose of the mission was to look at the progress of industriali-
sation in Taiwan and seek opportunities for increasing trade between
Singapore, Malaya and Taiwan.[58] This Mission ended the tour with high
praise for the KMT Government.

The Mission spent 15 days in Taiwan meeting ROC officials, visiting
different associations and business companies, and holding discussions
with President Chiang Kai-shek and Vice-President Chen Cheng.[59] Just
as the Chinese Government did with the trade mission in 1956, the ROC
government on Taiwan also brought the members of the mission on a
tour of Taiwan and her offshore islands. The mission also had discussions
with various trade associations and the Ministers of Finance and Economic Affairs. President Chiang, in particular, warned the mission on
6 August about the dangers of communism and viewed it as a threat to
internal security in Southeast Asia.[60] He certainly picked the right time
to say it — Malaya would become fully independent within 25 days.

The Mission revived old animosities. It was criticised by anti-KMT
elements in Singapore. One participant even remarked how a friend
mocked the Mission for trying to invade the mainland using American
dollars.[61] But although the ROC considered Lim to be a capitalist with
limited financial strength, he commandeered a considerable amount of
political clout among traders in Singapore. It was even thought that the

Mission would fail if Lim had not been its leader.[62] Upon landing in Taiwan, Lim said that the purpose of the Mission was to observe improvements in Taiwanese commerce and industry and to discuss with ROC officials the possibility of expanding trade links with Malaya and Singapore.[63] More importantly, as Malaya and Singapore were home to many nationalities, Lim observed that the Trade Mission included not only overseas Chinese, but also Malay, Indian, Indonesian, Ceylonese and British merchants. It was clear also that by the time of his visit to Taiwan, while he was anti-communist, Lim was no longer a member of the KMT.[64] However, he continued to maintain "a fragile connection with the Nationalist Government in Taiwan".[65] He noted that the value of Taiwan's imports of goods from Malaya and Singapore had risen from S$3,000,000 in 1951 to $8,200,000 in 1956. He felt that trade with Taiwan by Malaya and Singapore could be expanded, provided the twin obstacles of foreign exchange and shipping were tackled.[66]

While there are no records available on how the SCCA and the Sim Lim Siong Giap Kong Huay welcomed their returning members, the minutes of the SCTIEA notes that its four representatives were given a warm welcome by the association when they returned in July.[67] The SCTIEA was also introduced to a representative from the China-American Tea Company. The four representatives reported on the state of the Taiwanese tea industry and trade, informing members that they had kept the National Government abreast of the Singapore tea market and price hikes from mainland China. The representatives considered Taiwan teas as essentially Chinese but members were reminded that Taiwan teas were cheaper than China teas.[68] On his part, the representative of the China-American Tea Company was grateful to the SCTIEA for promoting the purchase of Taiwan teas. He gave a sample of current tea prices in Taiwan, mentioning that "Tian Dui tea" (天堆茶) cost S$2.80 per catty, "Shuang Tian tea" (双天茶) cost S$3.20 per catty, "Biao Zhun Dui tea" (标准堆茶) cost HK$1.90 to HK$2 per catty, and Taiwan Nankang tea (台湾南港茶) cost S$3 to S$3.20 per catty. The Taiwanese tea trade was conducted completely by private enterprise, and members needed to contact individual merchants in Taiwan to conduct any purchase. There was no government intervention in the Taiwanese tea trade. He also noted, however, that Taiwanese tea prices in 1957 had risen by 20% from the year before. Tea merchants in Singapore could make purchases in American currency and pay later in New Taiwan Dollars. Members were also told that the exchange rate had fallen slightly; one

American dollar now fetched NT$34.[69] The SCTIEA subsequently decided to postpone any decision on the allocation of tea purchases.

From the ROC point of view, the Trade Mission was an important public relations exercise in its political and ideological struggle against the PRC. Five merchants who were part of a Trade Mission to the PRC the year before were praised for visiting Taiwan and ignoring those who called them "double-headed snakes". The Mission included two British merchants with financial support from Jardine Matheson. The agency house had tried to trade with the PRC after 1949; not only was it unable to do so, it had to surrender all its assets to the Central People's Government in 1954. The ROC acknowledged the trouble taken by Lim and other merchants to organise a Trade Mission to Taiwan. Several merchants in Malaya and Singapore pulled out at the last moment due to political pressures and the "anti-KMT sentiments" of Tunku Abdul Rahman. But it also noted that the Trade Mission did not include any member of the KMT, and that the ROC needed to import more rubber from Malaya and export more sugar and tea to Malaya and Singapore.[70]

Judging from the report published a few months after the Mission returned home, Lim's political sympathies remained with the KMT; he continually noted progress and economic development on Taiwan, and expressed hope that there would be an improvement in trade between Taiwan and Malaya and Singapore.[71] The report described Taiwan as a base of anti-communism, a point Lim — who did not compile the report — could not possibly have overlooked.[72] For its part, the ROC Government also saw the importance of maintaining trade links with Malaya and Singapore. Chiang Kai-shek even invited the overseas Chinese to invest in Taiwan and members of the Mission stressed that better and more regular shipping between Taiwan and Malaya and Singapore should be encouraged in order to expand trade.[73] Lim, Chuang and "other Singapore Chinese businessmen" contemplated the formation of an electric tramways company in Taipei. But the Executive Yuan decided not to rush into the project as it required time to study the situation in Taipei, and the costs of building an electric tramway system.[74]

The trade mission received less publicity compared to the earlier mission to China because Taiwan, as a small island, was thought of as offering fewer trading opportunities compared to China. Furthermore, the island was governed by the KMT and it was possible that some business leaders refused to have anything to do with Taiwan because the KMT was seen to be the "loser" in the Chinese Civil War. For the delegates of this mission, the agenda of the KMT was no different from that of the PRC leaders the year before. In the face of "overseas Chinese" trade representatives from Malaya and Singapore, Chiang Kai-shek and his National Government continued in their attempts to win support from the "overseas Chinese" in their ideological struggle with the CCP. The leaders of this trade mission considered their work a success only because of their sympathies with the KMT. In reality, the trade with Taiwan by Malaya and Singapore remained small.

Conclusion

In the 1950s, there was a constant fear, not surprising with the continuing Cold War, that the overseas Chinese were potential "agents" for communist China. The merchants in Malaya and Singapore evidently did not fit into this picture, born out of intense suspicions of the overseas Chinese and their activities during the Cold War. The merchants in this article strove to avoid any political discussion with the PRC and ROC leadership — they ended up being sucked into the communism/anti-communism debate raging across East and Southeast Asia. Rather than subjecting themselves to act as "agents" for the PRC, the merchants went to China to see for themselves the socioeconomic changes that have taken place, and some of them returned to Singapore depressed over what they saw. These merchants, therefore, cannot be seen as merely brainwashed nationalists who would act on the orders of the Chinese Government.

Another study of the Chinese merchants has concluded that by the late 1950s, they had chosen to take on a political path and entered into local politics as a result. The 1958 Executive Committee elections in the SCCC resulted in the election of politically-minded officials.[75] This article proves that their foray into politics — local or international — had begun a few years before the 1958 SCCC Election. The merchants went to China and Taiwan acutely aware of the struggle against communism in Southeast Asia during the Cold War. They returned home to Singapore with the impression that while there were socioeconomic changes underfoot in China, the model of economic development used in the PRC was not meant for Malaya and Singapore.

In the end, what did the trade missions actually accomplish? Despite the publicity surrounding the missions as they departed for China and Taiwan, very little was done in terms of trade. Trade with China remained dependent on policies introduced by the Lim Yew Hock Government. The volume of trade with Taiwan remained largely unchanged. In terms of publicity, the mission to Taiwan in 1957 was a low-key affair in contrast to the trade mission to China the previous year. The Chinese newspapers carried reports on the mission to Taiwan but neither organised any extensive interviews with members of the mission nor gave extensive coverage to the activities of the mission in Taiwan. The obvious prejudice against the mission to Taiwan was so severe that a publishing house decided to publish a commemorative magazine on the trip in order to ensure that it would be remembered for posterity.[76]

What the missions succeeded in doing, however, was to polarise the Chinese community in Singapore even further on the question of citizenship. Those who contemplated not returning to China decided there was no longer the need to withhold their decision any longer since Premier Zhou "approved" it. If they were KMT sympathisers, they would not return to China for fear of persecution and death; taking on Singapore citizenship came naturally. It was those who admired China's progress after 1949 and had pro-communist ideals that had to decide whether they should stay in Singapore (and face persecution by right-wing regimes) or return to China (and be banished for good from Singapore).

Looking back at the work of both trade missions, it seems as if nothing concrete came out of them. The missions clearly had very little impact on the PRC and ROC regimes in Beijing and Taipei. If anything, they served as publicity stunts for both regimes. Both sides tried to persuade the missions of the "evils" of their opponents across the Taiwan Straits. Trade was never the primary issue for the leaders of either of the regimes who met the trade missions.

Notes

1.   C.M Turnbull, *A History of Modern Singapore, 1819–2005* (Singapore: NUS Press, 2009), p. 237.

2.   Ibid., pp. 247–8.

3.   Lennox A Mills *et al.*, *The New World of Southeast Asia* (Minneapolis: The University of Minnesota Press, 1949), p. 287.

4.   Singapore Chinese Chamber of Commerce and Industry, *Singapore Chinese Chamber of Commerce & Industry 60th Anniversary Souvenir* (Singapore, 1966), p. 325.

5.   Singapore Chinese Chamber of Commerce and Industry, *Singapore Chinese Chamber of Commerce & Industry 80th Anniversary Souvenir* (Singapore, 1986), pp. 360–1.

6.   *Singapore Legislative Assembly Debates Official Report: First Session of the First Legislative Assembly*, 6 June 1956, cols 1951–52.

7.   Kevin Y.L. Tan, *Marshall of Singapore: A Biography* (Singapore: Institute of Southeast Asian Studies, 2008), p. 365.

8.   Minutes of the Singapore Chinese Chamber of Commerce, 29 March 1956; and *Annual Report of the Singapore Chinese Chamber of Commerce and Industry 1956*, p. 11.

9.   Tan, *Marshall of Singapore*, p. 367.

10. National Archives of Australia (NAA), Series A1838, Item 766/3/40 Part 1, "Singapore and Malaya Trade Missions Arrive in Canton", enclosed copy of Hsinhua News Agency release with letter from the Australian Government Office in Hong Kong to the Department of External Affairs in Canberra, 3 September 1956.

11. National Archives of Singapore (NAS), accession number A000156/28, reel 13, interview with David Marshall by the Oral History Centre (OHC), 1984, transcript p. 140.

12. Ibid.

13. Institute of Southeast Asian Studies (ISEAS), David Marshall Papers, DM/157/31, "A Mission to China", letter from Marshall to the Editor of the Manchester Guardian, undated.

14. NAS, accession number A000156/28, reel 11, interview with David Marshall by the OHC, 1984, transcript p. 124.

15. Chan Heng Chee, *A Sensation of Independence: David Marshall, A Political Biography* (Singapore: Times Books International, 2001), p. 203; *Singapore (Tiger) Standard*, 21 July 1956.

16. David Saul Marshall, *Letters from Mao's China*, edited with an introduction by Michael Leifer (Singapore: Singapore Heritage Society, 1996), p. 43.

17. Ibid.

18. Chan, *Sensation of Independence*, p. 204.

19. *Renmin Ribao* (人民日报), 30 August 1956, 13 September 1956 and 30 September 1956. For more on Tan Kah Kee in post-1949 China, see C.F. Yong, *Tan Kah Kee: An Overseas Chinese Legend* (Singapore: Oxford University Press, 1989), pp. 328–43.

20. NAS, accession number A000156/28, reel 13, interview with David Marshall by the OHC, 1984, transcript p. 142.

21. NAS, accession number A000156/28, reel 14, interview with David Marshall by the OHC, 1984, transcript p. 156.

22. Ibid., transcript p. 157.

23. Chan, *Sensation of Independence*, pp. 209–10; and *Nanyang Siang Pau*, 5 October 1956.

24. Marshall, *Letters*, p. 119.

25. Ibid.

26. NAS, accession number A000156/28, reel 13, interview with David Marshall by the OHC, 1984, transcript p. 142.

27. Ibid.

28. Marshall, *Letters*, p. 97.
29. ISEAS, David Marshall Papers, DM/157/6, "Communism Must Be Kept Out of Singapore", *Singapore (Tiger) Standard*, undated.
30. Marshall, *Letters*, p. 55.
31. Chan, *Sensation of Independence*, p. 223.
32. Ibid.
33. Jason Lim, *Linking an Asian Trans-Regional Commerce in Tea: Overseas Chinese Merchants in the Fujian — Singapore Trade, 1920–1960* (Leiden and Boston: Brill, 2010).
34. NAA, Series A1838, Item 766/3/40 Part 1, Memorandum from the Australian Government Office in Hong Kong to the Department of External Affairs in Canberra, 5 October 1956.
35. *Nanyang Siang Pau*, 11 September 1956.
36. NAA, Series A1838, Item 766/3/40 Part 1, Memorandum from the Australian Government Office in Hong Kong to the Department of External Affairs in Canberra, 5 October 1956.
37. *The Straits Times*, 4 October 1956; and *Nanyang Siang Pau*, 4 October 1956.
38. NAS, accession number A000156/28, reel 14, interview with David Marshall by the OHC, 1984, transcript p. 158.
39. Ibid.
40. NAA, Series A1838, Item 766/3/40 Part 1, Letter from the Australian Commissioner's Office in Singapore to the Department of External Affairs in Canberra, 8 September 1956.
41. *Renmin Ribao* (人民日报), 21 September 1956.
42. Chan, *Sensation of Independence*, p. 219.
43. ISEAS, David Marshall Papers, DM/157/5, "Marshall's Peking Request: Singapore Citizenship for All Chinese", *China Mail*, 28 June 1956.
44. NAS, accession number A000156/28, reel 15, interview with David Marshall by the OHC, 1984, transcript p. 163.
45. Turnbull, *History of Modern Singapore*, p. 268.
46. Marshall, *Letters*, p. 57.
47. NAS, accession number A000052/24, reel 22, interview with Tan Keong Choon by the OHC, 1981, transcript pp. 187–8.
48. *Nanyang Siang Pau*, 6 October 1956; *Nanyang Siang Pau*, 7 October 1956; and *Nanyang Siang Pau*, 9 October 1956.
49. *Singapore Legislative Assembly Debates Official Report: Third Session of the First Legislative Assembly*, 22 April 1958, col. 53.
50. *Singapore Legislative Assembly Debates Official Report: Third Session of the First Legislative Assembly*, 24 April 1958, cols 191–2.
51. *Chung Hsing Jit Pao*, 21 May 1957.
52. *Singapore Legislative Assembly Debates Official Report: Third Session of the First Legislative Assembly*, 3 December 1958, col. 1111.
53. *Singapore Legislative Assembly Debates Official Report: Third Session of the First Legislative Assembly*, 16 December 1958, cols 1421–2.

54. NAA, Series A1838, Item 766/3/40 Part 1, Memorandum from the Australian Government Office in Hong Kong to the Department of External Affairs in Canberra, 5 October 1956.

55. Singapore and Malayan Trade Mission in Taiwan, *Xingma Kaochatuan Zai Taiwan* (*Singapore and Malayan Trade Mission in Taiwan*) (Singapore: Dacheng Tushu Zazhi Chubanshe, 1957), p. 10.

56. *Annual Report of the Singapore Chinese Chamber of Commerce and Industry 1957*, p. 9; and *Nanyang Siang Pau*, 30 March 1957.

57. *Nanyang Siang Pau*, 27 July 1957.

58. Xiao Liangzhang and Li Xiao, eds., *Zhonghua Minguo Shishi Jiyao Minguo 46 Nian 7 Zhi 9 Yue* (*Summary of Historical Events in the Republic of China from July to September 1957*) (Hsintien City: Academia Historica, 1992), pp. 233–4; and *Zhongyang Ribao* (*Central Daily News*), 25 July 1957. See also *Straits Times*, 24 July 1957. The "Singapore-Malaya Commercial and Industrial Mission to Formosa" was the name given to the Mission in this article.

59. Singapore and Malayan Trade Mission in Taiwan, *Xingma Kaochatuan Zai Taiwan*, pp. 13–5.

60. *Zhongyang Ribao*, 7 August 1957.

61. *Nanyang Siang Pau*, 27 July 1957. Communist propaganda never seemed to fail to paint Chiang Kai-shek and the KMT as "running dogs" of the United States. Hence, the reference to American dollars invading mainland China was tongue-in-cheek.

62. Academia Historica (AH), Personal Archives of Lim Keng Lian, accession number 1000008671-42156, document number 1560, "Lin Qingnian Yu Lin Wenzhi" (Lim Keng Lian and Lim Boon Tee), 2 August 1957.

63. Singapore and Malayan Trade Mission in Taiwan, *Xingma Kaochatuan Zai Taiwan*, p. 10; and Xiao and Li, eds., *Zhonghua Minguo Shishi Jiyao Minguo 46 Nian 7 Zhi 9 Yue*, p. 233.

64. Ibid.

65. Chui Kwei-chiang and Hara Fujio, *Emergence, Development and Dissolution of the Pro-China Organisations in Singapore* (Tokyo: Institute of Developing Economies, 1991), p. 22.

66. Singapore and Malayan Trade Mission in Taiwan, *Xingma Kaochatuan Zai Taiwan*, p. 10; and Xiao and Li, eds., *Zhonghua Minguo Shishi Jiyao Minguo 46 Nian 7 Zhi 9 Yue*, pp. 233–4.

67. The Singapore Contractors Association Ltd confirmed that they do not have the minutes of meetings for 1957 in an email to me on 16 January 2009. A letter to the Sim Lim Siong Giap Kong Huay on 9 January 2009 received no reply.

68. NAS, Microfilm No. NA 531, Records of the SCTIEA, Minutes of Annual General Meetings and Executive Committee Meetings, Executive Committee Meeting on 17 July 1957.

69. Ibid.

70. Xiao and Li, eds., *Zhonghua Minguo Shishi Jiyao Minguo 46 Nian 7 Zhi 9 Yue*, pp. 234–6.
71. Singapore and Malayan Trade Mission in Taiwan, *Xingma Kaochatuan Zai Taiwan*, p. 62.
72. Ibid., p. 11.
73. *Straits Times*, 16 August 1957.
74. Archives of the Institute of Modern History Academia Sinica (IMHA), Ministry of Economic Affairs Archives, Accession Number 30-01-026-02-015, Letter from the Industrial Committee of the Economic Stabilisation Commission of the Executive Yuan to the OCAC, 29 October 1957.
75. Sikko Visscher, *The Business of Politics and Ethnicity: A History of the Singapore Chinese Chamber of Commerce and Industry* (Singapore: NUS Press, 2007).
76. Singapore and Malayan Trade Mission in Taiwan, *Xingma Kaochatuan Zai Taiwan*.

References

Archival Materials and Oral History Interviews

Academia Historica, Sindian, New Taipei
Personal Archives of Lim Keng Lian

Archives of the Institute of Modern History Academia Sinica, Taipei
Ministry of Economic Affairs Archives

Institute of Southeast Asian Studies, Singapore
David Marshall Papers

Library of the Parliament of Singapore
Singapore Legislative Assembly Debates Official Reports

National Archives of Australia, National Reference Service, Canberra
Department of External Affairs (Series Number A1838)

National Archives of Singapore
Records of the Singapore Chinese Tea Importers and Exporters Association

Oral History Centre, National Archives of Singapore
Marshall, David, A000156/28, interview conducted in 1984
Tan, Keong Choon, A000052/24, interview conducted in 1981

Singapore Chinese Chamber of Commerce and Industry
Minutes of Meetings

Newspapers

Chuing Hsing Jit Pao [Singapore], 1957
Nanyang Siang Pau [Singapore], 1956–1957
Renmin Ribao [China], 1956
Singapore (Tiger) Standard [Singapore], 1956
The Straits Times [Singapore], 1956–1957
Zhongyang Ribao [Taiwan], 1957

Annual Reports

Annual Reports of the Singapore Chinese Chamber of Commerce and Industry, 1956–1957

Books

Chan Heng Chee. *A Sensation of Independence: David Marshall, A Political Biography*. Singapore: Times Books International, 2001.

Chui Kwei-chiang and Hara Fujio. *Emergence, Development and Dissolution of the Pro-China Organisations in Singapore*. Tokyo: Institute of Developing Economies, 1991.

Lim, Jason. *Linking an Asian Trans-Regional Commerce in Tea: Overseas Chinese Merchants in the Fujian-Singapore Trade, 1920–1960*. Leiden and Boston: Brill, 2010.

Marshall, David Saul. *Letters from Mao's China*. Edited with an introduction by Michael Leifer. Singapore: Singapore Heritage Society, 1996.

Singapore and Malayan Trade Mission in Taiwan 星马考察团在台湾. *Xingma Kaochatuan Zai Taiwan* 星马考察团在台湾 [*Singapore and Malayan Trade Mission in Taiwan*]. Singapore: Dacheng Tushu Zazhi Chubanshe, 1957.

Singapore Chinese Chamber of Commerce and Industry. *Singapore Chinese Chamber of Commerce & Industry 60th Anniversary Souvenir*. Singapore, 1966.

————. *Singapore Chinese Chamber of Commerce & Industry 80th Anniversary Souvenir*. Singapore, 1986.

Tan, Kevin Y.L. *Marshall of Singapore: A Biography*. Singapore: Institute of Southeast Asian Studies, 2008.

Turnbull, C.M. *A History of Modern Singapore, 1819–2005*. Singapore: NUS Press, 2009.

Visscher, Sikko. *The Business of Politics and Ethnicity: A History of the Singapore Chinese Chamber of Commerce and Industry*. Singapore: NUS Press, 2007.

Xiao Liangzhang 萧良章 and Li Xiao 李晓, eds. *Zhonghua Minguo Shishi Jiyao Minguo 46 Nian 7 Zhi 9 Yue* 中华民国史事纪要民国46年7至9月 [*Summary of Historical Events in the Republic of China from July to September 1957*]. Sindian: Academia Historica, 1992.

Yong, C.F. *Tan Kah Kee: An Overseas Chinese Legend*. Singapore: Oxford University Press, 1989.

10

Singapore and Its Neighbours

Nicholas Tarling

IN BRITAIN, WHEN MARY TURNBULL BEGAN HER research, public access to government archives was under a 50-year rule. The Wilson Labour government reduced the limit to 30 years, and the Major Conservative government of the 1990s initiated a re-examination of the documents that had been placed outside that limit, opening some wholly or partly to public view. Brown's New Labour government planned to reduce the limit to 20 years. The abandonment of the 50-year rule was, of course, largely welcomed, though some feared that it would lead officials to write and preserve — or not to write or preserve — with an eye to a future public rather than to current policymakers. A 20-year rule would run the same risks. Perhaps, too, more material would be placed in the "withheld" category.

By contrast to British practice, governments in Southeast Asia have been reluctant to open their archives, even under a 50-year rule. The late Chandran Jeshurun's account of Malaysian foreign policy had largely to do without such access, and it could hardly evidence the wonderful skill at reading official documents his earlier work had demonstrated. One result of this is, perhaps, somewhat paradoxical. Those writing accounts of the foreign policy of Southeast Asian governments have supplemented what has been published by resort to the archives of external powers, and have thus drawn on the reports of foreign diplomats, themselves often derived from what they could elicit from local officials and politicians, or what the latter saw fit to tell them. The paradox lies in the fact that we learn about the foreign policy of an independent country rather as we might have learned of the foreign policy of a pre-colonial regime.

In the case of Singapore, leading statesmen, such as Lee Kuan Yew and S. Rajaratnam, have been particularly articulate on foreign policy, that of other countries, in fact, as well as their own, and their remarks have always been worth reading. Singapore's foreign policy is not a particular focus of Mary Turnbull's history, even in its 2009 edition. But there is also a valuable secondary literature on Singapore's foreign policy, able to turn published material to account, though not to utilise the Republic's archives. The books of the late Michael Leifer, of N. Ganesan and of Amitav Acharya come readily to mind.

Like the statesmen, the authors often reflect on the vulnerability of Singapore, and analyse the measures the PAP Government has followed in its attempts to mitigate it. Much of the discussion relates to the Republic's anxiety to involve major powers in the region, with a view in particular to avoiding one-power dominance, meaning, of course, the dominance of the People's Republic of China. Also discussed is the relationship with Singapore's neighbours, in particular Malaysia, of which in the early 1960s it briefly formed a part, and Indonesia, by far the largest state in Southeast Asia. What is perhaps less readily discussed is the connexion between these two sets of relationships.

The relationship with the two neighbours is the more crucial inasmuch as they together constitute a "Malay world" surrounding a predominantly ethnic Chinese city-state. Very shortly after the separation from Malaysia in 1965, Lee pointed out that "[o]ur long-term survival demands that there's no government in Malaysia that goes with Indonesia. Life would be very difficult if I found myself between Malaysia and Indonesia."[1] The head of state took the same view a few months later. "So many of our neighbours and we ourselves would not have a separate existence if purely Asian forces were to settle the shape of decolonized Asia," he said, adding: "We must never be isolated and left friendless in Southeast Asia in a Singapore encircled by a hostile sea of communal obscurantist forces."[2]

If Singapore was vulnerable to the ganging-up of its neighbours, however, it also wished to avoid being defended by them. Keeping a number of major powers involved in Southeast Asia would not only avoid the dominance of any one of them, but also the need for the major regional power to defend Southeast Asia against such dominance. And that was undesirable, since it would require the counter-dominance of Indonesia.

The elaborate metaphor that Rajaratnam deployed in June 1976 seems to hint at this connexion: "Where there is a multiplicity of suns the gravitational pulls of each is not only weakened but also, by a judicious use of the pulls and counter-pulls of gravitational forces, the minor planets have greater freedom of navigation."[3] Certainly his speech in Bangkok about the same time suggests as much. "We in Singapore accept the fact of great powers and the fact of great power rivalry in Southeast Asia. We might wish things were otherwise but we console ourselves with the thought that if there were no great [power?] rivalries in the region, then, if pre-European history in the area is any guide, we might be confronted with less manageable small power rivalries."[4]

This chapter does not, of course, attempt a long-term history of Singapore's foreign policy. Instead it takes up three topics — West New Guinea, the early years of ASEAN, and Timor — and utilises some of the material in the archives of other powers in the hope of casting further light on that policy and demonstrating the value of unpublished material even if it was that of outside powers. It was indeed in the course of examining those documents that the author first became aware of the connexion between its policy towards its immediate neighbours and its attitude to great-power involvement.

West New Guinea

Singapore's sensitivity in regard to Indonesia was apparent even before the People's Action Party government took control of foreign affairs. As it advanced towards that goal, it sought to "live down" the role it had played in the late 1950s as "a support-base" for the rebellion in Sumatra and the charge that it was "an agent for British influence".[5] That led Lee to lend support to Indonesia's claim to West New Guinea. One might have thought that Singapore would not be keen to support Indonesia's expansion. But in West New Guinea it had a claim, and it could also be suggested that the early acceptance of the claim would perhaps diminish the violence with which the Indonesians began to use alongside their diplomatic pressure.

Visiting Jakarta in January 1960, Prime Minister Lee pledged support for Indonesia's struggle for West Irian.[6] The Singapore government's position was "logical," he said, "and based on the anti-colonialist instincts long felt among nations ruled for centuries under colonialism".[7] The Dutch Consul-General expressed concern, and Lord Selkirk, the British Commissioner-General, had Lee informed that the matter fell within Britain's responsibility and the statement could cause embarrassment. Prime Minister Djuanda wanted one, Lee replied, and in fact he agreed.

He would not mind if Britain disassociated itself: it would be "good for his prestige".[8] It did so.[9]

If Lee made "further undesirable incursions into Foreign Affairs," Selkirk commented, it would be necessary "to take more serious notice," but a press argument would only build up his prestige "and do us no good at all".[10] The Colonial Office in London thought that Selkirk should not get "too worried" by Lee's 'anti-colonial' noises ... the important thing being that there is a strong and popularly elected government in Singapore which is doing its best to focus the loyalty of the Singapore Chinese on Singapore and not on China and which accepts our presence there provided we do not advertise it too much".[11] Fred Warner, head of the Foreign Office's South East Asia Department, did not see what else Lee could have done. "The incident passed off very quietly ... it would be a mistake to stumble over this particular mole-hill."[12]

By late 1961, Sukarno's confrontation of the Dutch over West Irian had intensified. The British had committed themselves to offering logistic support, but were apprehensive lest that provoked opposition within Singapore or Malaysia. In the event of Indonesian-Dutch hostilities, most people in Malaya and Singapore would be emotionally moved in favour of Indonesia, Selkirk wrote. The Barisan Sosialis was planning a rally, and Lee Kuan Yew would find it "extremely difficult to act firmly for fear of himself being labelled a colonialist". Britain could not play an effective part even if it wanted to. New Guinea was 2,000 miles away; Singapore was within artillery range of Indonesian islands. "I would expect considerable difficulty if it became urgently necessary for us to provide repairs to Dutch ships or indeed logistic support if it were known that these were supplied from Singapore." The Malayan government would also be "greatly embarrassed".[13] The PAP had to show they were not stooges. If Britain supplied logistic support to the Dutch, its ministers might call out the service unions. And if it persisted, the British authorities thought, "we think this could well lead to a situation in which we had to suspend the constitution": the government might resign, or there might be violent demonstrations, against which it would not be prepared to use police and troops.[14]

Whatever they felt they had to say, Singapore's leaders were not now in fact in favour of the takeover of West Irian, if they ever had been. That was apparent when the Bunker proposal — a compromise very much in Indonesia's favour — was put forward. Lee told Harold Macmillan and Reginald Maudling in May 1962 that "it would be the greatest possible disservice to Indonesia to give them West Irian and the result of doing so would be that they would seek another grievance. There were two possible targets, West Borneo and East Timor". He thought they would pick on Borneo.[15]

That was, of course, what they did, though in the form of a further "confrontation", opposing the creation of Greater Malaysia. The negotiation of that had begun in 1961 during the West Irian crisis, and, though it is frequently presented in the literature as an anti-Communist move and an episode in Malayan politics, it should above all be seen in an Indonesian context. It seems clear that the Tunku and his colleagues in Malaya wished to keep Britain's Borneo territories out of Indonesia's hands, and that they accepted the inclusion of Singapore in the putative Malaysia at the instance of the British who were seeking a means to reconcile their strategic interests with its political advance.[16] At the time, that seemed to be also in the interest of Singapore, since it was not thought it could survive, economically or politically, without "merger".

Domestic politics, it is generally agreed, was the cause of the subsequent extrusion of Singapore, though it meant that the Tunku shed the territory he had least wanted to include, while he had ensured that Indonesia did not secure the Borneo territories. Sukarno was prompt to recognise the new state as a means of intensifying confrontation.[17] But when, after his fall, the Indonesians took steps to end confrontation, the Singaporeans were not included in the negotiations. It was in this period that they openly expressed their concern over the coming-together of their two neighbours.

The Early Years of ASEAN

The emergence of a regional grouping did not necessarily offer reassurance. Discussions about that reflected the tension between military and civilian elements in the leadership of Suharto's regime. In December 1966, Adam Malik, the Foreign Minister, stated publicly "that Indonesia would take the lead in establishing regional economic and cultural co-operation to achieve a united Southeast Asia. A week later, General Mariden Panggabean, deputy Army C-in-C, declared that Indonesia must, in face of China's ambitions in the region and aspirations towards nuclear capability", strengthen its armed forces so as to be able to join in a common defence effort with its neighbours. In January, Malik rejected a regional military alliance. He looked towards a different form of co-operation with Malaysia, the Philippines and Thailand. "What of Singapore?" asked the British ambassador, Horace Phillips. Malik "hastily" added he would include it, but apparently there were "mixed feelings" in Jakarta, and he was "in some difficulty with the Army" on the issue.[18]

Phillips discussed the British base in Singapore with Suharto himself. "Was it still necessary now that relations with Britain had improved?" the President asked. Or did HMG doubt his assurance that Indonesia had "no expansionist ambitions or aggressive intentions"? Phillips replied that the base existed to enable the UK to fulfil its obligations in Southeast Asia, and it contributed to employment on the island. Suharto said that he recognised the dangers from Communist China's expansionism, but that Singapore was a target for it. "The defence of South-East Asia ought to be a matter for the countries of the area themselves", and if the UK and the Western allies helped in the supply of arms, "Indonesia could play a leading role in this". Suharto did not press the point, though emphasising that, while he did not expect the base to be removed "overnight", he saw it as a gradual process to be aimed at. Malik dismissed what Suharto said. Southeast Asia could not defend itself in the foreseeable future. "He confided to us that he saw it simply as a gambit to equip the army ostensibly for regional defence but in fact for continuance of its control over the 100 million people of Indonesia."[19]

The draft agreement for the formation of ASEAN nevertheless described foreign bases in Southeast Asia as "temporary in nature". It was generally acceptable to Malik, Anwar Sani, the director-general of the Foreign Ministry, told Phillips, "because it made it clear that the proposed regional cooperation did not extend to defence". In deference to "Army thinking", he had been required to write in "something to the effect that foreign bases must be regarded as temporary". Malik and he did not want to pick a quarrel with the Army, "though they still believed that the soldiers' aim was to try to build up the strength of the armed forces on the pretext that South-East Asians (given a lead by Indonesia) should be able to defend themselves and thus get rid of foreign bases". That was "unrealistic, besides being undesirable from the domestic point of view".[20]

Discussing regional cooperation with Zainal Abidin Sulong, Principal Assistant Secretary for Southeast Asian affairs in the MFA in KL, the Australian High Commission observed that Singapore was generally left off the list of partners. "We said we thought this was a pity, especially as it carried an overtone of racism". Zainal said it was not the work of Malaysia, as some would think. "[F]eelers put to Singapore to seek membership of ASA [the Association of Asian Nations, Malaya, Thailand, the Philippines] had been cold-shouldered", and Jakarta was "less inclined

towards Singapore" than was KL. There was an element of racialism, he
thought, but it was more a matter of distrusting Lee Kuan Yew. If KL
came to feel that ostracism was primarily based on distrust and dislike of
the Chinese, it would have to try to counter that feeling. "It would be not
just a case of racism being bad in itself; there would also be a danger of
a racial gang-up against Singapore forcing the Republic into the hands
of Peking and creating serious morale and loyalty problems amongst
Chinese Malaysians."[21]

Singapore was leaving it to others to make the running, External
Affairs in Canberra concluded. If the advantages of membership were
mainly economic, and the group were not "identified with political
aims which might conflict with Singapore's "neutral" status", it would
probably join. It would favour the inclusion of Cambodia and Burma to
ensure the group's neutral appearance and "offset its domination by the
MAPHILINDO powers". Malaysia now favoured including Singapore,
so as "to assuage the fears of their own Chinese population about the
implications of closer cooperation with demonstrably anti-Chinese governments in Djakarta and Manila". The Indonesians saw Singapore's inclusion as "a means of diluting the pro-Western flavour" of the grouping.[22]

There was clearly a limit on the "ganging-up" that Singapore might
fear in a regional organisation. It could hardly avoid joining ASEAN:
it had to get along with its neighbours. The fact that their new-found
friendship did not amount to total identification made it easier. So, too,
did the fact that the regional organisation eschewed defence, and, though
Malik had to yield to the Army over the reference to foreign bases, the
agreement fell short of requiring their early removal. Nevertheless, the
agreement could provide a form of recognition of Indonesia's primacy in
the region. ASEAN was envisaged as "the vehicle through which a willing
acceptance of Indonesia's political primacy — as opposed to hegemony
— may be facilitated within Southeast Asia," Leifer wrote.[23] Singapore
stressed the economic aims of the ASEAN agreement. But stressing that
was itself a piece of politics.

Later in 1967, Lee warned the US against hastily rearming Indonesia.
He was not satisfied that the Americans had given up the idea of working
up nationalism against communism that they had followed after abandoning the subversion policy of the late 1950s. It would, he said, only
"provoke Muslim-Malay-Indonesian chauvinism".[24] He was concerned,
he said in January 1968, not with economics but with security. Who
might attack Singapore? He at first declined to answer, "then admitted

Indonesia was in his mind. As long as there was a stable non-Communist government in Indonesia, 'That's fine. But if there is not, and we get a general melee in which any colonel or brigadier has his own band of forces, my God, we are in for trouble.'"[25]

Insisting they were focused on economic challenges and maintained non-alignment, the generals had "probably not changed their ideas much on their own eminence as a big power in the area," Fred Emery suggested in *The Times*. They would favour a "purely regional" arrangement, provided everyone paid tribute, even if only psychologically, to the big-power status which one day they might have.[26] If Malaysia or Singapore were attacked, Indonesia would send in troops at once, a minister told Emery later in 1968. "When it was asked whether it was known in Kuala Lumpur and Singapore that they might be the recipients of such swift aid, the assurance came: 'Do not worry, they understand.'" It was, Emery thought, some kind of Monroe Doctrine, "commensurate with the basic Indonesian assumption that the country will one day come to be the leading power in a non-communist partnership in the area".[27]

In Singapore, two Indonesian marines found guilty of sabotage and murder during *konfrontasi* were hanged in October 1968.[28] The government rejected Suharto's personal plea for clemency. That hurt Singapore's "real interests," Mary Turnbull argued, since so much Indonesian trade flowed through it.[29] But it was done "in part to assert the rule of law and in part to assert Singapore's sovereignty and independence by a manifestation of strength".[30] In any case, Suharto resisted the retaliation that the ABRI advocated, and heeded Malik's advice not to break off diplomatic relations. But with that and the Sabah dispute, Zainal Sulong of the Malaysian foreign ministry commented, "ASEAN was now in a very bad way".[31]

Nevertheless, the third ministerial meeting was held at Cameron Highlands on 16–17 December 1969. The Tunku indeed announced the normalisation of relations between the Philippines and Malaysia, and Romulo welcomed it. Malik "stressed the importance of events in Vietnam and the likely effects of the British withdrawal and the possible disengagement of the United States from Asia". Thanat emphasised the importance of "increased mutual consultation", though adding "that it was no good trying to act too swiftly". Rajaratnam said that "trying to move too fast ... might lead to the creation of the wrong type of regional organisation". ASEAN needed the assistance of other countries. For that "a convincing display of internal stability in the region was necessary".

It should focus on promoting economic cooperation. "To try to use it to sort out ideological or military problems would be likely to introduce divisions between members." He added that "[n]othing should be done to discourage other non member countries from joining ASEAN at a future date".[32]

In Singapore's view, R.F. Stimson of the UK High Commission in Singapore reported in December, "for the foreseeable future A.S.E.A.N.'s usefulness to her depends on its objectives being strictly limited". Singapore's basic problems were the consolidation of its political position and the growth of its economy "in the midst of racially different and not necessarily well-disposed neighbours". Their attitude was at present "satisfactory", but might not always be so. "Therefore Singapore must seek to establish good working relations with as many other countries as she can. Regional collaborative arrangements may pay off; but the Singaporeans will continue to be wary of political alignments which might hamper their freedom of manoeuvre. This is particularly the case so far as the communist countries, with whom she wishes to establish workmanlike relations, are concerned."[33]

Rajaratnam's main concern was to "avoid political involvement in the Vietnam war", S.R. Nathan, then in Singapore's Ministry of Foreign Affairs, told J.K. Hickman in January, but also claimed that "an additional reason for Singapore's opposition to the expansion of ASEAN was that they were as much interested in developing cooperation with Burma and Cambodia as with South Vietnam or Laos, but that the two former countries did not at present regard membership as compatible with their neutral position. This was one reason for the emphasis which Singapore had placed on developing practical cooperation between countries in the region, if necessary on an informal or bilateral basis, as opposed to formal expansion of the organisation."[34]

Singapore was indeed seen as something of a "dampener" in ASEAN's earlier years.[35] "[T]here was a lot of circus at the cost of less and less bread," the Foreign Minister complained.[36] Its attitude to the organisation indeed related partly to its wider commercial ambitions, but it also related to its security concerns. That helped to make it assertive in respect of Indonesia, while its arming provoked Malaysia. Its policy began to shift after 1969. The endeavour to construct a Singapore identity reassured Malaysia, since that would make it even less likely that it would meddle on the peninsula: "building a perceptual fence separating transnational communal groups has helped make for good neighbours". And it increased its participation in ASEAN.[37]

The Zone of Peace, Freedom and Neutrality

Indonesia was supportive of Malaysia's proposed ZOPFAN, Anwar argues, but it was opposed to the outside guarantee Malaysia had included.[38] That "irked Indonesian leaders because it could only be realised at the expense of Jakarta's aspirations to achieve at least Middle Power status".[39] "No country with aspirations to big or middle power status could accept neutralization," as Tommy Koh of Singapore put it.[40] Great power guarantees would be "a new form of colonialism".[41] Nor were they anxious — least of all ABRI leaders — for the early resumption of relations with the PRC, "frozen" since 9 October 1967,[42] though that was the implication of the project. "We cannot ask Communist China to guarantee the neutrality of Southeast Asia," as Ismail put it, "and at the same time say we do not approve of her."[43] Again the differences between Malaysia and Indonesia could be welcomed in Singapore, which was, of course, opposed to neutralisation.

The 5th ASEAN ministerial meeting was held in Singapore on 13–14 April 1972. Ismail's reference to "national resilience" Chick of the FCO saw as "a polite bow in the direction of the Indonesians, who have expressed scepticism about the wisdom of Malaysian proposals for neutralisation, and who have sought to portray ASEAN as a body with a very limited political role". It was reported that ASEAN ministers had agreed to meet informally once a year "to review international developments," Chick added. If that were true, then Malaysia had "made some headway" in its endeavour to make ASEAN "an accepted clearing house for the exchange of views on political events".[44]

Lee Kuan Yew's opening speech dwelt on ASEAN's limitations: only a small proportion of the economic recommendations had been implemented. That was "to some extent ... inevitable", since the various economies were not complementary, and their consumers were extra-regional. Lee's aim, it seemed, was "to delineate what Singapore has always regarded as ASEAN's proper field of activity, economic cooperation", and to indicate that even in this field not too much should be expected.

Other speeches had "a high political content", including Rajaratnam's. Recent developments in international politics, it was agreed, "had enhanced the value of such regional groupings". The Singapore Foreign Minister put the point "most effectively; he argued that the change from a bipolar to a multipolar world and the detente between the US and China meant that the developed countries were no longer so concerned about the Third World. Developing countries would increasingly have to stand on their own feet — 'the big powers believe they can pursue their great-power game even if the Third World is permanently impoverished and increasingly turbulent.' The necessity of giving aid to poor countries to save them from communism was becoming less and less accepted". But, despite some pressure from other members to include political matters on the official agenda, Rajaratnam "reiterated Singapore's longstanding view that ASEAN is not the proper forum for political discussion, and suggested that periodic discussions among the foreign ministers of member countries should take place *'outside* the framework of ASEAN'. The suggestion was accepted."[45]

ASEAN had not grown in membership, J.L. Jones commented at the FCO in 1973, "but its stature gains little by little".[46] Despite earlier suspicious that it might be "a vehicle for Indonesia's regional ambitions, possibly in collusion with Malaysia",[47] the Singaporeans now appeared to think it had become useful for the exchange of views and consultation, the British High Commission reported. They had "particularly welcomed what they consider the realism of the general ASEAN agreement to discuss political and security matters, while sharing the ASEAN view that such discussions should not evolve into an internationalised form such as a pact".[48] "ASEAN must be strengthened," Rajaratnam declared.[49] No enthusiast for ZOPFAN, however, Singapore continued to want a US presence in the region.[50] A "Shangri-la Southeast Asia" — Lee Kuan Yew's derisive phrase — was not on.[51]

Timor

The question of Portuguese Timor was raised at the first ASEAN summit in Bali early in 1976. To the concern of the Singaporeans — among others — Indonesia had overtly intervened early the previous December. A long crisis on the island had been precipitated by the Carnation revolution in Portugal and the overthrow of the Caetano regime in 1974. By 1975, three main political groups were competing for power within the colony, UDT [the Timor Democratic Union], in favour of autonomy, the more left-wing pro-independence Fretilin, and Apodeti, which, the smallest, favoured integration with Indonesia. Early in August 1975, UDT had attempted to seize power, but they were overthrown by their main rivals, Fretilin. Would Indonesia openly intervene? So far, its intervention had been covert.

What were Singapore's views at that point? The question was put to the Minister of State by a diplomat in the British High Commission,

Peter Tripp. He did not think Indonesia would use force in attempting to control Timor. "They would, however, wish to exert control there since they could not accept a hostile regime or presence in the territory." He thought Sino-Soviet rivalry might operate: the PRC would not be able to tolerate a Soviet influence. He "agreed that any Indonesian military action against Portuguese Timor would set a very unfortunate precedent for ASEAN".[52] Tripp talked to Rajaratnam himself in October, by which time Indonesia's covert intervention had increased in face of Fretilin's dominance. The Foreign Minister feared its involvement might prompt others to intervene.[53]

Full-blown intervention began on 7 December. Two resolutions faced the Fourth Committee of UNGA in New York. One, supported by African states, condemned the intervention and called for the withdrawal of Indonesian troops. The other, supported by Asian states, was milder. Singapore, the British High Commission reported, had declined to sponsor the Asian resolution, though it was expected to vote in favour. "Not surprisingly it seems unlikely that Singapore will want to rock the ASEAN boat."[54] In the event, the Fourth Committee supported the African draft. Singapore, unlike its ASEAN colleagues, who voted against it, abstained.[55] The UN resolutions were to have an effect only in the longer term. More immediately, the Indonesians pushed ahead with the occupation of Timor and with its integration into the Republic.

"Would the communiqué from the Bali summit allude to Timor?" Australian diplomats asked the Principal Assistant Secretary Southeast Asia at the Singapore Ministry of Foreign Affairs after he had returned from the pre-summit Foreign Ministers meeting at Pattaya. Singapore, he said, hoped it would not. "Indonesia could not expect Singapore to acquiesce in any attempt to obtain formal ASEAN endorsement of its actions there. On the other hand, Singapore could not object to more general references to the right of member countries to protect their own territorial integrity."[56]

The Indonesians sought to give the incorporation of Timor the kind of local sanction given to their incorporation of West Irian in 1969, when an "act of free choice" had taken place and been noted by the UN. For that they sought the sanction of foreign presence. 28 members representing 13 regencies met on 31 May and unanimously approved a petition for integration. The ambassadors of India, Saudi Arabia and Iran were present, along with the chargé for Nigeria and representatives of Malaysia, Thailand and New Zealand. The Americans had been instructed they could go if the Australians did, and the Japanese if either did. None of them went.[57] ASEAN solidarity also crumbled, even though the Bali Summit had by now been held: neither Singapore nor the Philippines was represented.[58]

Indonesia proceeded to invite the embassies to send observers along with the parliamentary fact-finding mission that followed the petition for integration. Malaysia and the Philippines were among those who agreed to attend, Singapore and PNG were not.[59] No attempt was made by the mission on its one-day visit [24 June] to ascertain whether the Timorese wanted integration or independence.[60] Not a fact it wanted to find.

In his talk with Tripp, Rajaratnam had tended to discount the idea that Malaysia might find Indonesia's intervention in Timor a precedent for its own handling of Brunei. Under Prime Minister Razak, Malaysia was disposed to challenge the Sultanate's continued dependence on its British protectors. In 1975, it sponsored a Parta Rakyat Brunei delegation to the UN Committee on Decolonisation.[61] Indonesia's action might be more than a question of precedent.

Malaysia had indeed sent its man-of-all-work Ghazali bin Shafie to Jakarta during the August–September UDT-Fretilin conflict in Timor, when it seemed that the Indonesians might intervene in the guise of restorers of law and order in collaboration with Portugal and other states. Ghazali — on a secret mission uncovered by Michael Richardson — had come to offer Malaysia's help and held detailed discussions with Moerdani. "The Malaysians are said to have taken the attitude that 'what pinches Indonesia pinches Malaysia'", the British embassy in Jakarta reported. "It seems not to have been lost on the Indonesians that any assistance they seek from Malaysia over Portuguese Timor might involve some future quid pro quo over Brunei."[62]

Suharto resolved at that point still to focus on covert intervention. Perhaps there was an irony in the fact that he was anxious to avoid renewing the reputation his predecessor had gained for Indonesia in the latter stages of Confrontation. The Malaysians in fact thought he should act promptly. The Malaysian ambassador in Jakarta told his British counterpart, John Ford, that his government favoured incorporation, and that elements in it, such as Ghazali, thought the Indonesians were "being over-slow about the whole business".[63] The Prime Minister shared his view. In KL, the Under-Secretary [Khor] indicated in December that Malaysia's view was that, provided that self-determination went ahead, integration was the best solution. The PM's principal private secretary had told the British High Commissioner on 8 December that Razak's only criticism had been that the Indonesians "had not acted firmly earlier".[64]

In 1976, Malaysia sponsored a resolution in favour of elections in Brunei, the end of the ban on political parties, and the return of exiles; and in 1977, the resolution was adopted.[65] It was, as Leifer put it, seeking to destabilise the sultanate, "ostensibly from a fear that it would become a contagious source of insecurity in northern Borneo in much the same way as Indonesia's military establishment had contemplated the deteriorating situation in East Timor".[66] Such actions only made the sultanate more unwilling to relinquish Britain's protection. Razak's successor, Hussein Onn, took steps to improve relations, however, and, meeting in nearby Labuan in May 1978, he and Suharto expressed the hope that the sultanate would join ASEAN when it became independent.[67]

That line was supported by Singapore, "which had come to regard membership as a political asset".[68] Lee had sustained a close relationship with the sultans and stood aside from the challenge Malaysia had mounted in the UN.[69] In March 1979, he became the first ASEAN leader to visit Brunei. Attending the 1982 AMM as observer, Prince Md Bolkiah said Brunei was now "more confident of the support and cooperation of ASEAN countries", and stressed "mutual respect for the sovereignty, independence and territorial integrity" as "the basis for good relations".[70] ASEAN thus helped Brunei towards "full independence" in 1984, and itself moved a step towards regional inclusion on the basis of national sovereignty. Brunei retained a close connexion with Singapore: both were "wary of their giant neighbours", as V.G. Kulkarni put it.[71] "Timorization" remained a Singaporean concern, Indorf suggested in 1984.[72]

Whatever its attitude when still under British control to the future of West Irian, as an independent state, Singapore was concerned over the fate of the remaining small territories in the archipelago as they left the colonial sphere. Perhaps that reflected continuing doubts about its neighbours and even about ASEAN as a form of restraint and a source of security.

Does that possibility argue for the continued closure of the archives or for their opening at least on the restricted basis adopted in Britain? Politics may indeed turn access to account, even at 30 years' distance. And though the closure applies to a wide range of topics, if not to all, foreign policy is likely to be a particularly sensitive issue, both at home and in regard to other states, neighbouring and distant. Nevertheless, just as there may be dangers in too much openness, there is danger, too, in the reverse. Policies may be less well understood and their rationales misinterpreted.

Notes

1. Quoted in M. Leifer, *Singapore's Foreign Policy* (London: Routledge, 2000), p. 65.
2. Quoted in ibid., p. 36.
3. Quoted in ibid., p. 40; also in Bilveer Singh, *Singapore: Foreign Policy Imperatives for a Small State* (Singapore: Heinemann Asia, 1988), p. 33.
4. Quoted in ibid., p. 31.
5. Leifer, p. 59.
6. Telegram ex Mason, 27.1.60, 11. FO 371/152452 [DH 1081/5], National Archives, Kew. For the joint communique issued at the end of his visit, 19–26 January 1960, see CO 1030/1122, National Archives, Kew.
7. Telegram ex Fry, 28 January 1960, 28. DH 1081/5.
8. Telegram ex Selkirk, 27 January 1960. FO 371/152452 [DH 1081/7].
9. *The Times*, 2 February 1960.
10. Selkirk/Macleod, 16 February 1960. FO 371/152452 [DH 1081/13].
11. Wallace/Warner, 3 March 1960. Ibid.
12. Minute, 4 March 1960. Ibid.
13. Selkirk/Home, 30 December 1961. FO 800/897.
14. Ward/Roberts, 11 January 1962. CO 1030/1124 [10].
15. Record of Conversation at Admiralty House, 16 May 1962. CO 1030/1124 [104].
16. See N. Tarling, "The Tunku and West New Guinea", *Journal of the Malaysian Branch Royal Asiatic Society* 83, 1 (June 2010): 77–90.
17. Leifer, p. 58.
18. Phillips/Murray, 30 January 1967. FCO 24/16 [5].
19. Phillips/Murray, 30 January 1967. FCO 24/16 [6].
20. Telegram, 28 February 1967, 6S. FCO 24/16 [16].
21. Memorandum by C.E. McDonald, in McDonald/Bentley, 7 March 1967. FCO 24/16[19].
22. SAV.AP.63, 20 May 1967. FCO 24/16[54].
23. M. Leifer, *The Foreign Relations of New States* (Camberwell: Longman, 1974), p. 103.
24. *The Times*, 6 November 1967.
25. *The Australian*, 17 January 1968.
26. *The Times*, 15 January 1968.
27. Ibid., 9 July 1968.
28. Roger Irvine, "The Formative Years of ASEAN", in *Understanding ASEAN*, ed. A. Broinowski (New York: St Martin's Press, 1981), p. 20.
29. C.M Turnbull, *A History of Modern Singapore, 1819–2005* (Singapore: NUS Press, 2009), p. 329.
30. J. Haacke, *ASEAN's Diplomatic and Security Culture* (London: RoutledgeCurzon, 2003), p. 48.

31. S.A. Budd KL/Mound, 25 November 1968. FCO 24/341[2].

32. Clift/Le Breton, 31 December 1969. FCO 24/341[51].

33. Stimson/Le Breton, 31 December 1969. FCO 23/341[52].

34. Hickman/Aiers, 6 January 1970. FCO 24/620[3].

35. M. Antolik, *ASEAN and the Diplomacy of Accommodation* (Armonk: Sharpe, 1990), p. 35.

36. Quoted in W. Bucklin, "Regional Economic Cooperation in Southeast Asia", PhD thesis, Michigan State University, 1972, p. 40.

37. Antolik, p. 41.

38. Dewi Fortuna Anwar, *Indonesia and the Security of Southeast Asia* (Jakarta: CSIS, 1992), pp. 177–8.

39. Haacke, pp. 56–7.

40. Quoted in Dick Wilson, *The Neutralization of Southeast Asia* (New York, Washington, London: Praeger, 1975), p. 82.

41. Evelyn Colbert, "ASEAN as a Regional Organisation", in *ASEAN in a Regional and Global Context*, ed. Karl D. Jackson *et al.* (Berkeley: Institute of East Asian Studies, 1986), p. 202.

42. Rizal Sukma, *Indonesia and China* (London and New York: Routledge, 1999), p. 34.

43. Quoted in Sheldon W. Simon, *The ASEAN States and Regional Security* (Stanford: Hoover Institution Press, 1982), p. 94.

44. Minute, 27 April 1972. FCO 24/1269[20].

45. K.Q.F. Manning/B.R.T. Langridge SWPD, 12 May 1972. FCO 24/1269[22].

46. Ibid.

47. M. Leifer, *ASEAN and the Security of South-East Asia* (London: Routledge, 1989), pp. 18–9.

48. Hay-Edie/Paul, 25 May 1973. FCO 24/1530[44].

49. Quoted in A. Jorgensen-Dahl, *Regional Organization in South-East Asia* (New York: St Martin's Press, 1982), p. 80.

50. Tim Huxley, *ASEAN and Indochina* (Canberra: ANU, 1985), p. 29.

51. J.M. van der Kroef, "ASEAN's Security Needs and Policies", *Pacific Affairs* 47, 2 (Summer 1974): 164.

52. Memorandum, 20 August 1975. FCO 15/1705 [88].

53. Telegram, 18 October 1975, 658. FCO 15/1705 [135].

54. Telegram ex Singapore, 10 December 1975, 719. FCO 15/1707[247].

55. N. Ganesan, *Realism and Interdependence in Singapore's Foreign Policy* (London and New York: Routledge, 2005), p. 83.

56. Australian telegram, 13 February 1976, 7609. FCO 15/2173 [13].

57. Telegram, 1 June 1976, 171. FCO 15/1715[271]. Cf. Cablegram to Canberra, 30 May 1976. Wendy Way, ed., *Australia and the Indonesian Incorporation of Portuguese Timor* (Carlton, Victoria: Melbourne University Press, 2000), pp. 771–2.

58. Jones/Wallace, 4 June 1976. FCO 15/1715[280].

59. Cablegram to Peking, 21 June 1976. Way, pp. 795–6.
60. Ibid., p. 795.
61. Andrew T.H. Tan, *Security Perspectives of the Malay Archipelago* (Cheltenham: Elgar, 2004), p. 93.
62. Telegram, 5 September 1975, 333. FCO 15/1705[100].
63. Ford/Squire, 15 September 1975. FCO 15/1705[115].
64. Telegram, 10 December 1975, 441. FCO 15/1707[250].
65. Tan, p. 93.
66. Leifer, *Singapore*, p. 88.
67. Antolik, p. 87.
68. Leifer, *ASEAN*, p. 46.
69. Leifer, *Singapore*, pp. 88–9.
70. H. Indorf, *Impediments to Regionalism in Southeast Asia* (Singapore: Institute of Southeast Asian Studies, 1984), p. 45.
71. *Far Eastern Economic Review*, 26 January 1984.
72. Indorf, p. 13.

Bibliography of C.M. Turnbull

Books, Chapters, Academic Thesis

Turnbull, C.M. "The Movement to Remove the Straits Settlements from the Control of India Culminating in the Transfer to the Colonial Office in 1867". PhD thesis, University of London, 1962.

_____. "The Origin of British Control in the Malay States Before Colonial Rule". In *Malayan and Indonesian Studies: Essays presented to Sir Richard Winstedt*, ed. J.S. Bastin and R. Roolvink. Oxford: Clarendon Press, 1964.

_____. *The Straits Settlements, 1826–67: Indian Presidency to Crown Colony*. London: Athlone Press, 1972.

_____. *A History of Singapore, 1819–1975*. Kuala Lumpur: Oxford University Press, 1977.

_____. *A Short History of Malaysia, Singapore and Brunei*. Singapore: Graham Brash, 1980.

_____. "Melaka under British Colonial Rule". In *Melaka: The Transformation of a Malay Capital, c. 1400–1980*, 2 vols., ed. K.S. Sandhu and P. Wheatley. Kuala Lumpur: Oxford University Press, 1983.

_____. *A History of Singapore, 1819–1988*, 2nd ed. Singapore: Oxford University Press, 1989.

_____. "Imperial Svengali? Malcolm Macdonald and the Commonwealth". Lecture given to the Society of Fellows of Durham University, Durham, 27 April 1989.

_____. "Regionalism and Nationalism". In *The Cambridge History of Southeast Asia, Vol. 2: The Nineteenth and Twentieth Centuries*, ed. N. Tarling. Cambridge: Cambridge University Press, 1992.

_____. *Dateline Singapore: 150 Years of the Straits Times*. Singapore: Straits Times, 1995.

_____. "Formal and Informal Empire in East Asia". In *The Oxford History of the British Empire, Vol. 5: Historiography*, ed. R.W. Winks. Oxford: Oxford University Press, 1999.

_____. "The Malayan Civil Service and the Transition to Independence". In *Administering Empire: The British Colonial Service in Retrospect*, ed. J. Smith. London: University of London Press, 1999.

Articles, Book Reviews, etc. in Journals

Turnbull, C.M. "Governor Blundell and Sir Benson Maxwell: A Conflict of Personalities". *JMBRAS* 30, 1 (1957): 134–63.

———. "Communal Disturbances in the Straits Settlements in 1857". *JMBRAS* 31, 1 (1958): 94–144.

———. "Bibliography of Writings in English on British Malaya, 1786–1867" (with reprint of L.A. Mills, "British Malaya, 1824–1867"). *JMBRAS* 33, 3 (1960): 1–424.

———. "The European Mercantile Community in Singapore, 1819–67". *JSEAH* 10, 1 (1969).

———. "Convicts in the Straits Settlements, 1826–1867". *JMBRAS* 43, 1 (1970): 87–103.

———. "Internal Security in the Straits Settlements, 1826–1867". *JSEAS* 1, 1 (1970).

———. "Review of E. Hahn, *Raffles of Singapore*". *JSEAS* 1, 1 (1970): 110–1.

———. "British Planning for Post-War Malaya". *JSEAS* 5, 2 (1974).

———. "Review of C. Jeshurun, "The Contest for Siam: A Study in Diplomatic Rivalry". *JMBRAS* 51, 1 (1978): 125–6.

———. "Review of J. Kathirithamby-Wells, *The British West Sumatra Presidency (1760–85)*". *JMBRAS* 52, 1 (1985): 106–8.

———. "Review of Chan Heng Chee, *A Sensation of Independence: A Political Biography of David Marshall*". *JMBR* IS58, 2 (1985): 146–8.

———. "Britain and Vietnam, 1948–1955". *War & Society* 6, 2 (1988): 104–24.

———. "Review of E.C.T. Chew and E. Lee, eds., *A History of Singapore*". *JMBRAS* 65, 1 (1992): 101–3.

———. "From Colonial News to National Press: The Straits Times (Singapore)". Institute of Commonwealth Studies, University of London, Seminar Paper CH/95, 1996.

———. "Review of M.H. Murfett, J.N. Miksic. B.P. Farrell, and Chiang Ming Shun, *Between Two Oceans: A Military History of Singapore from First Settlement to Final Withdrawal*". *JMBRAS* 73, 1 (2000): 121–2.

———. "Review of J.N. Miksic and C.-A. Mei Gek, eds., *Early Singapore, 1300s–1819: Evidence in Maps, Text and Artefacts*". *JMBRAS* 78, 1 (2005): 122–4.

———. "British Colonialism and the Making of the Modern Johor Monarchy". *Indonesia and the Malay World* 37, 109 (2009): 227–48.

Introductions to Reprints

Earl, G.W. *The Eastern Seas*. Singapore: Oxford University Press, 1971. Reprint. Orig. publ. London, 1837.

Makepeace, W., G.E. Brooke and R. St. J. Braddell, eds. *One Hundred Years of Singapore*. Singapore: Oxford University Press, 1991. Reprint. Orig. publ. London, 1921.

Newbold, T.J. *Political and Statistical Account of the British settlements in the Straits of Malacca*, 2 vols. Singapore: Oxford University Press, 1971. Reprint. Orig. publ. London, 1839.

Oxford Dictionary of National Biography

Entries on:

Chambers, Rev. Walter (1824–1893), bishop of Labuan, Sarawak, and Singapore

Cooke, Sophia (1814–1895), missionary and schoolmistress

Crawfurd, John (1783–1868), orientalist and colonial administrator

Hose, Rev. George Frederick (1838–1922), bishop of Singapore, Labuan and Sarawak

Logan, James Richardson (1819–1869), lawyer and newspaper proprietor

McNair, John Frederick Adolphus (1828–1910), colonial official and penal reformer

Parkinson, Cyril Northcote (1909–1993), writer and historian

Raffles, Sir Thomas Stamford Bingley (1781–1826), colonial governor and founder of Singapore

Contributors

John BASTIN is Emeritus Reader in the Modern History of South-East Asia in the University of London. He was foundation Professor of History and Dean of the Faculty of Arts in the University of Malaya, and subsequently Reader in the Modern History of South-East Asia at the School of Oriental and African Studies, London. He has published numerous books and articles on the history of Indonesia, Malaysia and Singapore, and is the leading authority on Sir Stamford Raffles and his circle. His book, *The Founding of Singapore*, is to be published by the National Library Singapore in 2012.

Kevin BLACKBURN is an Associate Professor in History at the National Institute of Education, Nanyang Technological University, Singapore. He has published on oral history, heritage, the prisoner-of-war experience, and war memory. He recently co-authored with Karl Hack, *War Memory and the Making of Modern Malaysia and Singapore* (NUS Press, 2012), and authored *The Sportsmen of Changi* (New South Books, 2012).

Karl HACK is a Senior Lecturer in History at the Open University, United Kingdom. He moved there from the National Institute of Education, Nanyang Technological University, Singapore, at which he taught from 1995 to 2006. His recent books include (edited with Jean-Louis Margolin) *Singapore from Temasek to the 21st Century* (NUS Press, 2010), and (with Kevin Blackburn) *War Memory and the Making of Modern Malaysia and Singapore* (NUS Press, 2012). He is also Chair of the Open University's module — "Empires 1492–1975" — which is taken by several hundred students a year.

Jason LIM is a Lecturer in Asian History at the University of Wollongong, Australia. He is the author of *Linking an Asian Transregional Commerce in Tea* (2010) and is currently working on a project on the Cold War and the Chinese in Southeast Asia. His forthcoming book is *A Slow Ride* *into the Past: The Chinese Trishaw Industry of Singapore, 1942–1983* (Monash University Publishing, 2012).

Anthony MILNER is Basham Professor of Asian History, Australian National University, and wrote this volume's chapter while Pok Rafeah Professor at Universiti Kebangsaan Malaysia (2010–2011). His publications include *The Malays* (Wiley-Blackwell, 2008, 2011) and *The Invention of Politics in Colonial Malaya* (Cambridge University Press, 2002).

Kelvin W.K. NG is an officer in the Singapore Civil Service, and previously served in a staff appointment in the Ministry of Defence. His academic interests lie in the military history of empire, and more broadly in the history of warfare and strategic thought. He graduated with First Class Honours in Modern History from Oxford University, and completed his postgraduate studies in Imperial and Commonwealth History at St Antony's College, Oxford.

A.J. STOCKWELL is Emeritus Professor of Modern History, Royal Holloway, University of London. His publications include the volumes on Malaya and Malaysia in the series *British Documents on End of Empire*. He has served as editor of the *Journal of Imperial and Commonwealth History* and twice as President of the Royal Asiatic Society.

Nicholas TARLING (editor) was Professor of History at the University of Auckland from 1968 to 1997 and is currently a Fellow of the New Zealand Asia Institute. He is the author of a substantial number of books and articles on the history of Southeast Asia, including, most recently, *Britain and the Neutralisation of Laos*, and was editor of the *Cambridge History of Southeast Asia*.

P.J. THUM is coordinator of Project Southeast Asia, University of Oxford. He is a historian of modern Southeast Asia and has published on the vernacular perspectives of decolonisation in Singapore. His recent research focuses on intellectual, human, and disease networks in Southeast Asia, with particular reference to commonalities underpinning Southeast Asian identity and culture.

Index